D1529934

Nelson
Mathematics 5

Series Authors and Senior Consultants
Marian Small • Mary Lou Kestell

Senior Authors
Heather Kelleher • Kathy Kubota-Zarivnij • Pat Milot
Betty Morris • Doug Super

Authors
Andrea Dickson • Jack Hope • Mary Lou Kestell
Kathy Kubota-Zarivnij • Pat Milot • Marian Small • Rosita Tseng Tam

Assessment Consultant
Damian Cooper

THOMSON

NELSON

Australia   Canada   Mexico   Singapore   Spain   United Kingdom   United States

THOMSON

NELSON

Nelson Mathematics 5

Series Authors and Senior Consultants
Marian Small, Mary Lou Kestell

Senior Authors
Heather Kelleher,
Kathy Kubota-Zarivnij, Pat Milot,
Betty Morris, Doug Super

Associate Vice President of Publishing
David Steele

Publisher, Mathematics
Beverley Buxton

Project Manager, K–8
David Spiegel

Senior Program Manager
Shirley Barrett

Program Managers
Colin Bisset
Mary Reeve

Developmental Editors
David Hamilton
Brenda McLoughlin
Wendi Morrison
Bradley T. Smith
Michael Tabor
Susan Woollam

Developmental Consultants
Lynda Cowan
Jackie Williams

Authors
Andrea Dickson, Jack Hope,
Mary Lou Kestell,
Kathy Kubota-Zarivnij, Pat Milot,
Marian Small, Rosita Tseng Tam

Editorial Assistants
Matthew Griffin
Megan Robinson
John Rogers
Melinda Vander Ploeg
Michael Vo
Jenna Voisin
Linda Watson

Executive Managing Editor, Development & Testing
Cheryl Turner

Executive Managing Editor, Production
Nicola Balfour

Senior Production Editor
Linh Vu

Copy Editor
Julia Cochrane

Senior Production Coordinator
Sharon Latta Paterson

Production Coordinator
Franca Mandarino

Creative Director
Angela Cluer

Assessment Consultant
Damian Cooper

Art Director
Ken Phipps

Art Management
ArtPlus Ltd., Suzanne Peden

Illustrators
ArtPlus Ltd., Andrew Breithaupt,
Steven Corrigan, Deborah Crowle,
Sharon Matthews

Interior and Cover Design
Suzanne Peden

Cover Image
Wayne R. Bilenduk/Image Bank/
Getty Images

ArtPlus Ltd. Production Coordinator
Dana Lloyd

Composition
Valerie Bateman ArtPlus Ltd.

Photo Research and Permissions
Vicki Gould

Photo Shoot Coordinators
ArtPlus Ltd., Trent Photographics

Printer
Transcontinental Printing Inc.

Library and Archives Canada Cataloguing in Publication

Nelson mathematics 5 / Marian Small ... [et al.].

Includes index.
For use in grade 5.
ISBN 0-17-625970-8

1. Mathematics—Textbooks.
I. Small, Marian
II. Title: Nelson mathematics five.

QA135.6.N485 2004
510   C2004-903127-9

Advisory Panel

Senior Advisor

Doug Duff
Learning Supervisor
Thames Valley District School Board
London, Ontario

Advisors

Donna Anderson
Coal Tyee Elementary School
School District #68
Nanaimo-Ladysmith
Nanaimo, British Columbia

Keith Chong
Principal
School District #41
Burnaby, British Columbia

Attila Csiszar
Math Helping Teacher
Surrey School Board
Surrey, British Columbia

David P. Curto
Principal
Hamilton-Wentworth Catholic
District School Board
Hamilton, Ontario

Marg Curto
Principal of Programs, Elementary
Hamilton-Wentworth Catholic
District School Board
Hamilton, Ontario

Wendy Dowling
Vice Principal
Peel District School Board
Mississauga, Ontario

Lillian Forsythe
Regina, Saskatchewan

Peggy Gerrard
Dr. Morris Gibson School
Foothills School Division
Okotoks, Alberta

Mary Gervais
Consultant
Durham Catholic District
School Board

C. Marie Hauk
Consultant
Edmonton, Alberta

Rebecca Kozol
School District #42
Maple Ridge, British Columbia

A. Craig Loewen
Associate Professor
University of Lethbridge
Lethbridge, Alberta

Frank A. Maggio
Department Head of Mathematics
Holy Trinity Catholic
Secondary School
Halton Catholic District
School Board
Oakville, Ontario

Moyra Martin
Principal
Calgary Catholic School District
Calgary, Alberta

Meagan Mutchmor
K–8 Mathematics Consultant
Winnipeg School Division
Winnipeg, Manitoba

Mary Anne Nissen
Consultant
Elk Island Public Schools
Sherwood Park, Alberta

Darlene Peckford
Principal
Horizon School Division #67
Taber, Alberta

Kathy Perry
Teacher
Peel District School Board
Brampton, Ontario

Susan Perry
Consultant
Durham Catholic District
School Board
Oshawa, Ontario

Bryan A. Quinn
Teacher
Edmonton Public Schools
Edmonton, Alberta

Ann Louise Revells
Vice Principal
Ottawa-Carleton Catholic
School Board
Ottawa, Ontario

Evelyn Sawicki
Mathematics Consultant
Calgary, Alberta

Lorraine Schroetter-LaPointe
Vice Principal
Durham District School Board
Oshawa, Ontario

Nathalie Sinclair
Assistant Professor
Michigan State University
East Lansing, Michigan

Susan Stuart
Assistant Professor
Nipissing University
North Bay, Ontario

Doug Super
Principal
Vancouver School Board
Vancouver, British Columbia

Joyce Tonner
Learning Supervisor
Thames Valley District
School Board
London, Ontario

Stella Tossell
Mathematics Consultant
North Vancouver, British Columbia

Sandra Unrau
Principal
Calgary Board of Education
Calgary, Alberta

Gerry Varty
AISI Math Coordinator
Wolf Creek School Division #72
Ponoka, Alberta

Michèle Wills
Assistant Principal
Calgary Board of Education
Calgary, Alberta

Reviewers

Mary Adams
Thames Valley District School Board

Michael Babcock
Limestone District School Board

Nancy Campbell
Rainbow District School Board

Catherine Chau
Toronto District School Board

Deb Colvin-MacDormand
Edmonton Public Schools

William Corrigan
Lakeshore School Board

Anna Dutfield
Toronto District School Board

Susan Gregson
Peel District School Board

Susannah Howick
North Vancouver School District

Julie Keough
Waterloo Catholic District
School Board

Wendy King
Coley's Point Primary School

Gowa Kong
North Vancouver School District

Joanne Languay
Hamilton-Wentworth District
School Board

Joan McDuff
Faculty of Education
Queen's University

Ken Mendes
Ottawa-Carleton Catholic
School Board

Jennifer Peacocke
Ottawa-Carleton District
School Board

Rose Scaini
York Catholic District School Board

Lindy Smith
Peel District School Board

Mary Wallace
Peel District School Board

Triona White
Ottawa-Carleton Catholic
School Board

Aboriginal Content Reviewers

Brenda Davis
Education Consultant
Six Nations

Laura Smith
Educational Consultant
Abbotsford, British Columbia

Equity Reviewer

Mary Schoones
Educational Consultant/
Retired Teacher
Ottawa-Carleton District
School Board

Literacy Reviewer

Roslyn Doctorow
Educational Consultant

Thank you to the following teachers for testing the Chapter Tasks.

Shane Belknap
Peel District School Board

Sharon Bowerman
Rainbow District School Board

Sue Bowerman
Rainbow District School Board

Grace Brereton
Peel District School Board

Andrea Brown
Peel District School Board

Dianne Buja
Ottawa-Carleton Catholic
School Board

Dale Castellarin
Peel District School Board

Sherry Conroy
Rainbow District School Board

Malcolm DeLima
Peel District School Board

Janet Hedderson
Rainbow District School Board

David Mitchell
Rainbow District School Board

Bonnie Purdy
Peel District School Board

Dora Raymond
Rainbow District School Board

Triona White
Ottawa-Carleton Catholic
School Board

Contents

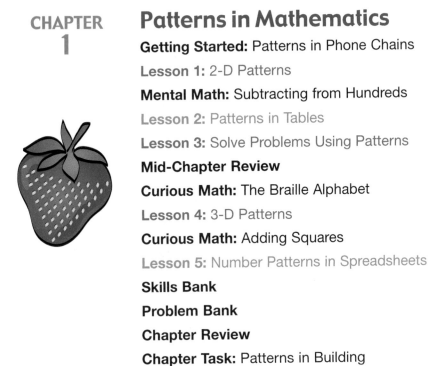

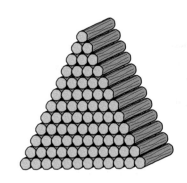

■	Guided Activity
■	Direct Instruction
■	Exploration

CHAPTER
3

Data Management   59

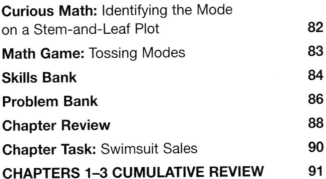

CHAPTER 4

Addition and Subtraction   93

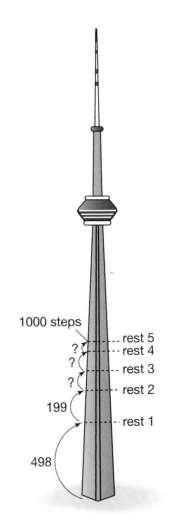

1000 steps

rest 5

? rest 4

? rest 3

? rest 2

199 rest 1

498

- Guided Activity
- Direct Instruction
- Exploration

CHAPTER 5

Measuring Length and Time 125

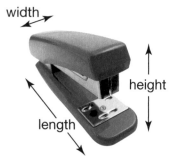

width

height

length

CHAPTER 6

Multiplication and Division 155

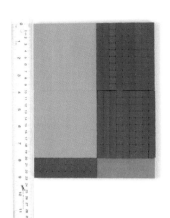

CHAPTER
7

2–D Geometry   187

- ◻ Guided Activity
- ◼ Direct Instruction
- ◼ Exploration

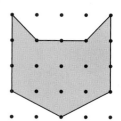

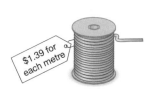

$1.39 for each metre

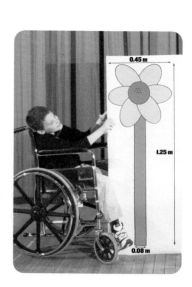

CHAPTER
10

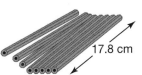

17.8 cm

Dividing Decimals   269

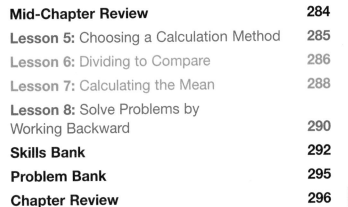

■ Guided Activity
■ Direct Instruction
■ Exploration

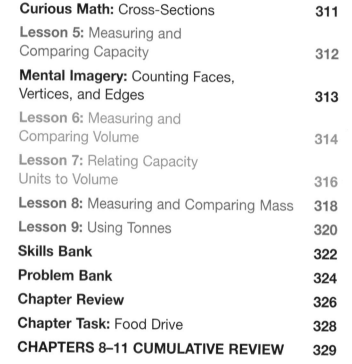

CHAPTER 13

Probability   357

■ Guided Activity
■ Direct Instruction
■ Exploration

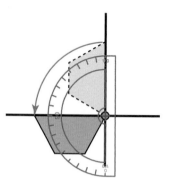

CHAPTER 14

Patterns and Motion in Geometry   381

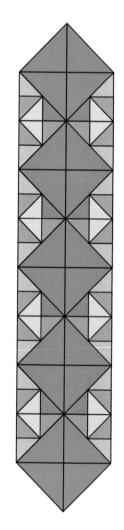

Patterns in Mathematics

Goals

You will be able to

- **use models and tables to identify patterns**
- **identify, extend, and create patterns**
- **analyze, represent, and describe patterns**
- **use patterns to solve problems**

Petal pattern

Getting Started

Patterns in Phone Chains

48 Grade 5 students entered a story-writing contest.
The judge tells Jasleen the results after school.
Jasleen volunteers to spread the news.

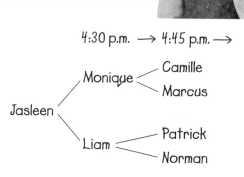

Jasleen's Phone Chain

At 4:30 p.m., I phone two students.

At 4:45 p.m., those two students each call two other students.

At 5:00 p.m., those four students each call two other students. Nobody is called twice.

4:30 p.m. ⟶ 4:45 p.m. ⟶

Jasleen
  Monique ⟨ Camille
            Marcus
  Liam ⟨ Patrick
         Norman

❓ **At what time will all 48 students know the winners of the story-writing contest?**

A. At 4:30 p.m., how many new calls are made?

B. How many new calls are made at 4:45 p.m.?
How many students know the winners after the calls are made at 4:45 p.m.?

Time	Number of new calls made	Total number of students who know
4:30 p.m.		
4:45 p.m.		

C. At 5:00 p.m., how many new calls are made?
How many students know the winners after the calls are made at 5:00 p.m.?

D. Write the next four clock times in this pattern:
4:30, 4:45, 5:00, 5:15, ...

E. What time will it be when all 48 students know the winners?

Do You Remember?

1. Match the patterns with the correct descriptions.
   a) 4, 8, 12, 16, ...
   b) 79, 78, 76, 73, 69, ...
   c) 3, 2, 6, 7, 3, 2, 6, 7, 3, 2, 6, 7, ...
   d) 110, 120, 135, 155, ...
   e) 81, 72, 63, 54, ...

   i) the pattern repeats
   ii) the pattern decreases by the same amount
   iii) the pattern decreases by different amounts
   iv) the pattern increases by the same amount
   v) the pattern increases by different amounts

2. Describe each pattern in words.
   Then write the next three numbers in the pattern.
   a) 1999, 2001, 2003, 2005, ...
   b) 44, 55, 67, 80, ...
   c) 275, 260, 245, 230, ...

3. Write a **pattern rule** for the pattern in Question 2 a).

4. Sketch picture 4 in the pattern.
   Complete a t-chart like the one shown.

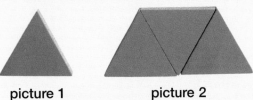

picture 1   picture 2

picture 3

Picture	Number of triangles
1	
2	
3	
4	

1 2-D Patterns

Goal Use models and t-charts to record, extend, and make predictions about number patterns.

Alain is a star! He is creating a design for his name to appear in lights.

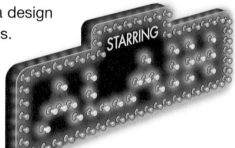

? How many light bulbs do you need for a letter design?

 Alain's Design

I will make a model with counters.

I start with the letter A.

To see what a larger letter looks like, I add counters.

Each time I make a larger size, I place the new counters red side up so I can see what I changed.

I add two counters to each arm of the A and two counters to the middle bar.

I record each size on grid paper and in a t-chart.

size 1

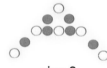
size 2

Size	Number of light bulbs
1	6
2	12
3	18

size 1

size 3

Now I can write the pattern rule.

Pattern rule:

Start with six bulbs and add six each time.

A. Pick a letter in your name. Make a design for the letter with counters. Record size 1 on grid paper and in a t-chart.

B. Make and record two larger sizes of the same letter.

C. Describe the changes you made to make your letter larger.

D. Each letter can use up to 50 bulbs. Predict the largest size of your letter that you can make. Test your prediction by extending the t-chart.

Reflecting

1. Why might it be easier to predict how the letter I grows than the letter N?

2. Which helps the most when you are predicting the number of bulbs in larger sizes of letters: the counters, the t-chart, or the drawings? Explain.

Subtracting from Hundreds

Think of numbers between 90 and 100 when subtracting a one-digit number from hundreds.

200 − 2 must be between 190 and 200.
200 − 2 = 198

A. How can you use addition to calculate 200 − 2?

Try These

1. Calculate.
   a) 100 − 6
   b) 300 − 3
   c) 400 − 4
   d) 500 − 5
   e) 600 − 6
   f) 700 − 7
   g) 800 − 8
   h) 900 − 9

2 Patterns in Tables

Goal Create tables to display, predict, and extend patterns.

Glynis is making Tangerine Twist with water and juice crystals for a class party. 27 people are coming to the party.

? **How much of each ingredient does Glynis need for 27 people?**

Glynis's Recipe

The recipe says I need five cups of water and three scoops of crystals for four people.

I'll use a table to see how many times I need to make the recipe.

Number of times I make the recipe	Number of cups of water	Number of scoops of crystals	Number of people served
1	5	3	4
2			

A. If Glynis makes two times the recipe, how many cups of water will she need?

B. If Glynis makes three times the recipe, how many scoops of crystals will she need?

C. Extend the table to show seven times the recipe. Write a pattern rule for each column.

D. How much of each ingredient does Glynis need for 27 people?

Reflecting

1. Explain how you can use Glynis's table to determine the amount of water needed and the number of people that can be served with 12 scoops of crystals.

2. a) How would you use Glynis's table to predict the amounts for 14 people?
   b) Why might there be more than one answer?

3. How can you predict the amounts for 40 people without extending the table?

Checking

4. a) Jack has a recipe for baked apples. Extend his table to show amounts for one to six apples.
   b) What does the fifth row of numbers tell you?
   c) How much brown sugar and butter are needed for six apples?

Jack's Baked Apples	
1	apple
25 mL	brown sugar
10 mL	butter

Number of apples	Brown sugar (mL)	Butter (mL)
1	25	10
2	50	20
3		

Practising

5. Grandpa's trail mix recipe calls for 250 mL of almonds, 125 mL of pumpkin seeds, 50 mL of raisins, and 1 handful of dried apricots. Make and extend a table to show amounts for five times the recipe.

6. 11 to 15 players and 2 coaches are needed to make a soccer team.
   a) Make and extend a table to show the number of coaches and the least and greatest number of players needed for one to five teams.
   b) 62 students want to play. How many teams can be made? How many coaches are needed? How many players will be on each team?

3 Solve Problems Using Patterns

Goal Identify patterns to solve problems.

? How many seeds are on the strawberry?

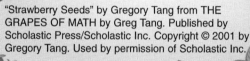
Jose's Solution

Strawberry Seeds

Strawberries grow along the ground.
A better treat cannot be found!
Their seeds reside in tiny rows.
From each of them a plant will grow.
Just how many seeds are there?
Count them only if you dare.
Here's a little trick of mine:
Pair the rows that sum to nine!

"Strawberry Seeds" by Gregory Tang from THE
GRAPES OF MATH by Greg Tang. Published by
Scholastic Press/Scholastic Inc. Copyright © 2001 by
Gregory Tang. Used by permission of Scholastic Inc.

Understand

I need to figure out the number
of seeds on the strawberry
without counting one at a time.

Make a Plan

I'll use the trick from the poem.
I'll look for pairs of rows that add to nine.

Carry Out the Plan

The top row has seven seeds and the bottom row
has two seeds.

$7 + 2 = 9$

The middle two rows have four seeds and five seeds.

$4 + 5 = 9$

I predict the other two rows will sum to nine, too.
I check my prediction.

$6 + 3 = 9$

I have three groups of nine.

$3 \times 9 = 27$

There are 27 seeds on the strawberry.

Reflecting

1. How can you check that there are 27 seeds?

2. Explain why finding a pattern is a good strategy for solving the problem.

3. a) How do you know that the number of seeds is the sum 2 + 3 + 4 + 5 + 6 + 7?
   b) How did Jose pair the numbers in part a) to add?
   c) How could you predict there would be three pairs?

Checking

4. a) Pair the top and bottom rows of this strawberry. How many seeds are in these rows combined?
   b) How many rows are there altogether?
   c) How many pairs of rows have the same sum?
   d) How many seeds are there altogether? Write a number sentence to show your work.

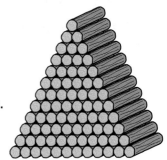

5. How can you use a pattern to add 20 + 30 + 40 + 50 + 60 + 70 + 80?

Practising

6. Ian is piling up firewood.
   a) Make a plan that uses a pattern to determine the number of logs in the pile.
   b) Use your plan to determine the number of logs in the pile.
   c) How many logs will there be in a similar pile that has 30 logs in the bottom row? How do you know?

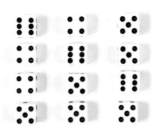

7. Use a pattern to add.
   a) 1 + 2 + 3 + 4 + 5 + 6 + ... + 18 + 19 + 20
   b) 1 + 2 + 3 + 4 + 5 + 6 + ... + 98 + 99 + 100

8. Determine the total on the dice. Show your work.

See if it jives, adding is fast if you count by fives.
Tricky to do? That depends.
It's even faster if you count by tens.

LESSON

Mid-Chapter Review

1

1. Chairs are being set up in the auditorium.
   a) Describe the changes for each new array.
   b) Make a t-chart to record the number of chairs in the first seven arrays. Write a pattern rule for the number of chairs.
   c) Predict the number of chairs in array 9. Show your work.
   d) Which array has 156 chairs in it?

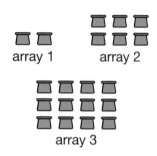

array 1   array 2

array 3

2

2. At the garden nursery, Peter makes bags of grass seed. To make a bag of grade A mix, he uses 2 cups of bluegrass seed and 3 cups of red fescue seed.
   a) How many cups of red fescue will he mix with 10 cups of bluegrass? How many bags of grade A mix will this make?
   b) How much of each kind of seed does he need to make 10 bags of grade A mix?

Number of bags of grade A mix	Number of cups of bluegrass seed	Number of cups of red fescue seed
1	2	3
2		

3

3. Write the first 10 numbers in each pattern.
   a) Start at 10 and add 10 each time.
   b) Start at 3 and add 4 each time.

4. a) Write the first 10 numbers in this pattern:
      Start at 1 and add 2 each time.
   b) Use a pattern to find the sum of the 10 numbers.

5. How many caps are there?
   Show your work.

   > Here's a hint to help you score:
   > Adding is fast with groups of four.

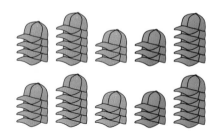

The Braille Alphabet

In 1824, Louis Braille invented a kind of writing that you read by touching.

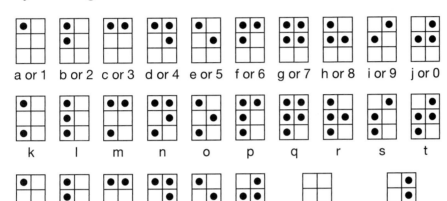

a or 1   b or 2   c or 3   d or 4   e or 5   f or 6   g or 7   h or 8   i or 9   j or 0

k   l   m   n   o   p   q   r   s   t

u   v   x   y   z   w   Capitalize the next letter.   Read the next word as a number.

You will need

• grid paper

• five-dot circles

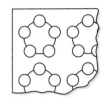

1 Compare the first two rows in the Braille alphabet. What pattern do you see?

2 How old will you be in 2012? Write your answer on grid paper using the Braille alphabet.

3 Use patterns to invent your own alphabet code with five-dot circles.

4 3-D Patterns

 Goal **Create a 3-D pattern and make predictions about its growth.**

Heather and Drake are stacking 100 boxes of food collected in a food drive.

❓ How many layers will there be in a stack of 100 boxes?

Heather's Plan

I make models of the stacks with linking cubes to represent boxes.

I record the numbers of boxes in a table and look for patterns.

Each time I make a new stack, I add the number of new boxes to the total.

stack 1   stack 2   stack 3

Number of layers	Number of new boxes	Total number of boxes
1	1	1
2	3	1 + 3 = 4
3	5	4 + 5 = 9
4		

A. Make the first three stacks. How is each new stack made from the one before? Where do you see this in the table?

B. Make stack 4. Complete a table like Heather's for stack 4.

C. Predict the number of new boxes and the total number of boxes for stack 6. Explain how you know.

D. Describe the pattern in the total number of boxes. Write a pattern rule.

E. How can you determine the total number of boxes if you know only the number of layers?

F. How many layers will there be for a stack of 100 boxes?

1. How does knowing the number of boxes in the bottom layer help you to fill in the table?

2. Describe the strategies you used to relate the total number of boxes to the number of layers.

Curious Math

Adding Squares

picture 1

picture 2

picture 3

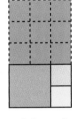

picture 4

You will need

• grid paper

1 How do you know what side length of square to add each time in this picture pattern?

2 Draw pictures 5 and 6 on grid paper.

3
a) Make a t-chart to record the side length of the square that is added for each new picture.
b) Extend the t-chart to determine the side length of the square that would be added to picture 9 to make picture 10.

4 How is this pattern like the flower petal pattern on page 1?

5 Number Patterns in Spreadsheets

You will need

- spreadsheet software
- Yoshi's spreadsheet

Goal Create and identify patterns in spreadsheets.

Yoshi and his sisters are having a garage sale. Small items cost $1.50 each, medium items cost $2.50 each, and large items cost $4.50 each.

? **How can Yoshi use the spreadsheet to calculate prices?**

B6	▼		=	B5 + 1.50

	A	B	C	D
1	Garage sale prices			
2		small	medium	large
3	Number of items	$1.50	$2.50	$4.50
4	1	$ 1.50	$ 2.50	$ 4.50
5	2	$ 3.00	$ 5.00	$ 9.00
6	3	$ 4.50	$ 7.50	$ 13.50
7	4	$ 6.00	$ 10.00	$ 18.00
8	5	$ 7.50	$ 12.50	$ 22.50
9	6	$ 9.00	$ 15.00	$ 27.00
10	7	$ 10.50	$ 17.50	$ 31.50
11	8	$ 12.00	$ 20.00	$ 36.00
12	9	$ 13.50	$ 22.50	$ 40.50
13	10	$ 15.00	$ 25.00	$ 45.00

Yoshi's Spreadsheet

When I look for the price of three small items, I see **4.50** in **cell** B6. The top line says B6 = B5 + **1.50**. This tells me how to get the number in cell B6 from the number in cell B5.

4.50 = **3.00** + **1.50**

cell

A box in a spreadsheet

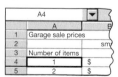

Cell A4 is in column A and row 4.

A. How can you get the number in cell B7 from other cells? How can you get the numbers in cells B8 and B9 from other cells?

B. Write a pattern rule for each pattern in columns B, C, and D.

C. Calculate the total price of three small items.
Calculate the total price of two medium items.
How can you use the spreadsheet to calculate the total price of five items?

D. Late in the day, Yoshi thinks that he won't sell all of the items, so he wants to reduce the prices. Change Yoshi's spreadsheet to show reduced prices of small $0.95, medium $1.95, and large $2.95.

Reflecting

1. Explain how the spreadsheet is useful for calculating prices at the garage sale.

2. What happened to the cells in the spreadsheet when you reduced the prices?

Checking

3. Use Yoshi's spreadsheet to calculate the reduced sale price.
   a) three small items
   b) five small items and three medium items
   c) four small items, three medium items, and five large items

Practising

4. Use Yoshi's spreadsheet to calculate the reduced sale price.
   a) ten small items
   b) five small items and four medium items
   c) one small item, four medium items, and nine large items

5. a) Each student ticket to the Fall Fair costs $6.00 and each adult ticket costs $9.50. Create a spreadsheet to show the cost of 1 to 10 Fall Fair tickets.
   b) Write the pattern rule for each column in the spreadsheet.

Skills Bank

1 1. Sketch the next two shapes in the pattern.
   Make a t-chart to record the number of squares in each shape.

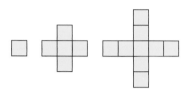

2. Diane's class is setting up tables for the school barbecue.
   6 people can sit around 1 rectangular table.
   When 2 tables are pushed together, 10 people can be seated.
   14 people can sit around 3 tables.

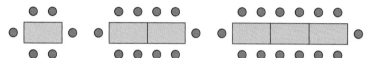

   a) How many people can sit around 4 tables?
      5 tables? Show your work.
   b) How many people can sit around 15 tables?

2 3. **a)** Which row of the chart has a repeating pattern?
      Which column of the chart has a repeating pattern?
   b) Write pattern rules for the patterns in the third
      column, the fifth column, and the second row.
   c) Describe the patterns in the first row, the third row,
      and the fifth row. Write the next three numbers for
      the patterns in the first row and the third row.
   d) Describe how the numbers in the second column are
      related to the numbers in the first column.

1	2	7	8	13	14
2	4	6	8	10	12
3	6	5	8	7	10
4	8	4	8	4	8
5	10	3	8	1	6

4. Serge is ordering hats and gloves for the ski team.
   a) Make a table to show the number of skiers, the number
      of gloves for each skier, and the number of hats and
      gloves for each skier.
   b) Describe the patterns you see in the table.
   c) What is the number of hats and gloves for 12 skiers?

2 5. a) Describe how each picture is made from the
   one before.
   b) Make a table to record the number of triangles,
   the number of squares, and the total number of
   triangles and squares in each picture.
   c) Which picture has 15 triangles? How many triangles
   and squares does it have altogether?

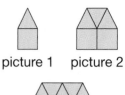

picture 1   picture 2

picture 3

3 6. Find the sum of the first 100 even numbers, starting at 2.

7. How many labels are there?
   Show your work.

4 8. a) Describe how each display of cans is made
   from the one before.
   b) Make a table to record the number of cans
   added each time and the total number of
   cans in each display.
   c) Predict the number of cans on the bottom
   row of display 6. How many cans are
   there altogether?

display 1   display 2   display 3

9. a) Mona is building a staircase of blocks.
   She says she needs exactly 47 blocks to make
   a staircase 9 blocks high. Can you tell if she's right
   without building the staircase? Explain.
   b) Predict the height of the staircase Mona could make
   with 25 blocks. Test your prediction.

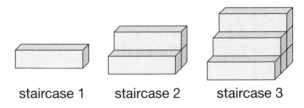

staircase 1   staircase 2   staircase 3

5 10. a) Create a spreadsheet to show the **multiples** of 6 from
   6 to 90.
   b) Create another column in your spreadsheet to show
   the multiples of 4 from 4 to 60.
   c) Identify the multiples that are on both lists.

Problem Bank

1 1. a) Describe how each design is made from the one before.
   b) Sketch design 4.
   c) Make a t-chart to record the number of green triangles in each design.
   d) How many green triangles will there be in design 5? Explain how you know.

design 1   design 2   design 3

2 2. Stella likes two kinds of invitations.
   One kind of invitation costs $8.75 for a box of 8.
   The second kind costs $5.50 for a box of 4, or $1.50 each.
   What is the least amount Stella could pay for 10 invitations?

3 3. a) Calculate each product. Use a calculator.
      $15 \times 15 = \blacksquare$ $25 \times 25 = \blacksquare$ $35 \times 35 = \blacksquare$ $45 \times 45 = \blacksquare$
   b) Describe the pattern in the last two digits of your answers.
   c) Describe the pattern in the other digits.
   d) Use the patterns you found to determine each product below without multiplying. Use a calculator to check.
      $75 \times 75 = \blacksquare$ $85 \times 85 = \blacksquare$ $95 \times 95 = \blacksquare$

4. Create a number pattern that increases by the same amount. Find the sum of the first 20 numbers in the pattern.

5. a) Ashley created a pattern using green and white triangle tiles. Make a table to record the number of green triangle tiles and the total number of triangle tiles in each design.
   b) Describe how to use a pattern to determine the total number of triangle tiles in each design.
   c) What is the total number of triangle tiles in design 3?
   d) Predict the total number of triangle tiles in designs 4 and 5. Explain your thinking.

design 1   design 2

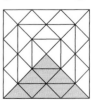

design 3

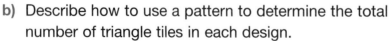

6. Leela is using cubes to build models of the letter L.
   a) How many cubes high will model 4 be?
      How many cubes wide will it be? How many cubes will it use altogether?
   b) Predict the total number of cubes in model 6. Explain how you know.

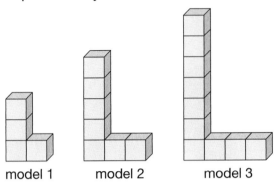

model 1   model 2   model 3

7. Heather made growing stacks of linking cubes. She used this table to record information about each stack.
   Create models of her first four stacks.

Number of layers	Number of new cubes	Total number of cubes
1	2	2
2	4	6
3	6	12

8. Company A charges $0.12 per minute for long-distance calls. Company B charges $0.07 per minute for long-distance calls.
   a) Make a spreadsheet to compare the long-distance rates for both companies. In your spreadsheet, show time going up in 5-minute steps.
   b) Company B also charges a network fee of $1.95 each month. Add a column to your spreadsheet to show the cost of long distance plus the network charge for company B.
   c) If you normally make 30 minutes of long-distance calls each month, which company should you use?
   d) Company C charges $6.00 each month for any amount of long distance. How many long-distance minutes would you need to use each month to make company C a better choice than company A or B?

Chapter Review

1
1. a) Look for a pattern in the designs.
      Sketch the next two designs in the pattern.
   b) Predict the number of squares in design 7.
      Use a t-chart.

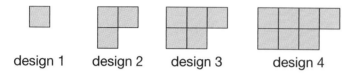

design 1   design 2   design 3   design 4

2
2. a) Describe the patterns you see in the designs.
   b) Sketch the next two designs in the pattern.
   c) Make a t-chart to record the number of dots
      in the designs.
   d) Write a pattern rule for the number of dots.

design 1   design 2   design 3

3. A shop sells wrapping paper by the metre.
   1 m costs $1.50, 2 m cost $2.00, and
   3 m cost $2.50. This pattern continues.
   How many metres can you buy for $5.00?

Number of metres	Cost
1	$1.50
2	

4. Philip lives in the eighth house on Emma Street.
   The first house on Emma Street is numbered 1,
   the second is numbered 5, the third and fourth are
   numbered 9 and 13. This pattern continues.
   What is Philip's house number?

5. Nick's father gave him this challenge:
   "At camp, do one pushup on day 1. Try to double the
   number of pushups you do each day."
   a) Make a t-chart to show the number of pushups Nick
      will try to do each day for a seven-day camp.
   b) How many pushups will he try to do on day 4?
   c) It takes about four seconds to do each pushup.
      How many minutes will the pushups take on day 7?
      Show your work.

3

6. While walking home through a park, Avril noticed bags of leaves lined up along a road in a pattern.
   a) How many bags would be in the group with 7 bags in the back row?
   b) How many bags would be in the back row of a group with 25 bags altogether?

group 1   group 2

group 3

7. Trapezoid and square tables are set up in a classroom as shown. Describe a plan to determine the total number of tables without having to count each one.

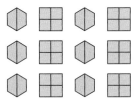

4

8. Sam is gluing wooden cubes together to make towers for a model of a city. The bottom of each tower doesn't need to be painted, so a single cube has five faces to paint.
   a) How many faces need to be painted when two cubes are glued together? when three cubes are glued together?
   b) Make a table to record the number of faces that need to be painted when up to six cubes are glued together.
   c) Predict the number of faces that need to be painted when eight cubes are glued together. Check your prediction by making a model and counting the faces.

5

9. Yvonne signed up for a charity walk-a-thon.
   a) Complete the table for 1 km to 10 km.
   b) Yvonne walked 7 km. How much will she collect from her mother, who pledged $0.75 for each kilometre?
   c) One neighbour pledged $0.25 for each kilometre, another pledged $0.75 for each kilometre, and a third offered to pay $10.00 no matter how far Yvonne walked. How much will Yvonne collect from all three neighbours?

Number of kilometres	Amount pledged at $0.25 for each kilometre	Amount pledged at $0.75 for each kilometre
1	$0.25	$0.75
2	$0.50	$1.50

Chapter Task

Patterns in Building

Patrick volunteered to build doghouses for the Humane Society. He said he would work for free if they paid for the materials.

These are the shapes of wood that Patrick needs for one doghouse.

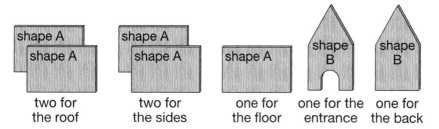

two for the roof   two for the sides   one for the floor   one for the entrance   one for the back

At the end of each month, the Humane Society pays Patrick for the materials for each doghouse he completes.

? How many doghouses did Patrick build in the first month?

A. How many pieces of each shape does Patrick need for 10 doghouses?

B. In his first order, the lumberyard delivers all of the pieces of shape B that Patrick needs, but only 24 pieces of shape A. How many doghouses can he make? Explain.

C. The materials for each doghouse cost $30. For every doghouse that Patrick completes in the first two weeks, the Humane Society pays him a $10 bonus. At the end of the first month, Patrick is paid $250. How many doghouses did he build?

Task Checklist

- ☑ Did you use charts to identify patterns?
- ☑ Did you describe the patterns?
- ☑ Did you show all your steps?
- ☑ Did you explain your thinking?

Numeration

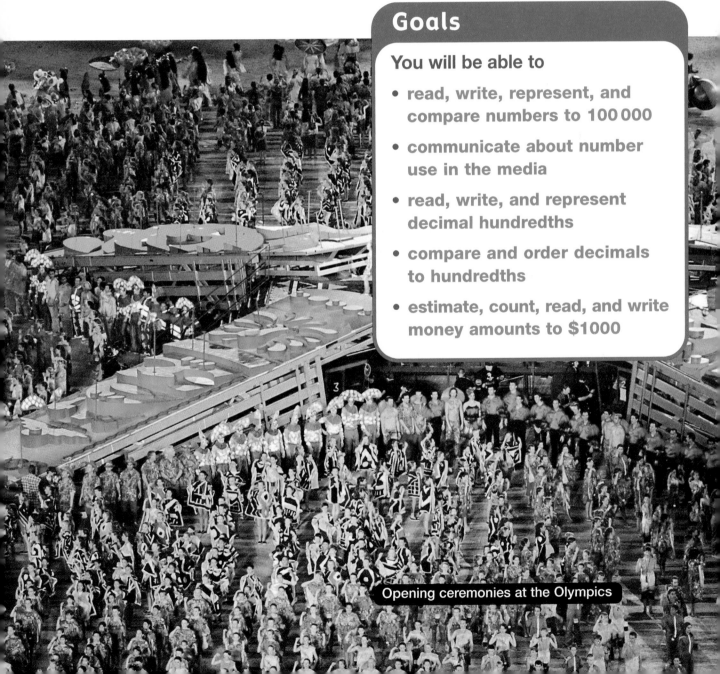

Goals

You will be able to

- read, write, represent, and compare numbers to 100 000

- communicate about number use in the media

- read, write, and represent decimal hundredths

- compare and order decimals to hundredths

- estimate, count, read, and write money amounts to $1000

Opening ceremonies at the Olympics

Getting Started

Modelling and Comparing Numbers

Monique read that it is healthy to walk about 10 000 steps each day.

Monique and three of her friends counted their steps one day.

Healthy Walking

Name	Number of steps
Monique	7423
Patrick	8917
Marcus	6023
Anna	7447

? **How can Monique use models to show who is closest to 10 000 steps?**

Monique's Model

I showed my number with a base ten block tower.

I started with the largest blocks.

I sketched my tower on grid paper.

top view   side view

A. Say the words for the number of steps Monique took.

B. How does Monique's tower show that
7423 = 7000 + 400 + 20 + 3?

C. If you built towers for all four numbers, which do you think
would be tallest? Explain your prediction.

D. Build all four towers. Sketch each tower on grid paper.

E. Whose tower is tallest? Was your prediction in Part C correct?

F. Whose tower is shortest?

G. What do you notice about the heights of the other two
towers? Explain your observations.

H. Which student walked closest to 10 000 steps?
Explain how you know.

Do You Remember?

1. a) Write each number on a place value chart.
   b) Write each number in **expanded form**:
      ■000 + ■00 + ■0 + ■
   c) Order the numbers from least to greatest.

   847
   5037
   1003
   3420

2. Write the numeral for each.
   a) three thousand four   b) three thousand fourteen

3. What decimal describes the green part of the grid?
   a) 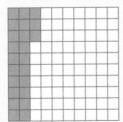   b)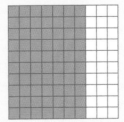

4. How much money is this?

Estimating 50 Thousand

 Use numbers you know to estimate 50 thousand objects.

You will need

- pennies

- a shoebox

- a calculator

Dan's school is having a penny drive. Their goal is to collect 50 thousand pennies for charity.

? How many shoeboxes does Dan's school need to hold the pennies?

A. Count out two sets of 100 pennies.

B. Do you think 200 pennies will fill a shoebox? How do you know?

C. Combine your 200 pennies with the pennies from four other students. How many pennies are there altogether?

D. About how many pennies will fill one shoebox? How did you decide on that number?

E. About how many shoeboxes are needed to hold 50 thousand pennies? Explain your answer.

Reflecting

1. You started with sets of 100 pennies. Was this a good strategy for estimating the number of pennies that would fill a shoebox? Explain your answer.

2. Describe two other ways to estimate 50 thousand pennies.

3. Do you think 50 thousand is a lot? Explain why.

Keep On Doubling

How many times must you double to get to at least 10 000?

1 Start with the number 100. Predict the number of times you must double to get to at least 10 000. Test your prediction.

2 Repeat Question 1 with 200, 300, 400, 500, 600, 700, 800, 900, and 1000.

3 What is surprising about your answers to Question 2?

Lots of Money

1
a) How many $100 bills are in 50 thousand dollars?
b) How many $50 bills are in 50 thousand dollars?

2
a) How many $10 bills are in 50 thousand dollars?
b) How many $5 bills are in 50 thousand dollars?

2 Reading and Writing Numbers

 Goal Read, write, and model five-digit numbers.

Aaron's friend asked him how he was doing with his two-page social studies report.

Aaron checked the information box on his computer. He said, "So far, it's only one page long, but that's 8427 bytes!"

? **How can Aaron represent the possible number of bytes for a two-page report?**

You will need

- base ten blocks

- a place value chart

Ten thousands	Thousands	Hundreds	Tens	Ones

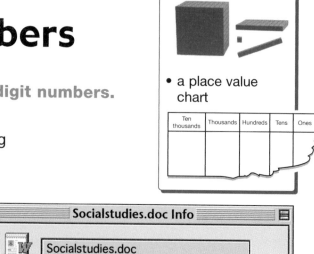

Socialstudies.doc Info

Socialstudies.doc

Show: General Information ▲▼

Kind: Word document
Size: 8427 bytes
Where: HD

Aaron's Models

I can model 8427 with base ten blocks.

I'll show this amount twice to estimate the number of bytes for a two-page report.

Thousands	Hundreds	Tens	Ones
8	4	2	7
8	4	2	7

Now I'll regroup.

I know that I always regroup 10 blocks in a column as 1 block in the next column. I will need a new column.

The new column must be the **ten thousands** column.

Ten thousands	Thousands	Hundreds	Tens	Ones
1	6	8	5	4

I have 1 ten thousand, 6 thousands, 8 hundreds, 5 tens, 4 ones.

This is 10 000 + 6000 + 800 + 50 + 4 in **expanded form**.

This is 16 854 in **standard form**.

I can read it as "sixteen thousand eight hundred fifty-four."

Reflecting

1. Juanita's report was 35 004 bytes long. Write this number in expanded form. How many numbers did you add to show the expanded form? Explain.

2. 16 854 is a five-digit number. It represents the number of bytes in a two-page report. How many digits might it take to represent the number of bytes for a four-page report? Explain.

3. What is the greatest possible five-digit number? What is the least?

standard form

The usual way in which we write numbers.

When numbers greater than 9999 are written in standard form, the thousands part is separated from the rest of the number with a space to make it easier to read.

16 854
↑
space

Checking

4. A file on your computer is 33 284 bytes long.
   a) Write this number in words.
   b) Write this number in expanded form.
   c) Describe or sketch a block model for 33 284.

Practising

5. Write each number in words and in expanded form.
   a) 21 341   c) 10 000 greater than 42 003
   b) 50 120   d) 1000 less than 30 004

6. Write each number in standard form.
   a) thirty thousand thirteen   b) 20 000 + 8000 + 30 + 5

7. There were 10 651 athletes at the 2000 Summer Olympic Games.
   a) Write 10 651 in words and in expanded form.
   b) Model this number with base ten blocks. Sketch the model.
   c) How is this number like 1651? How is it different?

Multiply Numbers Close to Tens and Hundreds

You can multiply numbers close to tens and hundreds by multiplying and then subtracting.

Liam's Method

To multiply 6 by 98, I think of six hundreds instead of six ninety-eights.

I calculate $6 \times 100 = 600$. Then I subtract 12.

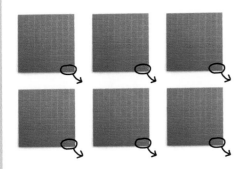

$600 - 12 = 588$, so $6 \times 98 = 588$.

A. Why did Liam subtract 12?

B. What are some ways to subtract 12 from 600?

Try These

1. Multiply by thinking of tens and hundreds.
   a) $6 \times 99 = $ ■
   b) $3 \times 98 = $ ■
   c) $3 \times 49 = $ ■
   d) $2 \times 79 = $ ■
   e) $4 \times 199 = $ ■
   f) $5 \times 198 = $ ■
   g) $6 \times 299 = $ ■
   h) $5 \times 899 = $ ■

3 Renaming Numbers

Goal Rename numbers with up to five digits.

The largest milkshake ever made would fill 22 712 one-litre containers.

Imagine that containers are available in the following sizes.

V	**W**	**X**	**Y**	**Z**
10 000 L	1000 L	100 L	10 L	1 L

? **What containers could you fill with all of the largest milkshake?**

A. What is the least number of full containers you could use? What are they?

B. What 23 containers could you fill with the milkshake?

C. What 32 containers could you fill with the milkshake?

D. Write five other sets of full containers that would hold the largest milkshake.

Reflecting

1. How could you use your answer from Part A to answer Part D?

2. Why did you always need to fill at least two of the Z containers?

3. How is using the containers to hold 22 712 L like using base ten blocks to model 22 712?

4. How is estimating 22 712 as ■ hundreds related to using only the X containers to hold the milkshake?

Curious Math

Easy as 1, 2, 3

12 312 is a five-digit number using the digits 1, 2, and 3.

1 What other numbers between 10 000 and 20 000 use all of the digits 1, 2, and 3?

2 Are more of these numbers closer to 10 000 or to 15 000? Explain why.

4 Comparing and Ordering Numbers

Goal Compare and order numbers with up to five digits.

Heather is a Blue Jays fan. She collected data about attendance at Toronto games.

? Which opponent team drew the greatest attendance in Toronto?

Baseball Attendance

Blue Jays' opponents	Average attendance in Toronto
Orioles	20 572
Devil Rays	20 459
Expos	31 571
Yankees	27 205
Angels	20 106

Heather's Comparison

I will start by comparing the Expos and the Yankees.

31 571 is greater than 31 thousand.

27 205 is less than 28 thousand.

31 is greater than 28, so more people came to see the Expos than the Yankees.

A. Do you agree with Heather? Explain how to compare the two numbers using base ten blocks.

B. Show how to compare the numbers using a number line.

27 000 28 000 29 000 30 000 31 000 32 000

C. Use **inequality signs** to compare the attendance for the Expos and the Yankees.

D. Order the five attendance numbers from least to greatest. Which team had the greatest average attendance in Toronto?

inequality signs

> and < are inequality signs.

8 > 5 is read as "eight is greater than five."

5 < 8 is read as "five is less than eight."

Reflecting

1. Would a number line be a good way to compare the Angels and Orioles numbers? Explain why or why not.

2. How does knowing how to compare four-digit numbers help you to compare five-digit numbers?

Checking

3. Heather also collected data for attendance at Blue Jays games at opponents' stadiums.
   a) Which team drew a greater attendance: the Orioles or the Yankees? Explain your strategy.
   b) Order the attendance numbers from least to greatest.

Baseball Attendance

Blue Jays' opponents	Average attendance at opponent's stadium
Expos	12 782
Orioles	27 955
Devil Rays	9 048
Yankees	33 916
Angels	41 088

Practising

4. Complete each number sentence using < or >.
   a) 10 999 ■ 10 100
   b) 4587 ■ 4576
   c) 56 091 ■ 58 091
   d) 32 231 ■ 23 321
   e) 30 000 ■ 29 999
   f) 97 560 ■ 70 650

5. Write an attendance number for each description.
   a) a bit greater than 50 000
   b) between 20 000 and 45 000, but closer to 45 000

6. Order these numbers from least to greatest.
   78 420   78 402   78 024   7842

7. Attendance at a Montreal Canadiens hockey game was posted using number cards. The cards fell down.
   a) The arena holds 21 273 people. What might have been the attendance? List five numbers made up of these digits. Explain your thinking.
   b) Order your numbers from least to greatest.
   c) How did you decide which number was greatest?

8. Yoshi says it's easier to compare 13 100 to 18 143 than to 13 216. Do you agree? Explain.

5

Rounding Numbers

 Goal Round numbers to the nearest ten thousand, thousand, and hundred.

This is a welcome sign that might have been put up after the 2001 Canadian census.

? **In what other ways can the population of Sudbury be shown on the sign?**

Welcome to Sudbury
Population 85 354

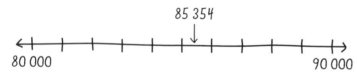

Jasleen's Rounding

I don't think the population of Sudbury stays at exactly 85 354. I think the sign should use an estimate.

85 354 is between 80 000 and 90 000.

I'll use a number line for rounding.

85 354

←+——+——+——+——+——+——↓——+——+——+——+——+→
80 000   90 000

I think the sign should say 90 000.

A. Jasleen estimated by rounding 85 354 to the nearest ten thousand. Explain why 90 000 is the nearest ten thousand.

B. Round the population to the nearest thousand.

←+——+——+——+——+——+——+——+——+——+——+→
85 000   86 000

C. Round the population to the nearest hundred.

←+——+——+——+——+——+——+——+——+——+——+→
85 300   85 400

D. If the population had been 95 354, why might you have rounded it to 100 000? How would you read this number?

Reflecting

1. Jasleen thought the population should be rounded to the nearest ten thousand. Do you agree? Why?

2. You rounded 85 354 to the nearest ten thousand, nearest thousand, and nearest hundred.
   For each rounding, how did you decide whether to round up or round down?

Checking

3. Round each number. Use a number line.
   a) 17 235 to the nearest ten thousand
   b) 28 356 to the nearest thousand
   c) 16 534 to the nearest hundred

10 000

Practising

4. a) Round the population of Gravenhurst to the nearest ten thousand, nearest thousand, and nearest hundred.
   b) Why might you round the population of Ajax to 74 000 or 70 000 but not to 73 000?
   c) Which two populations round to the same ten thousand? Do they round to the same thousand?

Ontario Populations

Place	Population in 2001
Ajax	73 753
Belleville	45 986
Cornwall	45 640
Gravenhurst	10 899

5. Round each number to the nearest ten thousand, nearest thousand, and nearest hundred.
   a) 32 456   b) 40 117   c) 35 648

6. The population of Kanata was about 59 000 in 2001.
   a) Do you think the actual population was more likely to be 57 947 or 58 947? Explain.
   b) What is the least the population might have been? What is the greatest the population might have been?
   c) Repeat part b) for a city with a population of about 60 000. Is there more than one set of answers? Explain why or why not.

6 Communicate About Numbers in the Media

Goal Evaluate the use of numbers in the media.

A wildlife protection group has this information on its Web site.

? **What should Camille say in a letter to the group about how numbers are used on its Web site?**

Wildlife Populations		
Species	**Status**	**Population**
polar bear	stable	between 22 000 and 27 000
sea otter	threatened (off California)	between 44 500 and 69 400
blue whale	endangered	1987
humpback whale	endangered	6000
grey whale	threatened (western Pacific)	about 21 000

Camille's Letter

I asked Akiko to help me with my letter.
She gave me some suggestions to improve my letter.

I think your Web site mixes up exact numbers and ← You used math language.

rounded numbers. ←

This is very confusing. → How do you know some numbers were rounded?

You didn't include ranges for all of the populations.

I think you should present all the numbers in the same way. ← How should they present the numbers?

I don't agree with how you round your numbers. ← You used math language.

The numbers for the sea otters are rounded to the

nearest hundred. I think the numbers should have been → You included a specific example.

rounded to the nearest thousand like the numbers

for polar bears. ←

I don't think the way you showed your numbers → You explained your thinking.

raises enough concern about these species. ← You made an important conclusion.

A. Do you agree with Akiko's suggestions? Explain using the Communication Checklist.

B. What other suggestions would you make about Camille's letter?

Communication Checklist

- ☑ Did you explain your thinking?
- ☑ Did you use math language?
- ☑ Did you include the right amount of detail?

Reflecting

1. Suppose you are writing a report. What should you keep in mind if you are using number information from a Web site?

2. Suppose you are giving advice on the way numbers are presented on a Web site. What can you include to make your advice convincing?

Checking

3. The wildlife protection Web site also includes animal fact charts.
Martin wrote a letter to the organization about the numbers on this chart.
   a) Identify at least one strength in Martin's letter.
   b) What questions would you ask Martin to help him improve his letter?

Martin's Letter

For the mass of blue whales, you say "more than 100 000 kg." How much more? I think you should have given the average mass or told how you rounded to get 100 000. I didn't think you needed to give the speeds of whales to decimal tenths. For the calf, I think it should say "about 2000 kg."

Blue Whale	
Size	• measures between 21 m and 24 m • has a mass of more than 100 000 kg
Food	• eats up to 35 000 kg of krill each day
Lifespan	• about 80 years
Swimming speed	• swims 22.5 km each hour with bursts as fast as 48.5 km each hour
Diving	• can dive as deep as 500 m • dives last between 10 minutes and 20 minutes
Pod size	• groups up to 60
Offspring	• average calf is 7 m long and has a mass of 1998 kg at birth

Practising

4. Jessica found this chart on a Web site about Canada. Write a letter about the use of numbers in the chart. Use the Communication Checklist to help you write the letter.

Canadian Facts 🍁	
Parks	Canada has more than 100 national parks and historic sites.
Dollar	The Canadian dollar is divided into 100 cents.
Tallest peak	Mount Logan in the Yukon is Canada's tallest peak at 6050 m above sea level.
Largest lake	Great Bear Lake is the largest lake in Canada with an area of about 30 000 km².
Longest river	The Mackenzie River is the longest river in Canada, flowing 4241 km through the Northwest Territories.
Coldest capital	Ottawa has the lowest average temperature of any capital city in the world.
Maple leaf	The maple leaf has been associated with Canada since the 1700s. The Canadian flag was adopted as the national flag in 1965.

Mental Math

Adding by Bridging

You can add a group of numbers by bridging tens and ones.

$$12 + 23 + 18$$
$$= 12 + 20 + 3 + 10 + 8$$

Teresa's Adding

First I add 12 and 20, that's 32.
… plus 3 is 35.
… plus 10 is 45.
… plus 8 is 53.

A. What are some other ways to add $12 + 23 + 18$?

Try These

1. a) $25 + 23 + 22 = \blacksquare$ c) $25 + 15 + 15 = \blacksquare$ e) $15 + 12 + 13 + 25 = \blacksquare$
   b) $16 + 18 + 12 = \blacksquare$ d) $17 + 13 + 15 = \blacksquare$ f) $12 + 25 + 13 + 35 = \blacksquare$

Mid-Chapter Review

1 1. Markers come in boxes of 10.
A case of markers has 200 boxes.
How many cases are needed for 20 000 markers?

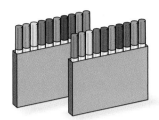

2 2. A candy company put on an egg hunt in
Niagara Falls using 11 340 kg of chocolate eggs.
a) Write this number in words.
b) Write this number in expanded form.
c) Sketch a model for this number.

3. Use words to write the number of bytes in each file.
a) 10 000 bytes more than 56 712
b) 1000 bytes more than 29 112
c) 100 bytes less than 17 098

4. Write each number in standard form.
a) 80 000 + 9000 + 500 + 20 + 6   b) 60 000 + 200 + 5

3 5. Write each number in standard form.
a) 12 thousands 12 hundreds 12 ones   b) 20 thousands 20 hundreds

4 6. Create two numbers for each description.
Use only the digits 3, 3, 4, 4, and 7 for each number.
a) between 33 000 and 33 500   c) greater than 37 000
b) between 43 000 and 44 000   d) between 60 000 and 80 000

7. The same digit goes in each blank.
8■327 < 851■9
How many answers are possible?
How do you know?

5 8. Round each number.
a) 57 107 police officers in Canada
b) 22 176 police officers in Ontario
c) 17 648 volunteer firefighters
   in Ontario

Nearest ten thousand	Nearest thousand	Nearest hundred

7 Decimal Hundredths

Goal Read, write, and represent decimal hundredths.

Jose and two of his friends are practising high jump.

? **How can Jose represent the heights of the jumps?**

High Jump

Jose	1.35 m
Martin	0.95 m
Norman	1.02 m

Jose's Jump

I jumped 1.35 m.

This is one and thirty-five hundredths metres.

I can write this on a place value chart that shows decimals.

Ones	Tenths	Hundredths
1	3	5

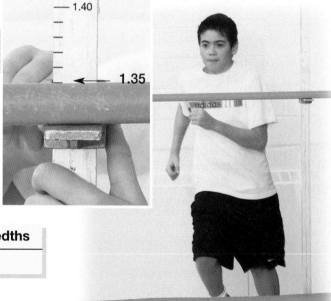

— 1.40

← 1.35

A. Use two metre sticks to model the heights of Martin's and Norman's jumps. Represent each number on a metre stick number line.

B. Write each number from Part A in words.

C. Liam jumped as well. His jump was one and twenty hundredths metres. Write this number in decimal form.

Reflecting

1. Explain why one and two hundredths metres is the same as one metre and two centimetres.

2. In what ways can you read 1.55?

3. Why is one and two hundredths written as 1.02 and not as 1.2?

Checking

4. Nick found these results for high jump.
   a) Use words to represent each height.
   b) Mark each height on a metre stick number line.

**Women's High Jump
2002 Commonwealth Games**

Gold	Hestrie Cloete (S.A.)	1.96 m
Silver	Susan Jones (Eng.)	1.90 m
Bronze	Nicole Forrester (Can.)	1.87 m

5. Write the decimal for each.
   a) six and seven hundredths
   b) five and ten hundredths
   c) fourteen and fifteen hundredths
   d) twenty-six hundredths

Practising

6. Represent each decimal on a metre stick number line.
   a) 1.04   b) 0.85   c) 1.50   d) 1.16

7. Copy and complete the chart.

	3.01	1.3	5.20	10.52
Value in the tenths place				
Value in the hundredths place				

8. Write a decimal in standard form for each description.
   a) one tenth greater than 3.59
   b) one greater than 3.59
   c) one hundredth greater than 3.59

9. Each of these distances uses the digits 2, 0, and 5.
   a) Use words to represent each distance.
   b) Describe each distance in metres and centimetres.
   c) Explain why 2.50 m and 2.05 m are not the same distance even though they use the same digits.

2.05 m

2.50 m

0.52 m

8

Exploring Equivalent Decimals

Goal Rename a decimal tenth as a decimal hundredth.

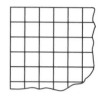
? **Which portions of the decimal grid can be named using two different decimals?**

A. Place a penny in each space of the first three columns of a decimal grid.

B. Write a decimal tenth to describe the part of the grid that is covered.

C. Write a decimal hundredth to describe the part of the grid that is covered.

D. Use the grid and penny model to explain why you can read 0.30 as three tenths and zero hundredths. What other way can you read it?

E. Add more pennies to the grid. Represent three other numbers that can be named as either tenths or hundredths. Record each number in two ways.

F. Place 16¢ on the grid. What decimal of the grid is covered? Why can't you name this as a decimal tenth?

G. For what numbers of pennies are there two decimal names for the portion of the grid that is covered?

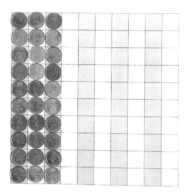

decimal grid

Reflecting

1. What number of pennies can you use in Part E to show that 0.7 = 0.70?

2. How can you tell whether a decimal hundredth can also be named as a decimal tenth?

3. Why can a decimal tenth always be renamed as a decimal hundredth?

Decimal Snap

Number of players: 2
How to play: Call out "snap" when you see two cards with matching values.

Step 1   Shuffle the cards.
Deal out cards face down into two equal draw piles.

Step 2   Both players turn over their top cards at the same time.
If the two cards have the same value, the first person
to call "snap" wins the two cards.

Step 3   Continue to turn over cards. If you run out of draw cards,
make a new draw pile with the cards you've won.

Continue to draw and call "snap" until one player has all the cards.

You will need

- Decimal Snap
cards

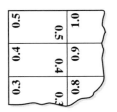

Snap!

9 Rounding Decimals

Goal Interpret rounded decimals, and round decimals to the nearest whole and to the nearest tenth.

Sofia is measuring the height of her room for a new bookcase. She says it is about 2.8 m high.

? **Sofia rounded the height of the room. If she gave a more precise measure, how might she describe the height?**

Karin's Solution

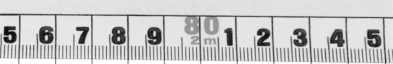

I want to find numbers that round to 2.8 m.

Sofia rounded the height to the nearest tenth, so I will look for numbers measured in hundredths.

First I will look for numbers that round up to 2.8.

All of the numbers from 2.75 to 2.80 round up to 2.8.

2.75 2.76 2.77 2.78 2.79 2.80 2.81 2.82 2.83 2.84 2.85

Now I will look for numbers that round down to 2.8.

All of the numbers from 2.80 to 2.85 round down to 2.8.

The height of the room could be any number from 2.75 m to 2.85 m.

Reflecting

1. Suppose Sofia rounded the height to the nearest whole number. What number would she use to describe the height?

2. Why might Sofia have rounded to the nearest tenth?

3. How can you round a decimal to the nearest tenth without using a metre stick or a number line?

Checking

4. Katrina is having new curtains made for a window in her room. She needs 1.56 m of fabric. Fabric is sold in lengths of whole metres and tenths of metres. How much fabric should she buy? Why?

Practising

5. An electrician needs 6.23 m of wire. Round that length to the nearest tenth of a metre. Should the electrician buy that amount or a different amount? Explain.

6. Round each number to the nearest whole number and to the nearest tenth.
   a) 2.78   b) 0.65   c) 8.04   d) 6.90

7. a) A number rounded to the nearest tenth is 3.9. What might the number be? List three possibilities.
   b) A number rounded to the nearest whole number is 5. What might the number be? List three possibilities.

8. Fiona says her canoe is about 3 m long.
   Meir says his canoe is about 3.2 m long.
   Can you be sure whose canoe is longer? Explain.

9. Name two numbers with decimal hundredths that round to the same whole number but to different tenths.

10. Name a number with decimal hundredths that rounds up to the nearest whole number but down to the nearest tenth.

10 Comparing and Ordering Decimals

Goal Compare and order numbers to decimal hundredths.

These are some of the results of the women's long jump qualifying and final jumps at the 2000 Sydney Olympics.

? **Did each competitor do better in the qualifying jump or the final jump?**

Women's Long Jump 2000 Olympics

Competitor	Qualifying (m)	Final (m)
Drechsler	6.84	6.99
Jones	6.78	6.92
Rubleva	6.65	6.79
Tiedtke	6.65	6.74
Vaszi	6.70	6.59

Drake's Comparison

I'll use base ten blocks to model Drechsler's jumps.

I'll use a flat block to represent 1.

I'll use a place value chart that shows decimals.

Qualifying Jump

Ones	Tenths	Hundredths
6	8	4

Final Jump

Ones	Tenths	Hundredths
6	9	9

A. Drake used a flat block to represent 1. Explain why it makes sense that the rod is used for 0.1 and the small cube for 0.01.

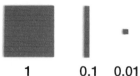

1   0.1   0.01

B. Which of Drechsler's jumps was better? Explain how the model shows that.

C. In an earlier practice jump, Drechsler jumped 6.92 m. Order her three jumps from least to greatest.

D. Compare the qualifying and final jumps of the other competitors.

Heike Drechsler

Reflecting

1. How can you compare numbers like 2.■■ and 1.■■, even when you don't know the number of hundredths?

2. Explain how you can compare Jones's jumps without using base ten blocks.

Checking

3. This chart shows the winning lengths for Olympic women's long jump for various years.
   a) In which years was the winning jump less than 7.00 m?
   b) Order the jumps from least to greatest.

Women's Long Jump

Year	Winning jump (m)
1948	5.69
1960	6.37
1972	6.78
1984	6.96
1988	7.40
1992	7.14
1996	7.12
2000	6.99

Practising

4. Complete each number sentence using < or >.
   a) 6.92 ■ 6.99   b) 29.04 ■ 28.04   c) 10.70 ■ 10.07

5. Order each set of numbers from least to greatest.
   a) 0.14, 3.56, 8.12, 0.97, 3.65   c) 2.12, 1.22, 0.21, 12.01
   b) 0.51, 0.15, 0.05, 0.01   d) 3, 3.03, 3.1, 3.75, 3.5

6. a) Complete each number with any digit from 4 to 9. Use the same digit in each number. Order the numbers from least to greatest. Which is greatest?
   b) Replace the missing digits with 0. Repeat with 1, 2, and 3. Which number is greatest each time?
   c) Why were your results in parts a) and b) different? How could you have predicted that?

0.4■
3.4■
3.44
3.■4
■.43
■.34

11 Counting Money

 Goal Estimate, count, read, and write money amounts to $1000.

Two Grade 5 classes are raising money for charity. Juanita's class raised the amount shown.

Patrick's class raised $10 more, but they had five fewer coins.

? **What bills and coins might be in the amount for Patrick's class?**

 ## Juanita's Estimate

First I'll estimate the total for my class.

I'll count the bills first: 20, 30, 35, 40.

I see five $2 coins.

I estimate the total is about $50.

A. Count the amount for Juanita's class. Record the amount in dollars and cents.

B. Compare your answer to Juanita's estimate. Is your answer reasonable?

C. Record the amount for Patrick's class in dollars and cents.

D. What bills and coins might be in the amount for Patrick's class? His class had five fewer coins than Juanita's.

Reflecting

1. Describe how Juanita counted the bills. Why might she have counted this way?

2. Juanita didn't count all of the coins when she estimated. How do you decide which coins to count when estimating?

Checking

3. Roger's class raised this amount of money.
   a) Estimate the total. Explain your estimate.
   b) Count and record the amount.

4. Another class raised $185.75. Describe two sets of coins and bills that make $185.75.

Practising

5. Estimate the amount of money. Then count the total.

   a)

   b)

6. How would you make each amount?
   a) $75.63   b) $374.50   c) $985.98

7. a) Show or describe three different sets of coins and bills that make $625.47.
   b) How would you make this amount using the fewest bills and coins possible?

Skills Bank

1. Complete each equation.

    a) 20 thousands = ■ hundreds   **b)** 40 thousands = ■ hundreds

2. Write the number in standard form for each model.

a)

Ten thousands	Thousands	Hundreds	Tens	Ones
			I	.....

b)

Ten thousands	Thousands	Hundreds	Tens	Ones
				.....

3. Sketch or describe a model for each number.

    a) 18 100   **b)** 30 010   **c)** 22 310   **d)** 41 002

4. Write each number in words.

    a) 12 305   **c)** 8017   **e)** 52 931   **g)** 80 006

    b) 23 008   **d)** 11 111   **f)** 30 900   **h)** 99 999

5. Write each number in expanded form.

    a) 31 004   **c)** 72 307   **e)** 54 321   **g)** 30 400

    b) 91 123   **d)** 80 003   **f)** 22 020   **h)** 60 302

6. Complete each number sentence using < or >.

    a) 12 146 ■ 15 315   **c)** 26 043 ■ 20 643   **e)** 30 043 ■ 29 847

    b) 6512 ■ 65 120   **d)** 10 803 ■ 18 003   **f)** 55 545 ■ 55 455

7. Order each set of numbers from least to greatest.

    a) 8439, 18 439, 19 384, 3479   **c)** 98 123, 93 128, 97 314, 97 413

    b) 40 007, 7004, 33 217, 23 172   **d)** 50 030, 50 300, 50 003, 53 000

8. Use all of the digits 1, 0, 2, 3, and 4 to create a number for each description.
   a) greater than 24 000, but less than 30 000
   b) greater than 34 000
   c) 100 greater than 32 040
   d) the greatest number possible

9. The chart shows average home and away attendance at Ottawa Senators hockey games.
   a) Which team drew the greatest attendance in Ottawa?
   b) Which team drew the least attendance in Ottawa?
   c) Which team drew the greatest attendance when Ottawa played away?
   d) Which team drew a greater attendance in Ottawa than at home?

Hockey Attendance

Senators' opponents	Attendance in Ottawa	Attendance at opponents' arenas
Canadiens	17 106	21 043
Maple Leafs	18 268	18 422
Sabres	16 648	11 322

10. Round each number to the nearest ten thousand, nearest thousand, and nearest hundred.
   a) 12 305
   b) 34 297
   c) 37 367
   d) 81 034
   e) 67 666
   f) 40 096

11. The population of a town is reported to be about 70 000.
   a) What is the greatest number the population could be?
   b) What is the least number the population could be?

12. Represent each number on a metre stick number line.
   a) 1.20
   b) 1.02
   c) 1.43
   d) 0.45

13. Copy and complete the chart.

	3.56	2.4	12.06	6.52
Value in the tenths place				
Value in the hundredths place				

7 **14.** Write a decimal to fit each description.

    a) one tenth greater than 4.17   **c)** one hundredth greater than 4.17

    b) one tenth less than 3.06   **d)** one hundredth less than 3.60

8 **15.** Rename each number as a decimal tenth or a decimal hundredth.

    a) 3.40   **b)** 2.6   **c)** 12.50   **d)** 4.2

9 **16.** Round each decimal to the nearest whole number and to the nearest tenth.

    a) 2.06   **c)** 16.81   **e)** 7.83   **g)** 3.89

    b) 7.72   **d)** 5.45   **f)** 22.70   **h)** 6.04

17. Baseboard is sold in tenths of a metre. How much baseboard should a carpenter buy for a wall that is 3.67 m long?

10 **18.** Complete each number sentence using < or >.

    a) 1.3 ▇ 2.4   **c)** 2.81 ▇ 3.16   **e)** 1.43 ▇ 2.6

    b) 0.43 ▇ 1.23   **d)** 3.0 ▇ 0.35   **f)** 2.14 ▇ 2.40

19. Order each set of numbers from least to greatest.

    a) 3.91, 1.9, 1.39, 9.3   **c)** 7.05, 5.07, 7.5, 0.57

    b) 1.13, 3.11, 1.3, 1.33   **d)** 10.03, 1.30, 3.01, 3.31

11 **20.** Estimate each amount of money. Then count the total.

    a)

    b)

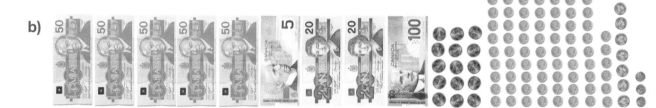

21. What bills and coins can you use to make these amounts with the fewest number of bills and coins possible? You can use $20 bills, $10 bills, $5 bills, and any coins.

    a) $100.75   **b)** $29.35   **c)** $135.17   **d)** $220.21

Problem Bank

1

1. Estimate the number of pencil cases needed to hold 10 thousand pennies. Show your work.

2. Estimate the height of a stack of 50 thousand pennies. Show your work.

3

3. The population of Orillia was reported as 27 954 in 1996. Describe or sketch three ways to model this population with fewer than 100 base ten blocks.

4

4. What five-digit numbers can you create using all of the digits 3, 3, 5, 5, and 5? Which number is the greatest?

5. The number of fast food restaurants Canada reported in 2003 fits these clues:
   • The sum of the digits is 17.
   • It is an even number between 17 000 and 18 000.
   • There are two pairs of digits that have a difference of 6.
   • No digit is greater than 7.
   • The number is less than 17 100.
   How many fast food restaurants were there in 2003?

6. In these two numbers, each digit between 0 and 9 appears only once. Complete the numbers. Determine all possible answers.
   ■■ 249 > ■■ 173

5

7. A number is increased by 3 when it is rounded to the nearest ten thousand or to the nearest thousand. What could the number be?

10

8. Shade your first and last initials on 10-by-10 grids. What decimal hundredth is shaded for each letter? Which number is greater?

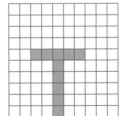 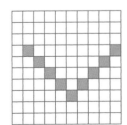

11

9. What set of 5 bills and 16 coins is worth $152.90?

Chapter Review

1 1. 40 000 beads are needed to decorate a powwow outfit. A jar holds 200 beads. A box holds 10 jars of beads. How many boxes are needed?

2 2. A heart pumps about 47 880 L of blood in a week.
   a) Describe or sketch a block model for this number.
   b) Write this number in words.
   c) Write this number in expanded form.

3. Write each number in standard form.
   a) 30 000 + 300
   b) 20 000 + 3000 + 80 + 3
   c) fifty-five thousand six
   d) thirty thousand two hundred twelve

3 4. A barn swallow migrated 14 226 km. Sketch or describe three different block models for this number.

barn swallow

4 5. There are 36 114 km of railroad track in Canada and 33 819 km in Australia. Which country has more kilometres of railroad track? Explain how you know.

6. The chart shows the total area of the Great Lakes.
   a) Which Great Lake covers the greatest area?
   b) Which Great Lake covers the least area?
   c) Order the areas from least to greatest.

Area of Great Lakes

Great Lake	Total area (km^2)
Ontario	18 960
Superior	82 100
Erie	25 700
Huron	59 600
Michigan	57 800

5 7. The diameter of Earth is 12 756 km. Round the number to the nearest ten thousand, nearest thousand, and nearest hundred.

8. A number can be rounded to 30 000, 32 000, and 31 900. What is the least number it could be? What is the greatest?

9. A newspaper says "a large crowd" attended a meeting of the school board and that the crowd filled the room. What is good about the way the newspaper reported the size of the crowd? What could be better?

10. Mark each number on a metre stick number line.
   a) 1.05   **b)** 0.89   **c)** 1.2

11. Copy and complete the chart.

	7.08	21.43	3.25	14.06
Value in the tenths place				
Value in the hundredths place				

12. Write a decimal in the form ■.■■ for each description.
   a) between 3.4 and 3.45   **c)** one hundredth less than 32.46
   b) one tenth greater than 29.12   **d)** one hundredth greater than 29.49

13. Kyle says his height is 1.5 m. Ben's height is 1.50 m. Can you be sure who is taller? Explain.

14. Round each number to the nearest whole number and to the nearest tenth.
   a) 16.72   **b)** 0.92   **c)** 2.03   **d)** 9.99

15. An electrician needs 9.45 m of wire. Wire is sold in lengths of whole metres. How much wire should the electrician buy?

16. Complete each number sentence using < or >.
   a) 0.58 ■ 0.56   **b)** 12.21 ■ 12.12   **c)** 5.06 ■ 5   **d)** 0.01 ■ 0.10

17. Estimate the amount of money. Then count the total.
   a)   **b)**

Chapter Task

Guess That Number

Marcus is using the facts from this poster to create a game called Guess That Number. This is one of his questions:

What was the speed of the fastest skateboarder in kilometres each hour?

These are his clues:

- I am a decimal hundredth.
- I have a zero in the tens place.
- When rounded to the nearest whole number, I am 101.
- My decimal part can be read as sixty-six hundredths.

Largest four-leaf clover collection 72 928

Greatest racehorse speed 69.62 km each hour

Greatest wingspan on an aircraft 66.65 m

Speed of fastest skateboarder _____ km each hour

? **What clues can you create so the players can find each number?**

A. What is the speed of the fastest skateboarder?

B. Make clues for the other three facts on the poster.

C. Test your clues. Do they lead you to one and only one number?

D. Marcus wants to ask the questions starting with the fact with the least number. Order the four numbers from least to greatest.

Task Checklist

☑ Do your clues lead to only one answer?

☑ Did you use a variety of math words?

☑ Did you include the right amount of detail?

Data Management

Goals

You will be able to

- **create a survey and interpret the results**

- **make broken-line graphs, bar graphs, and pictographs**

- **interpret circle graphs**

- **recognize accuracy in graphs**

- **calculate the mean and identify the mode of a set of data**

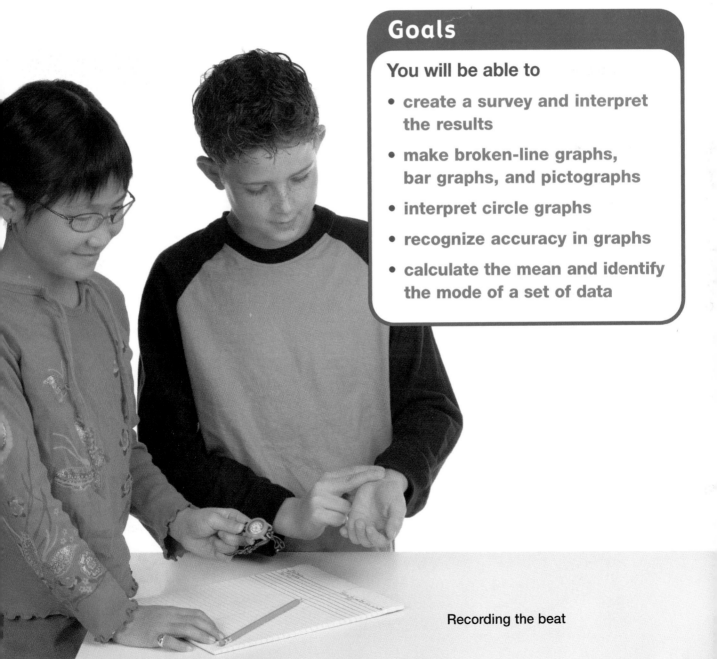

Recording the beat

Getting Started

Graphing Favourite Authors

Jasleen and her friends asked the students in their school to name the author of their all-time favourite book.

? **How can you present the survey results?**

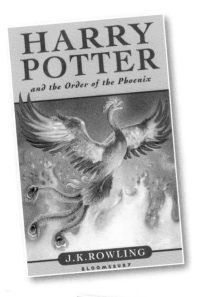

Students' Top 5 Choices

Author	Number of students
J.K. Rowling	260
J.R.R. Tolkien	120
Roald Dahl	90
C.S. Lewis	40
Lemony Snicket	30

A. Graph the results using a bar graph or a pictograph.

B. Explain why you chose that type of graph.

C. Explain how you chose your **scale**.

D. Do you think the survey results would be the same if an equal number of adults were asked to name the author of their favourite book? Give a reason for your answer.

Do You Remember?

1. The bar graph shows the number of pencil crayons in students' desks in a Grade 5 class.
   a) What is the size of each **interval** for the number of pencil crayons?
   b) How many students have 20 or more pencil crayons in their desks?
   c) Is it possible to determine the greatest number of pencil crayons in a desk using the graph? Explain how you know.

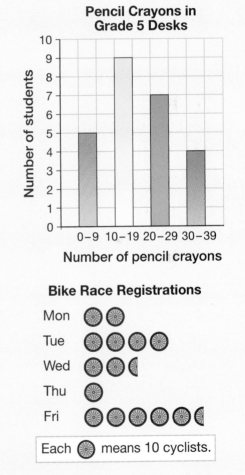

2. Ali registered cyclists for a long-distance bike race.
   a) Calculate the total number of riders who signed up each day. Use the pictograph.
   b) About how many riders registered for the race in total?
   c) Write two more things you can read from the graph.

Bike Race Registrations

3. Sketch a bar graph using the data from the pictograph in Question 2. Show a scale and include labels.

1 Evaluating Survey Results

You will need
- grid paper

or
- graphing software

 Goal Decide whether the results of a survey would likely apply to other groups of people.

Liam is preparing a report on technologies that students in his school think are the most important.

Liam's Survey

I asked 25 students in my Grade 5 class this question:

Which technology would you choose if you could have only one?
a) television
b) radio
c) Internet
d) telephone

? **How can you decide whether the results of Liam's survey might apply to other groups of people?**

A. Are the results of Liam's survey of 25 students likely to apply to all Grade 5 students in his school? Explain.

B. Why might the results of Liam's survey be **biased**?

C. Conduct a survey of the students in your class using Liam's question. Use his list of technologies or your own.

D. Show the results of your survey in a graph. Explain why you chose that type of graph.

E. Are the results of your survey likely to apply to all students in your school? Explain.

biased results
When survey results for part of a group are not likely to apply to the rest of the group

Reflecting

1. How might the results of your survey be different if you surveyed each group below?
   a) the same number of students in a local high school
   b) the same number of senior citizens
   c) a class of Grade 5 students in another country

2. Would your survey results be the same if you surveyed another Grade 5 class 20 years from now? Explain.

3. What are some reasons that the results of a survey for one group might not apply to another group? Explain your thinking.

Mental Math

Multiply Numbers by Five

Think of 10 when you multiply by 5.

$5 \times 12 =$ one half of 10×12
$10 \times 12 = 120$
one half of $120 = 60$
$5 \times 12 = 60$

A. How can you calculate 10×12?

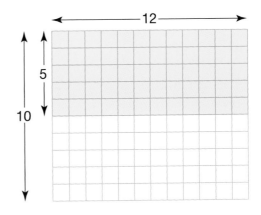

Try These

1. a) 5×14 c) 5×22 e) 5×48
   b) 5×16 d) 5×28 f) 5×64

2 Broken-Line Graphs

Goal Make and use a broken-line graph to identify trends.

Karin is studying climate. Her town gets most of its precipitation as snow in the winter and just a bit of rain during the rest of the year. She wondered if it's the same in India.

? **Are there similar trends for precipitation in Calcutta, India?**

Karin's Graph

I recorded the monthly precipitation in Calcutta.

Monthly Precipitation in Calcutta, India (mm)

Jan	Feb	Mar	Apr	May	Jun	Jul	Aug	Sep	Oct	Nov	Dec
0	20	30	40	110	300	330	260	290	110	30	10

I'll make a **broken-line graph**.

Step 1 The **horizontal axis** will show the months.

The **vertical axis** will show the amount of precipitation in millimetres.

The **range** in the amount of precipitation is **0** to **330**, or 330.

For the scale on the vertical axis, 1 unit will represent 50 mm.

I will draw 7 units of 50 mm for the scale on the vertical axis.

trend

The general direction of data in a graph. The data can increase, decrease, or stay about the same over time.

increase

decrease

stays about the same

broken-line graph

A graph in which data points are connected point by point

Step 2 I draw a point at 0 for January, 20 for February, and so on.

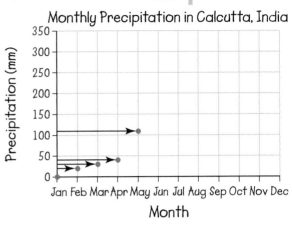

Monthly Precipitation in Calcutta, India

Step 3 I use line segments to connect the points in order.

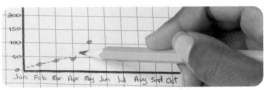

Step 4 I look for trends in my graph. Precipitation in Calcutta is different. The amount of precipitation increases each month from January to July. The amount decreases each month after July, except for September.

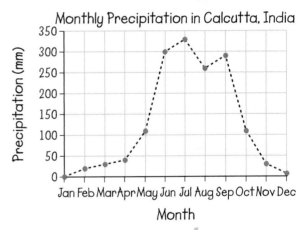

Monthly Precipitation in Calcutta, India

Reflecting

1. a) Why did Karin draw 7 units of 50 mm on the scale for the vertical axis?
   b) Explain how to locate the point that shows the amount of precipitation in July.
   c) Suppose Karin chose a scale of 1 unit for 100 mm. How would the height of the point for July change?

Checking

2. a) Make a broken-line graph of monthly precipitation for either Cairns or Prince Rupert. Use the same scale as in Karin's graph.
   b) What trends do you see in your graph?

Monthly Precipitation (mm)

	Jan	Feb	Mar	Apr	May	Jun	Jul	Aug	Sep	Oct	Nov	Dec
Cairns, Australia	400	410	430	190	90	40	20	20	30	30	90	170
Prince Rupert, B.C.	240	190	210	160	130	100	120	130	190	310	310	280

Practising

3. a) Compare your broken-line graph in Question 2 to Karin's graph. How are they similar? How are they different?
   b) Can you compare two graphs that use different scales? Explain your answer.

4. The table shows the highest recorded temperature for each month in Ottawa.

Monthly Temperatures in Ottawa (°C)

Jan	Feb	Mar	Apr	May	Jun	Jul	Aug	Sep	Oct	Nov	Dec
10	12	23	30	32	35	35	33	32	27	20	16

   a) Create a broken-line graph for the monthly temperatures in Ottawa.
   b) Explain how you chose the scale for the vertical axis.
   c) Describe any trends you see in the graph.
   d) Give a reason for the trends.

5. a) Collect some data about the climate of another city or town.
   b) Make a broken-line graph of the data.
   c) Describe any trends you see in your graph.

3 Interpreting Circle Graphs

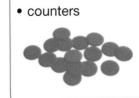

Goal Calculate the number represented by each part of a circle graph.

24 students in Grade 5 answered a survey about eye colour and glasses. The circle graphs show the results.

Eye Colour

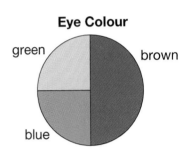

green   brown

blue

? **What do the graphs tell you about the students?**

A. Describe what each circle graph shows.

B. What fractions represent each part in the Eye Colour graph?

C. Use 24 counters to model the number of students surveyed. How many students are represented by each colour in the Eye Colour graph?

D. How many students are represented by each fraction in the Wears Glasses graph?

E. Suppose the survey results apply to all Grade 5 students. How would your answers to Parts C and D change if half as many Grade 5 students were surveyed?

F. How would your answers to Parts C and D change if 100 Grade 5 students were surveyed?

G. Choose different numbers for the total number of Grade 5 students surveyed. Calculate the number of students represented by each fraction in both graphs.

Wears Glasses

yes

no

Reflecting

1. Which numbers could you choose in Part G to get a whole number of students in each part of the circle graphs?

2. How does knowing the number of students in one part of a circle graph help you to calculate the number of students in the other parts?

4 Bar Graphs with Intervals

Goal Use the range to estimate the size of intervals to construct a bar graph.

Akiko collected the heart rates for the 28 students in her class.

Heart Rates (beats in one minute)

70	60	53	76	84	68	62
80	74	70	84	60	76	68
70	72	78	66	54	72	56
68	72	70	60	78	80	76

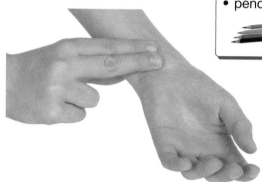

? **What intervals can Akiko use for a heart-rate bar graph?**

Akiko's Method

I'll use the **range** and number of **intervals** to estimate the size of each interval on my bar graph.

The range in heartbeats is 53 to 84, or about 30.

I think I'll choose three or four intervals and make three or four bars on my bar graph. Each interval will be 10. The first will be 50 to 59.

A. What other intervals and endpoints can Akiko use for her bar graph?

B. Make a tally chart with intervals to organize the heart-rate data.

C. Use your tally chart to make a bar graph.

interval

The distance between two endpoints on a graph scale. Intervals on a graph should be equal.

This graph shows intervals of 5.

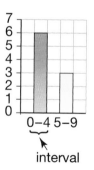

The endpoints of this interval are 0 and 4.

Reflecting

1. a) How can you determine the range of the data?
   b) How can you use the range and number of intervals to determine the size of each interval?

2. Describe how a bar graph changes if you increase the size of the intervals.

Checking

3. A veterinarian recorded the heart rates of 20 hamsters in a petting zoo.
   a) What is the range of the data?
   b) How many intervals or bars would you use for a bar graph of the data? Explain how to use the range to estimate the size of each interval on a bar graph.

Hamster Heart Rates (beats in one minute)

450	410	400	450	460
470	430	435	450	450
440	480	499	455	450
450	450	460	470	400

Practising

4. a) Make a tally chart and a bar graph of the hamster heart-rate data. Use the intervals you chose in Question 3.
   b) Would it make sense to choose an interval size of 5 to graph the data? Why or why not?

5. Fawn showed her class a baby blanket that her mother made. She asked the 22 students to look at the blanket and estimate the number of rhombus patches. She recorded the 22 estimates.

Estimates of Number of Rhombus Patches

150	75	300	84	95	150	160	300	100	115	150
250	120	120	180	204	123	125	240	240	145	150

   a) What is the range of the data?
   b) Choose a number of bars for a bar graph of the data. Explain how to use the range to determine the size of each interval on your bar graph.
   c) Make a tally chart and a bar graph of the data.

5 Pictographs

Goal Use whole and partial symbols
to display data on a pictograph.

Jose is making a pictograph of data for some cities in Canada
with high numbers of lightning flashes.

**Number of Lightning
Flashes Each Year**

City	Lightning flashes each year
Toronto, ON	200
Windsor, ON	251
Regina, SK	113

? **How can Jose show his data
on a pictograph?**

Jose's Pictograph

Step 1 For my scale, I chose each 🗲 means
20 lightning flashes.

I chose 20 because I don't want too many
symbols.

I can show 10 as a half symbol and 5 as a
quarter symbol.

Step 2 Toronto gets 10 whole symbols.

Step 3 For Windsor, I use 12 whole symbols and
1 half symbol. That's close to 251.

Step 4 To figure out the number of symbols for Regina, I keep multiplying by 20.

$4 \times 20 = 80$ 4 symbols are not enough.

$5 \times 20 = 100$ 5 symbols are not enough.

$6 \times 20 = 120$ 6 symbols are too many.

I'll use 5 whole symbols and a partial symbol.

$113 - 100 = 13$

I'll show 15 more flashes. I can use a half symbol to represent 10 and a quarter symbol to represent the other 5.

Step 5 I made this pictograph.

Number of Lightning Flashes Each Year

Windsor, ON ⚡⚡⚡⚡⚡⚡⚡⚡⚡⚡⚡

Toronto, ON ⚡⚡⚡⚡⚡⚡⚡⚡⚡⚡

Regina, SK ⚡⚡⚡⚡⚡⚡

Each ⚡ means 20 lightning flashes.

Reflecting

1. How did Jose decide how many whole and partial symbols to use for Toronto and Windsor?

2. Is it possible to use Jose's pictograph to determine the exact number of lightning flashes for each city? Explain.

3. a) What other scale could Jose use for the lightning-flash data?

   b) Would a scale of 25 lightning flashes be a good choice? Explain your thinking.

Checking

4. a) Make a pictograph for the data.

Number of Lightning Flashes Each Year

City	Lightning flashes each year
Hamilton, ON	191
Kitchener, ON	164
Winnipeg, MB	80
Calgary, AB	79
Saskatoon, SK	71

b) Explain how your pictograph would change if you used a different scale.

Practising

5. A Grade 5 class counted the number of birds on a lake in Saskatchewan one day in May.

Number of Birds on the Lake

Type of bird	Number of birds
American white pelican	105
redhead duck	154
blue-winged teal	192
ruddy duck	95

ruddy duck

For each scale, how many whole and partial symbols do you need to show each type of bird?

a) Each ● means 20 birds.   b) Each ■ means 40 birds.

6. Pete's Pizza Zone recorded the number of pizzas sold over five days.

a) Draw a pictograph of the data using whole and partial symbols. Make sure you show the scale.

b) Explain how you decided on the number of whole and partial symbols to represent the number of pizzas sold on Wednesday.

Pizzas Sold in Five Days

Day	Number of pizzas
Monday	165
Tuesday	180
Wednesday	145
Thursday	198
Friday	230

Mid-Chapter Review

LESSON

1

1. Olivia surveyed 120 Girl Guides in her town about their favourite camping activity. Are the results of her survey likely to apply to 120 people in each of these groups? Why or why not?
   a) Sparks (Girl Guides who are 5 to 6 years old)
   b) senior citizens
   c) Grade 5 students

2

2. This broken-line graph shows the amount of fresh fruit eaten each year by the average Canadian.
   a) What is the scale on the vertical axis?
   b) What trend do you see?

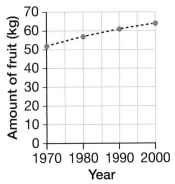

Fresh Fruit Eaten by Canadians Each Year

4

3. Philip collected the breathing rates of the 28 students in his class. He wants to draw a bar graph with at least three bars.
   a) What is the range of the data?
   b) What interval size can you use to graph the data?
   c) List the endpoints of the intervals.
   d) Use your intervals to organize the breathing-rate data in a tally chart.

Breathing Rates
(breaths in one minute)

22	26	25	25	15	15	9
17	15	14	19	22	20	20
9	13	10	14	16	9	19
12	11	14	14	25	20	19

5

4. The average Canadian adult drinks these amounts of beverages in one year.
   a) Make a pictograph of the data.
   b) Explain how you chose your scale.
   c) Explain how you decided on the number of whole and partial symbols for pop.

Amount of Beverages in One Year

Beverage	Amount (L)
pop	113
coffee	101
tea	70
bottled water	28

6 Changing the Appearance of a Graph

Goal Explain how changing the scale of a graph can affect its appearance.

Drake made two graphs to show the results of a survey about favourite types of cheese for sale at a food fair.

Favourite Cheese

Cheese	Number of people
gouda	951
cheddar	987
brie	955

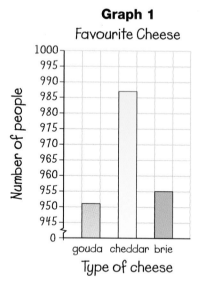

Graph 1
Favourite Cheese

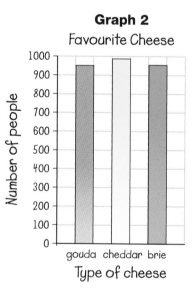

Graph 2
Favourite Cheese

? How does changing the scale of a graph change its appearance?

A. Which graph seems to show that about the same number of people like cheddar, gouda, and brie?

B. Which graph seems to show that many more people like cheddar than gouda or brie?

C. Do the graphs use the same data? Explain how you know.

D. How are the two graphs different?

E. How do the differences affect the appearance of the graphs?

Reflecting

1. What is the meaning of the symbol ⸕ on the vertical axis of graph 1? Explain your reasoning.

2. Why didn't Drake use the same scale to make both graphs?

3. a) Describe what would happen to the bars on graph 1 if the scale on the vertical axis started at 900.
   b) What if the scale started at 960?
   c) How can you make graphs that display data well, but don't use too much paper?

Checking

4. A vendor at a stadium collected data about favourite hot-dog toppings. She used the data to create a bar graph.

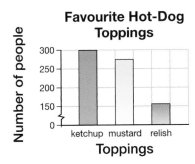

Favourite Hot-Dog Toppings

Ketchup	Mustard	Relish	Hot peppers
300	275	155	42

   a) What does the graph appear to show about the popularity of the toppings?
   b) Make a bar graph with a different scale to show less of a difference between the bars.

Practising

5. These two broken-line graphs show the number of students participating in provincial science fairs over several years.

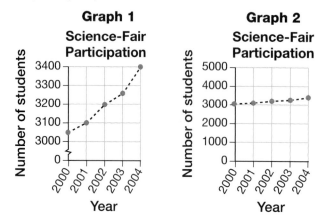

Graph 1
Science-Fair Participation

Graph 2
Science-Fair Participation

a) Which graph seems to show a greater increase in attendance?

b) Do the graphs appear to show the same data? Explain your reasoning.

c) Which graph might the organizers of the science fair prefer to show sponsors? Explain your choice.

6. Sagitha used data about the amount of pop the average Canadian drinks in a year to make a bar graph.

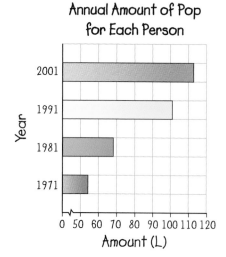

Annual Amount of Pop for Each Person

Year	1971	1981	1991	2001
Amount (L)	54	68	101	113

a) Draw another graph that appears to show smaller increases from decade to decade.

b) Describe how your scale differs from Sagitha's scale.

7 Graphing with Technology

Goal Use graphing software to organize and display data.

Two fruit pits were tossed in a game played by First Nations people. One pit was marked with 2 dots on one side and 3 dots on the other side.

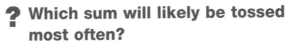

The other pit had 4 dots on one side and 5 dots on the other side. Players tossed the pits and found the sum of the dots.

? **Which sum will likely be tossed most often?**

A. What are the possible sums?

B. Predict which sum might be tossed most often.

C. Place a piece of masking tape on each side of two counters.

Draw 2 dots and 3 dots on one counter.

Draw 4 dots and 5 dots on the other counter.

D. Toss your counters 25 times and use a tally chart to record the number of times each sum is tossed.

E. Combine the results of all the students in your class. Make a bar graph of the class results using software.

F. Use the class results to create a circle graph.

Reflecting

1. Explain how your bar graph can be used to check your prediction.

2. Describe what you notice about the size of the parts in your circle graph.

8 Mean and Mode

Goal Calculate the mean and identify the mode of a set of data.

The manager of a new movie theatre is giving theatre discount coupons to 10 friends.

? **What discount will each friend get?**

Alain's Solution

We each get one discount coupon.

I wonder which discount most of us will get.

I'll list the discounts to see which appears most often.

Monique's Solution

I think we should share the total value of all 10 coupons equally.

I wonder which discount we'll each get.

I make cube towers showing each discount.

Then I move cubes from one tower to another until all the towers have the same number of cubes.

mode

The number that occurs most often in a group of numbers

0, 5, <u>1, 1</u>, 3

The mode of these numbers is 1.

A. Alain decided to identify the **mode**. Complete Alain's solution.

B. Monique decided to calculate the **mean**.
Use linking cubes to complete her solution.

Reflecting

1. How can the friends use Alain's solution?

2. How can the friends use Monique's solution?

mean

Numbers rearranged to make equal shares

0, 5, 1, 1, 3

The mean of these numbers is 2.

Checking

3. What would be the mode and mean solutions if the friends were offered these discount coupons instead?

Practising

4. Calculate the mean and identify the mode discount for three coupons of $3, $3, and $6. Describe your steps.

5. Create a set of three discount coupons for each description.
   a) The mode is 1 and the mean is 2.
   b) The mode is 0 and the mean is 3.

6. a) What is the mean of 3, 4, and 5?
   b) What is the mean of 8, 9, and 10?
   c) What do you notice about the mean of each set of three consecutive numbers?
   d) Predict the mean of 21, 22, and 23.
      Calculate the mean to check your prediction.

7. Paul solved one crossword puzzle each week for a month. These are the hours he spent solving the puzzles: 10, 10, 10, and 2.
   a) What are the mode and mean number of hours?
   b) Which number would likely impress his friends about his ability to solve crossword puzzles? Explain your thinking.
   c) Which number better represents the number of hours that he usually takes to solve a puzzle? Explain your thinking.

9 Communicate About Graphs

Goal Evaluate the accuracy of a graph and suggest ways to present data accurately.

Anna's school can buy more equipment for only one sport. The Grade 5 students were asked to choose their favourite sport from a list.

A student made this pictograph to show the results.

Our Favourite Sports

baseball	59
soccer	35
basketball	29
floor hockey	21

Our Favourite Sports

soccer

basketball

floor hockey

? **How well does the graph represent the data?**

Anna's Evaluation

The graph is not accurate. The symbols are all different sizes. It looks like basketball is the favourite sport, but the data in the chart show that it isn't. The graph should show symbols that are the same size.

A. What can you add to Anna's evaluation? Use the Communication Checklist.

Communication Checklist

☑ Did you check the scale?

☑ Did you include all of the data?

☑ Did you draw and label the graph correctly?

Reflecting

1. How did the Communication Checklist help you to improve Anna's evaluation of the pictograph?

2. Why might the Our Favourite Sports chart be more useful to the school than a pictograph?

Checking

3. Marcus evaluated this graph. What can you add to Marcus's evaluation of the graph? Use the Communication Checklist.

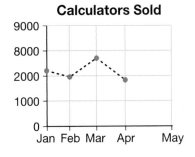

Calculators Sold

Marcus's Evaluation

The graph is not accurate. The distances between the months on the horizontal axis are not the same.

Calculators Sold

Month	Jan	Feb	Mar	Apr	May
Sales ($)	1500	2000	8000	1800	1000

Practising

4. The bar graph represents 20 five-pin bowling scores in a tournament.
   a) Evaluate the graph. Use the Communication Checklist.
   b) Sketch a more accurate graph.

Bowling Scores

267	157	244	174	216	260	197	248	211	154
178	200	209	249	180	209	185	192	227	152

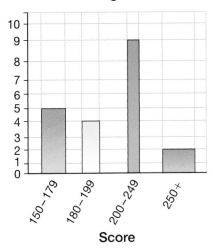

Bowling Scores

Identifying the Mode on a Stem-and-Leaf Plot

Stella made a **stem-and-leaf plot** to display the heights of the 22 students in her class.
Stella's height is **124** cm.

stem-and-leaf plot

A way to organize data in groups.
The stem shows the beginning of the number and the leaf shows the rest.

Height (cm)										
11	8	9								
12	1	4	7	8	9					
13	0	0	0	0	0	1	1	1	1	5	9
14	0	2	2	3						

1
a) What is the height of the shortest student in the class? What is the height of the tallest student?
b) What is the range of heights?
c) What is the mode height?

2
Three new students join the class.
Their heights are 145 cm, 131 cm, and 131 cm.
a) Draw a new stem-and-leaf plot for all 25 students.
b) Which answers to Question 1 will change? What are the new answers?

Tossing Modes

Number of players: 2 to 4

How to play: Toss a die six times and identify the mode.

Step 1   Decide who goes first. Player 1 tosses a die six times and records each number.

Step 2   Player 1 identifies the mode. Player 1's score is the mode. If there is more than one mode, score zero.

Step 3   Take turns tossing the die and identifying the mode. Add each score to the player's total. Play until one player reaches a total of 20.

Camille's Turn

I rolled 6, 4, 4, 1, 2, 4.

The mode is 4.

I score 4 points.

Heather's Turn

I rolled 1, 3, 3, 1, 5, 6.

1 and 3 each came up twice.

There are 2 modes. I get 0 points.

Skills Bank

LESSON

2

1. Vincent measured the height in millimetres of his bean plant. Describe any trends you see in the broken-line graph.

Height of Bean Plant

Height (mm) vs. Day (Mon, Tue, Wed, Thu, Fri)

2. The data show the amount of bottled water the average Canadian drank each year.
   a) Make a broken-line graph to show the data.
   b) Describe any trends that you see in your graph.

Amount of Bottled Water Each Year

Year	1995	1996	1997	1998	1999	2000
Amount of water (L)	18	20	21	23	25	28

4

3. Chantal tossed a red die and a white die to make a two-digit number. She used the number on the red die to represent tens and the number on the white die to represent ones. She recorded the results for 50 tosses.

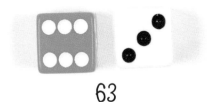

63

Results for 50 Tosses

21	63	55	41	65	53	26	33	52	36
45	22	33	22	44	31	54	66	51	23
12	53	52	33	55	12	43	62	43	15
34	51	24	12	25	34	21	12	43	54
45	61	33	26	43	35	41	23	44	61

   a) What is the range of the data?
   b) Chantal wants her graph to show about six bars. What intervals can she choose for the graph?
   c) Use Chantal's data to create a tally chart and a bar graph.

5 **4.** The chart shows the results of a survey of several homes.

Sergei wants to use blue recycling bins for the symbols on his pictograph.

For each scale, estimate the number of whole and partial symbols needed to represent each item.

a) Each 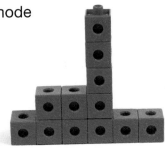 means 20 homes.

b) Each 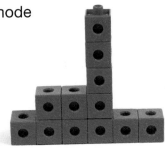 means 40 homes.

c) Each 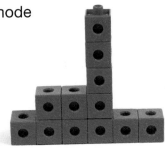 means a number of homes of your choice.

What People Recycle

Item	Number
paper	212
metal cans	215
glass bottles	230
plastics	218
no recycling	199

6 **5.** Simone kept track of the number of minutes she spent travelling each day in a week.

Time Spent Travelling This Week

Mon	Tue	Wed	Thu	Fri	Sat	Sun
35	22	21	23	40	21	23

She used the data to make a bar graph.

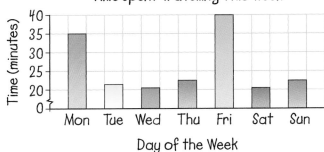

a) What does the graph appear to show about the time Simone spent travelling?

b) Sketch a graph with a different scale that shows less of a difference between the bars.

8 **6.** Calculate the mean and identify the mode for each set of numbers.

a) 1, 2, 2, 5, 1, 1

b) 0, 3, 0, 0, 7

c) 1, 5, 5, 0, 5, 2

Problem Bank

2

1. Elvin recorded the high temperatures for one week in July. On Monday the high temperature was 24°C. Each day after was 2°C warmer than the previous day.
   a) Draw a broken-line graph showing the temperatures for that week.
   b) Describe any trends you see in the graph.
   c) Predict how the graph would change if each day was 3°C warmer than the day before.

4

2. The graph shows the number of students at each of the 100 schools in a city.
   a) What number of schools might each bar represent? Explain your reasoning.
   b) What do you think is the scale on the vertical axis? Explain your reasoning.

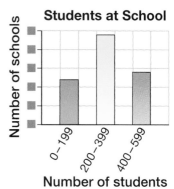

Students at School

5

3. Mona surveyed all the students in her school about how they travelled to school. She made a pictograph of the results, but forgot to complete the scale.
   a) What is the scale if 210 students walked to school? Explain your reasoning.
   b) Show how to use the pictograph to estimate the total number of students in the school.

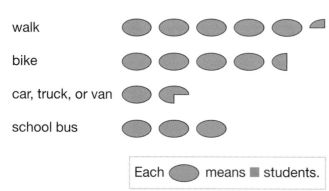

Travelling to School

walk

bike

car, truck, or van

school bus

Each ⬭ means ■ students.

6

4. *Fish Owner* magazine asked its readers how many fish they owned. They graphed the results of their survey.
   a) Describe what happens to the graph if the scale on the vertical axis is kept the same, but includes numbers from 0 to 800.
   b) Show how to use the graph to estimate the number of people who answered the survey.

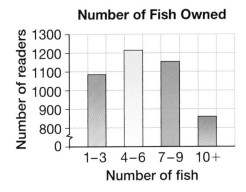

Number of Fish Owned

8

5. a) Determine the mode and mean of five numbers of your choice.
   b) Add 2 to each of your numbers. Determine the mode and mean of these new numbers.
   c) How do the mode and mean in part b) compare to the mode and mean in part a)?
   d) Predict the mean and mode if you added 3 to each of your numbers from part a). Test your prediction.

6. Alain shared linking cubes to calculate the mean of four numbers.
   a) What number of linking cubes might have been in each of the four groups before Alain began sharing?
   b) How would your answer to part a) change if the mode of the four groups was 0?

7. Choose three numbers that have a mode of 2 and a mean of 3.

Chapter Review

2

1. On a day in May, Monika recorded the length of her shadow each hour.

Length of Shadow Each Hour

Time	8:00 a.m.	9:00 a.m.	10:00 a.m.	11:00 a.m.	noon	1:00 p.m.	2:00 p.m.	3:00 p.m.	4:00 p.m.	5:00 p.m.	6:00 p.m.
Shadow length (cm)	354	246	171	131	110	105	121	143	228	280	360

a) Make a broken-line graph of her data.
b) Explain how you chose the scale on the vertical axis.
c) Describe any trends that you see in the graph.

4

2. Malik found the age when each of Canada's first 21 prime ministers was first elected.

a) Determine the range of the data.
b) What interval size would you choose for a bar graph?
c) How many bars will be on the graph?
d) Make a tally chart and a bar graph of the age data.

Age When First Elected

52 51 70 48 70 74 54

57 46 47 60 66 61 65

48 39 55 45 46 59 65

5

3. a) Make a pictograph using whole and partial symbols for the lifespan data.

Animal Lifespans

Animal	Lifespan (years)
alligator	56
box turtle	123
crocodile	45
Galapagos land turtle	193

box turtle

b) Explain how you chose your symbol and scale.
c) Explain how you determined the number of whole and partial symbols to show each animal lifespan.

4. The chart shows the number of passengers riding on special-needs buses each month in a city.

Passengers Each Month

Month	Passengers
December	4106
January	4178
February	4317
March	4576

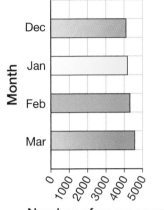

Graph 1
Passengers Each Month

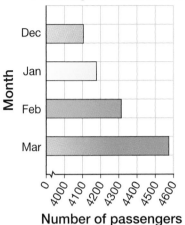

Number of passengers

Graph 2
Passengers Each Month

Number of passengers

a) What does each graph appear to show?
b) Do the graphs use the same data? Explain your reasoning.
c) Which graph would you use to persuade the bus operators to provide the same number of buses each month? Explain your choice.

5. Students are reading at four tables in the library.
   a) Which problem can be solved by calculating the mean?
   b) Which problem can be solved by identifying the mode?
   c) What are the mean and mode?

Problem A

If you count the number of students at each table, what number will you get most often?

Problem B

If you want each table to have the same number of students, how many students will be at each table?

Chapter Task

Swimsuit Sales

The table shows the number of swimsuits sold each month at Swimsuit Village.

The manager of the store plans to make a broken-line graph of the data to help him decide which months require the most staff.

Swimsuit Village Sales

Month	Jan	Feb	Mar	Apr	May	Jun	Jul	Aug	Sep	Oct	Nov	Dec
Swimsuits sold	450	559	89	145	243	513	856	938	136	107	84	356

? **In which months should the store have the most staff?**

A. Why do you think the manager chose a broken-line graph instead of another type of graph?

B. Make a broken-line graph to show the swimsuit data.

C. Describe some trends that you see in the broken-line graph.

D. Give a reason why you might expect to see these trends.

E. In which months should the store have the most staff?

Task Checklist

☑ Did you explain how you chose the scale?

☑ Did you include all the data in your graph?

☑ Did you use math language?

Cumulative Review

Cross-Strand Multiple Choice

1. How many rhombuses and triangles are in the seventh flower of this pattern?
   A. 7 rhombuses, 14 triangles
   B. 8 rhombuses, 16 triangles
   C. 7 rhombuses, 16 triangles
   D. 8 rhombuses, 14 triangles

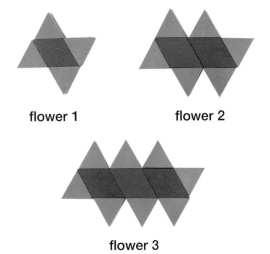

flower 1 flower 2

flower 3

2. Which does *not* represent ninety-four thousand one hundred four?
   A. 94 104
   B. 100 more than 94 004
   C. 90 000 + 4000 + 100 + 4
   D. 9 ten thousands, 1 hundred, 4 ones

3. Which set of numbers is in order from least to greatest?
   A. 0.9, 0.92, 0.29, 0.90, 1.09
   B. 0.1, 1, 1.03, 1.31, 1.33
   C. 2.8, 2, 1.98, 1.88, 1.8
   D. 0.06, 0.56, 0.5, 0.6, 0.60

4. Which best describes the trends in this graph?
   A. the temperature increases
   B. the temperature decreases
   C. the temperature decreases and then increases
   D. the temperature increases and then decreases

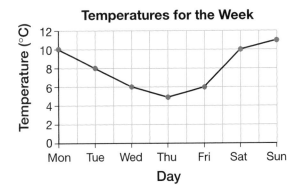

Temperatures for the Week

5. Yoshi went for a hike each Saturday for a month. He hiked 6 km, 5 km, 8 km, and 5 km. What is the mean distance that he hiked each day?
   A. 6 km   B. 24 km   C. 5 km   D. 7 km

Cross-Strand Investigation

Hot Off the Press!

When People Get Together

When people get together, they can do amazing things. In 2003, 10 240 students in China all brushed their teeth at the same time! Why do people like to set records? Because it's fun!

Here are some team records:

In 1996, 72 000 people danced the chicken dance together at a fair.

In 2002, 48 824 people got together for the world's largest aerobics class.

In 2000, a team of students stacked 9455 cans in a pyramid.

Some Really Big Animals!

Animal	Length (m)
elephant seal	6.52
polar bear	2.61
tiger	2.80
giraffe	5.83
camel	3.58

6. **a)** Find a number in the magazine that is between 30 000 and 50 000. Represent the number in three ways.
   b) Order the animal lengths from least to greatest. Sketch a base ten model to represent the least and the greatest length.
   c) Choose a number from the magazine. Do you think the number is rounded? Explain why or why not.

7. **a)** Make a graph to show the data for new magazine subscribers. Explain how you decided what scale to use.
   b) Describe what the graph shows about the magazine. Who might use these data? How?
   c) Create a problem you can solve with the data. Solve your problem.

New Magazine Subscribers

Month	New subscribers
March	152
April	181
May	203
June	251
July	289

8. Martin and Rosa wanted to find out how long it would take to collect cans to make a pyramid. They started collecting cans on October 1. Martin started with 18 cans and collected 4 more each day. Rosa started with 8 cans and collected 5 more each day.
   a) Write pattern rules for Rosa's and Martin's patterns.
   b) How many days will it take Martin and Rosa to collect at least 100 cans altogether?

Addition and Subtraction

FREE
END PARKING

CLEARANCE 1.9 M

VEHICLES OVER
IN HEIGHT ONLY ↑

4.1 m
↓

DURHAM

FARM FRESH

WILLOWTREE FARM
5.5 km →

SPADEMAN TREE FARM
→

REGULAR UNLEADED
PER LITRE 79⁹

DIESEL
PER LITRE 65⁹

PROPANE
PER LITRE 57⁹

WELCOME TO THE

TOWN OF TABER

TABER
LAND OF THE LOOONG SUN

POPULATION 6400

ELEVATION 806 M

Signs all around

Goals

You will be able to

- add and subtract mentally
- estimate sums and differences
- use addition and subtraction to solve one-step and two-step problems
- add and subtract four-digit whole numbers and decimals
- calculate the total cost of purchases and the amount of change

Getting Started

Going to the Movies

You enter a contest and win these movie gift certificates.

You want to use them to take some adults, some classmates, and yourself to a movie.

? **What group of people can you take to a movie?**

Admission
Adults $12.95
Children $ 7.50

A. Use estimation to decide on a group of people you can take to a movie. Show your work.

B. Calculate the cost of taking that group to a movie.

C. Did you use mental math, pencil and paper, or a calculator to calculate the cost of taking your group to a movie? Explain your choice.

D. Compare your answer to Part B to your estimate in Part A. Is your answer reasonable?

E. What combination of gift certificates can you use? Explain how you decided on that combination.

F. What change would you get if you used the gift certificates from Part E?

G. Create and solve a problem about taking some adults and some classmates to two movies.

Do You Remember?

1. The population of a town is just over 6000.
   The number of children living in the town is 767.
   About how many adults live in the town?
   Explain how you estimated.

2. Show two ways to subtract 775 from 1000.

3. Estimate and then calculate. Show your work.
   a) $4566 + 1837 = \blacksquare$ c) $3000 - 865 = \blacksquare$
   b) $2756 + 4248 = \blacksquare$ d) $3299 + \blacksquare = 6348$

4. Use mental math.
   a) $75 + 26$ b) $15 + 69$ c) $100 - 15$ d) $80 - 18$

Adding and Subtracting Using Mental Math

Goal Use mental math strategies to add and subtract.

The CN Tower has 1769 steps that the public may climb. Aaron set a goal to climb 1000 of the steps.

? **How many more steps do you have to climb after each rest to reach a goal of 1000 steps?**

A. Use mental math to calculate the number of steps Aaron has left to climb after rest 1. Describe your strategy.

B. Use mental math to calculate the number of steps Aaron has left to climb after rest 2. Describe your strategy.

C. Climbing stairs is tiring. After rest 2, Aaron climbs fewer steps between rests. How many steps might he climb between the remaining rests?

D. Use your numbers from Part C to calculate the number of steps Aaron has left to climb after rests 3 and 4.

E. Aaron will reach his goal with five rests. Describe how you would reach the same goal with five rests. How many steps would you have left to climb after each rest?

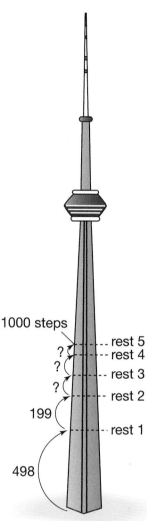

Reflecting

1. Compare your mental math strategy for Part B to the strategies of your classmates.

2. Did the numbers you chose for Part E allow you to use mental math? Explain why or why not.

Open Sentences

An open sentence or equation contains one or more symbols that represent numbers. The sentence may always, sometimes, or never be true when numbers replace the symbols.

Liam's Open Sentence

I'll work with this sentence.

$5 + \blacksquare > 12$

I replace $\blacksquare$ with 8.

$5 + 8 > 12$ true

I replace $\blacksquare$ with 2.

$5 + 2 > 12$ not true

The open sentence $5 + \blacksquare > 12$ is sometimes true.

1 If the missing number is a whole number, is each open sentence always true, sometimes true, or never true? Give a reason for each answer.

a) $222 + \blacksquare = 227$
b) $25 + \blacksquare = \blacksquare + 25$
c) $100 > 105 + \blacksquare$
d) $123 - \blacksquare < 200$

2 Explain why the open sentence $\blacksquare - 99 = \blacksquare - 100 + 1$ is always true.

3
a) Write an open sentence that is always true.
b) Write an open sentence that is never true.
c) Write an open sentence that is true for only one value of the missing number.

2 Estimating Sums and Differences

You will need

• a calculator

Goal Estimate sums and differences and justify your strategy.

Monique's ringette coach is comparing the number of ringette players in different provinces. She knows there are 2475 players in Quebec. The chart shows data for Ontario players.

Ontario Ringette Players

Group	Players
Bunny (ages 4–6)	1198
Novice (ages 7–9)	1510
Petite (ages 10–11)	1454
Tween (ages 12–13)	1354

? **How many more ringette players are there in Ontario than in Quebec?**

The coach used a calculator to figure out the total number of players in Ontario. Some team members thought the calculation was unreasonable.

Monique's Estimate

I round each number down to a lower thousand and calculate the total.

$1000 + 1000 + 1000 + 1000 = 4000$

I round each number up to the next thousand and calculate the total.

$2000 + 2000 + 2000 + 2000 = 8000$

I estimate that the total is between 4000 and 8000.

I can **justify** this estimation strategy. It gives me a range for the total, and I only have to add digits in the thousands place.

Akiko's Estimate

I estimate that the total is about 5600.

Jasleen's Estimate

I estimate that the total is about 5000.

A. What strategies might Akiko and Jasleen have used to estimate?

B. Calculate the total number of players in Ontario.

C. Estimate how many more ringette players there are in Ontario than in Quebec. Show your work.

D. Calculate how many more ringette players there are in Ontario than in Quebec.

E. Compare your calculated answer to your estimate. Is your answer reasonable? Explain.

Reflecting

1. a) Are all three estimates for the total number of players in Ontario reasonable?
   b) What estimation strategy would you have used? Justify your choice.

2. Justify your choice of estimation strategy for Part C.

Checking

Alberta Ringette Players

Group	Players
Bunny	511
Novice	710
Petite	701
Tween	585

3. a) Estimate the total number of players in Alberta. Justify your choice of estimation strategy.
   b) Calculate the total number of players in Alberta. Compare your answer to your estimate. Is your answer reasonable?
   c) Calculate how many more players there are in Ontario than in Alberta. Is your answer reasonable?

Practising

Soccer Players

Group	Players
youth indoor	3304
senior indoor	1281
youth outdoor	6254
senior outdoor	6303

4. The chart shows data for soccer players in a city. How many more outdoor soccer players are there than indoor soccer players? For each step, estimate to check the reasonableness of your calculation. Justify your choices of estimation strategies.

5. Estimate to determine which calculations are reasonable. Show how you estimated. For one estimate, justify your choice of estimation strategy.
   a) $7003 - 3567 = 4436$
   b) $1259 + 745 + 5567 = 7571$

3 Adding Whole Numbers

Goal Add 3 four-digit whole numbers using paper and pencil.

A forklift operator wants to lift several crates at one time. The forklift can safely lift up to 7000 kg at once.

? **Which combination of three crates can the forklift safely lift?**

Capacity 7000 kg

1899 kg Screws

3045 kg Nuts

2357 kg Rivets

1289 kg Nails

Teresa's Addition

I'll try the screws, nuts, and rivets first.

Their total mass is about 7000 kg.

I can calculate the actual mass by adding from left to right.

```
    1 8 9 9
    3 0 4 5
+   2 3 5 7
    6 0 0 0
    1 1 0 0
```

Martin's Addition

The total mass of the screws, nuts, and rivets is about 7300 kg.

I can calculate the actual mass by regrouping.

```
        2
    1 8 9 9
    3 0 4 5    9 + 5 + 7 = 21
+   2 3 5 7    21 = 2 tens + 1 one
          1
```

A. Explain why Teresa wrote 6000 and 1100 in her first two steps.

B. Complete Teresa's addition. Show your work.

C. Complete Martin's addition. Show your work.

D. Can the forklift safely lift the screws, nuts, and rivets together? Why or why not?

E. Calculate the total for other combinations.
   What combinations can the forklift safely lift?

Reflecting

1. a) Why might Martin and Teresa have estimated first?
   b) Show how you would have estimated.

2. Which addition method do you prefer for this problem? Explain.

3. Should forklift operators underestimate or overestimate the mass of the crates they want to lift? Why?

Checking

4. The forklift operator needs to move the original four crates, as well as these washers and bolts.
   a) Determine two new combinations of three crates that can be lifted together safely.
   b) Is there a combination of four crates that can be lifted together safely? Explain.

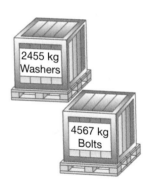

2455 kg
Washers

4567 kg
Bolts

Practising

5. Estimate and then add. Show your work.

   a)   4273   b)   5689   c)   1657
         2539   1291   2657
       + 1203   + 389   + 4089

6. Add. Show your work.
   a) 1259 + 3618 + 987   b) 8963 + 2364 + 1221

7. A larger forklift lifts four crates with a total mass of 9600 kg. What might the mass of each crate be? Explain your reasoning.

4 Solve Two-Step Problems

Goal Select operations and solve two-step problems.

On the day Glynis turns 12, her aunt will turn 25.

? **About how many days older is Glynis's aunt than Glynis?**

Glynis's Solution

Understand

I have to find the difference between age 12 and age 25 in days.

Make a Plan

I'll calculate my age and my aunt's age in days by multiplying each of the number of years by 365. I'm going to ignore leap years.

Then I need to calculate the difference.

A. Carry out Glynis's plan and solve the problem. Show your work.

Reflecting

1. Explain how Glynis might have known that the problem needed more than one step to solve.

2. Describe how you can solve the problem using a different set of steps.

Checking

3. Glynis's brother is 2453 days older than her.
   Glynis's sister is 1562 days younger than her.
   How many years older is Glynis's brother than her sister?
   a) Which two operations will you perform to solve this problem? Justify your choices.
   b) Solve the problem.
   c) For each calculation, did you use mental math, pencil and paper, or a calculator? Justify your choices.

Practising

4. In October 1984, astronaut Marc Garneau became the first Canadian in space, aboard the *Challenger* shuttle. In January 1992, astronaut Roberta Bondar become the second Canadian in space, aboard the *Discovery* shuttle. How many months passed between the first and second Canadians in space? Show your work.

Roberta Bondar

5. Dieter sleeps about 9 hours each day. About how many hours is he awake for each period of time?
   a) one week   b) one month   c) one year

6. James Naismith of Canada is the inventor of basketball. He was born in 1861 and invented the game of basketball at the age of 30. How many years ago did he invent basketball?

7. Create and solve a two-step problem about comparing the ages in days of two people you know.

8. Each bag contains 124 red and black candies. Altogether, there are 3173 red candies in 50 bags. How many black candies are in the bags? Show your solution.

Mid-Chapter Review

LESSON

1. 1. Use mental math to calculate each answer.
   Show your strategy for two of your answers.
   a) 45 + 55   c) 9500 + 205   e) 1250 + 751
   b) 2000 + 455   d) 98 + 299   f) 1499 + 499

2. Explain how knowing that 200 + 300 = 500 can help
   you to calculate each answer.
   a) 199 + 299 = ■   c) 500 − 199 = ■   e) 198 + 302 = ■
   b) 205 + 325 = ■   d) 250 + 350 = ■   f) 500 − 301 = ■

2. 3. Use estimation to decide which answers are reasonable.
   Correct the unreasonable answers.
   a) 3176 + 2857 = 6033   d) 8087 − 1935 = 6152
   b) 6655 − 1596 = 3059   e) 256 + 118 + 978 + 253 = 1605
   c) 5965 + 3582 = 9547   f) 4508 + 497 + 3504 = 7509

3. 4. Calculate. Show your work.
   a) 1567 + 2366 + 3856   d) 1089 + 1789 + 2768
   b) 1249 + 5555 + 2643   e) 7234 + 1198 + 987
   c) 5488 + 1098 + 2387   f) 6243 + 1112 + 482

   5. a) Use estimation to determine the reasonableness of
      two of your calculations from Question 4.
      b) Justify your choice of strategy for each estimate in
      part a).

4. 6. Three crates with masses of 1099 kg, 1050 kg, and 1285 kg
   are in a freight elevator. The elevator can safely carry 5000 kg.
   A fourth crate is about to be loaded onto the elevator.
   What is the greatest mass it can safely be?

   7. A town has a population of 9000.
   The circle graph shows the number of
   people living in three areas of the town.
   How many people live in Eastside?
   Show your solution.

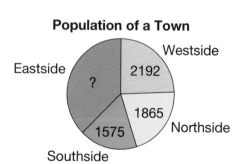

Population of a Town

Calculating Sums and Differences

You will need

- a calculator

Number of players: 4

How to play: Estimate sums and differences of four-digit numbers.

Step 1 Each player writes a four-digit number.

Step 2 Each player estimates the sum of all four numbers and the difference between any two of the numbers. Players record their estimates.

Step 3 Use a calculator or pencil and paper to calculate the sum and differences.

Step 4 Each player scores this number of points for each estimate:

> **Estimate within 1000: 1 point**
> **Estimate within 500: 2 points**

Continue for five turns. The player with the most points wins.

Norman's Turn

I estimate that the total is about 25 000.

I estimate 9841 − 7426 is about 2400.

How many points do I get?

5 Communicate About a Choice of Calculation Method

 Goal Justify your choice of calculation method and explain each step in solving a problem.

A bird sanctuary has a fence that is 8567 m long. What is the length of the side along the river?

? **How can Drake justify his calculation methods and explain how he found the length?**

1750 m

1875 m

1250 m

 Drake's Rough Copy

I used mental math to calculate the total length of the three sides that I know. The length is 4875 m.

I used pencil and paper to subtract the length of the three sides from the perimeter: $8567 - 4875 = 3692$

 Drake's Good Copy

I used mental math to add the three sides because it was easy to do.

To add 1750 and 1250, I thought: $\overbrace{1000 + 1000}^{2000} + \overbrace{750 + 250}^{1000} = 3000$

Then I added the length of the last side: $3000 + 1875 = 4875$

To subtract the total length of the three sides from the perimeter, I used pencil and paper. The numbers were too hard to use mental math.

The length of the side along the river is 3692 m.

$$\begin{array}{r} {\scriptstyle 14} \\ {\scriptstyle 7\ \,14\ \,16} \\ 8\,5\,6\,7 \\ -\ 4\,8\,7\,5 \\ \hline 3\,6\,9\,2 \end{array}$$

Reflecting

1. Describe the differences between Drake's rough copy and his good copy. Use the Communication Checklist.

Checking

2. Last year, 7929 people visited the bird sanctuary from May to August. The chart shows the number of visitors so far this year. About how many visitors are needed in August to match last year's attendance?

   Marcus wrote a rough copy justifying his calculation method and explaining his steps. Write a good copy. Use the Communication Checklist.

Visitors to Bird Sanctuary

Month	Visitors
May	1228
June	1875
July	1765

Marcus's Rough Copy

The problem asks "about" how many people, so I'll estimate.

The total this year is about 5000.

They need about 3000 visitors in August to match last year's attendance.

Practising

3. Amanda had 8356 reward points and traded them for these items. How many reward points does she have left?
   a) Solve the problem.
   b) Make a rough copy to justify your calculation method and explain your steps.
   c) How can you improve your rough copy? Use the Communication Checklist. Then write a good copy.

Reward Points Trade

Item	Points
DVD player	2500
watch	500
telescope	2300
donation to bird sanctuary	1700

6 Adding Decimals

Goal Add decimal tenths and hundredths using base ten blocks and pencil and paper.

You will need
- base ten blocks

- a decimal place value chart

Tens	Ones	Tenths	Hundredths

Yoshi's class is sending a wool sweater with a mass of 0.45 kg and an inukshuk sculpture with a mass of 1.76 kg to a class in Australia.

? **What is the total mass of the two gifts?**

Yoshi's Addition

I estimate that the total mass is between 2.00 kg and 2.50 kg.

I'll use blocks to represent these amounts.

| 1 | 0.1 | 0.01 |

Step 1 I model 1.76 and 0.45.

```
  1.76
+ 0.45
```

Step 2 I add the hundredths.
I regroup 11 hundredths as 1 tenth and 1 hundredth.

```
   1
  1.76
+ 0.45
     1
```

NEL

Step 3 I add the tenths.
I regroup 12 tenths as
1 one and 2 tenths.

$$\begin{array}{r} {\scriptstyle 1\,1} \\ 1.76 \\ +\ 0.45 \\ \hline 21 \end{array}$$

Ones	•	Tenths	Hundredths

Step 4 I add the ones.

$$\begin{array}{r} {\scriptstyle 1\,1} \\ 1.76 \\ +\ 0.45 \\ \hline 2.21 \end{array}$$

Ones	•	Tenths	Hundredths

The total mass of the gifts is 2.21 kg.

Reflecting

1. How is adding decimals like adding whole numbers?

2. If the class sent gifts with masses of 10.76 kg and 0.45 kg, how would you line up the numbers to calculate the total with pencil and paper?

Checking

3. Over the year, the class sent other packages to Australia. Each package contained several items. Estimate and then calculate the total mass of each package.

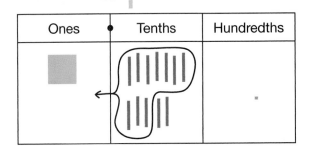

a) 0.85 kg and 5.38 kg   b) 1.25 kg, 1.65 kg, and 0.90 kg

Practising

4. Estimate and then add. Show your work.
   a) 5.9 + 4.9   c) 4.7 + 2.5
   b) 5.76 + 3.98   d) 3.66 + 2.34 + 0.85

5. Create a problem that involves the addition of two decimal numbers. Solve your problem.

7 Adding Money

Goal Use various methods to calculate the cost of purchases.

The class has this much money to buy magazine subscriptions.

They voted to buy *National Geographic for Kids* and *Owl*. They want to buy one more.

Magazine Subscriptions

Magazine	Cost
Boys' Life	12 issues: $54.74
Owl	10 issues: $29.95
National Geographic for Kids	10 issues: $35.95
Girls' Life	6 issues: $27.50
Sports Illustrated for Kids	12 issues: $29.90

Get your magazines here!

? Which other subscription can they buy?

Patrick's Method

First I'll calculate the cost of the subscriptions to *National Geographic for Kids* and *Owl*.

I'll regroup the cents so it's easier to add.

5¢

35.95 + 29.95

35.90 + 30.00

Juanita's Method

To get an exact cost, I'll add cents, dimes, and dollars.

$$\begin{array}{r} 1 \\ 35.95 \\ + 29.95 \\ \hline 0 \end{array}$$

5¢ + 5¢ = 10¢
10¢ = 1 dime + 0¢

$$\begin{array}{r} 1\,1 \\ 35.95 \\ + 29.95 \\ \hline .90 \end{array}$$

10¢ + 90¢ + 90¢ = 190¢
190¢ = $1 + 9 dimes

A. Use mental math to complete Patrick's method. Explain what you did.

B. Complete Juanita's method.

C. How much money does the class have left to spend after buying these two subscriptions?

D. Which other subscription can the class buy? How do you know?

Reflecting

1. Teresa used Patrick's method, but she transferred 5¢ from $29.95 to $35.95 instead. Would you transfer like Patrick or like Teresa? Why?

2. Juanita regrouped 190¢ as $1 and 9 dimes. How did this step help with the final step of the calculation?

3. Would you use Patrick's method or Juanita's method to calculate the total cost of subscriptions to *Boys' Life* and *Girls' Life*? Give a reason for your choice.

Checking

4. Estimate and calculate the total cost of each set of subscriptions. Show your work.
   a) *Boys' Life* and *Owl*
   b) *Boys' Life* and *National Geographic for Kids*
   c) *Owl*, *Girls' Life*, and *Sports Illustrated for Kids*

Practising

5. Estimate and then add. Show your work.

a) $\begin{array}{r} 1.99 \\ + \ 2.01 \\ \hline \end{array}$ c) $\begin{array}{r} 4.25 \\ + \ 15.75 \\ \hline \end{array}$ e) $\begin{array}{r} 9.99 \\ + \ 1.75 \\ \hline \end{array}$

b) $\begin{array}{r} 45.67 \\ 24.79 \\ + \ 16.87 \\ \hline \end{array}$ d) $\begin{array}{r} 28.63 \\ + \ 12.88 \\ \hline \end{array}$ f) $\begin{array}{r} 85.20 \\ 1.75 \\ + \ 10.93 \\ \hline \end{array}$

8 # Making Change

You will need
- a calculator

- play money

Goal Calculate change from purchases.

Karin's family plans to use earthworms to turn their garbage into food for plants. They have $100 to spend.

? **How much change will they receive after buying these items?**

Prices (tax included)
compost bin: $28.75
kitchen compost carrier: $24.24
bag of red wiggler worms: $14.38
Worms Eat My Garbage, book by Mary Appelhof: $26.39

Karin's Method

The total cost is $93.76.
I count on from $93.76
to $100 to calculate
the amount of change.

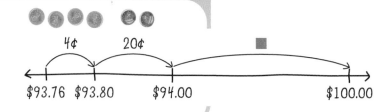

4¢   20¢

$93.76 $93.80 $94.00 $100.00

Norman's Method

The total cost is $93.76. I use mental math to calculate
the amount of change by subtracting in parts.

$100.00 − $93.76 = $100.00 − $90.00 − $3.00 − 76¢

$7.00 − 76¢

A. Complete Karin's method. Use a number line.

B. Check your answer by completing Norman's method.

Reflecting

1. Karin and Norman calculated the total cost. Would you use mental math, pencil and paper, or a calculator to calculate the total? Justify your choice.

2. Which method of calculating the amount of change do you prefer? Explain your choice.

Checking

3. Yasmina's class has $90 to purchase these materials.
   a) What is the total cost of the purchase?
   b) Use Norman's method to calculate the change.
   c) Use Karin's method to check your answer.

Prices (taxes included)

Worms Eat Our Garbage, activity book: $45.94

Mini-Muncher bin with red wiggler worms: $40.25

Practising

4. Calculate the total cost and the amount of change.

a) 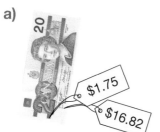 $1.75 $16.82

b)  $12.50 $13.75

c)  $27.89 $32.50

5. You have $100 to spend at a store with these items.
   a) Choose two items. Calculate the total cost of the items. Show your work.
   b) Calculate the amount of change you will receive. Show your work.

6. What is the cost of Yoshi's purchase? How much change did he receive? Show your work.

Prices (tax included)

watch: $43.75
calculator: $24.26
lunch box: $12.98
inline skates: $78.65
book: $29.98
CD: $26.75

 Yoshi's Purchase

25¢ more is $18.00 and $2.00 makes $20.00.

9 Subtracting Decimals

Goal Use base ten blocks and pencil and paper to subtract decimal tenths and hundredths.

Sofia's dog eats 0.75 kg of dog food each day.
She has 3.00 kg of dog food.

? **How much dog food will be left after one day?**

Sofia's Subtraction

First I'll estimate. 3.00 − 0.75 is close to 3 − 1 = 2,
so there will be more than 2 kg of food left.

Next I'll subtract 7 tenths 5 hundredths from 3.

I'll use blocks to represent these amounts.

| 1 | 0.1 | 0.01 |

Step 1 I model 3.00 kg.

$$\begin{array}{r} 3.00 \\ -\ 0.75 \end{array}$$

Ones	Tenths	Hundredths

Step 2 I regroup 1 one as 10 tenths, so I can take away 7 tenths. Now I have 2 ones and 10 tenths.

$$\begin{array}{r} {\scriptstyle 2\ 10} \\ 3.\cancel{0}0 \\ -\ 0.75 \end{array}$$

Ones	Tenths	Hundredths

Step 3 I regroup 1 tenth as 10 hundredths, so I can take away 5 hundredths. Now I have 2 ones, 9 tenths, and 10 hundredths.

$$\begin{array}{r} \overset{9}{2}\;\cancel{10}\;10 \\ 3.00 \\ -\,0.75 \end{array}$$

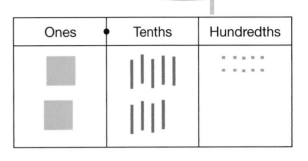

Ones	•	Tenths	Hundredths

Step 4 Now I can subtract 7 tenths and 5 hundredths.

$$\begin{array}{r} \overset{9}{2}\;\cancel{10}\;10 \\ 3.00 \\ -\,0.75 \\ \hline 2.25 \end{array}$$

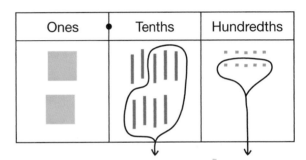

Ones	•	Tenths	Hundredths

There will be 2.25 kg of dog food left after one day.

Dan's Subtraction

To calculate the amount of dog food, I'll count up from 0.75 to 3.00.

Step 1 I add 0.25 to 0.75 to get to 1.00.

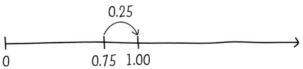

Step 2 I count 2.00 to get from 1.00 to 3.00.

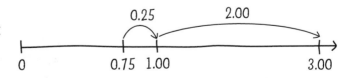

I need to add 2.00 to 0.25.

There will be 2.25 kg of dog food left after one day.

Reflecting

1. a) Can Sofia use a small cube instead of a flat to represent 1 kg? Explain.
   b) Can she use a large cube or a stack of 10 flats to represent 1 kg? Explain.

2. How can subtracting 75 from 300 help with subtracting 0.75 from 3.00?

3. Can Dan use another way to count up from 0.75 to 3.00? Explain.

Checking

4. How many days will the dog food last? Use subtraction to calculate how much food will be left after each day. Record your answers in a table.

Dog Food Amounts

Number of days	1	2
Mass of dog food left (kg)	2.25	

Practising

5. The height of a truck is 3.85 m. How much clearance does the truck have when it goes under a sign that is 5.00 m above the ground?

6. Lynne starts from school and runs 1.85 km north.
   She then runs another 2.50 km north.
   She turns around and runs 1.45 km south.
   How far does she have to run to return to school?

7. Estimate and then calculate. Show your work.
   a) $1.5 - 0.7 = \blacksquare$
   b) $1.65 - 0.88 = \blacksquare$
   c) $4.35 - 1.70 = \blacksquare$
   d) $4.00 - 2.85 = \blacksquare$
   e) $\blacksquare + 0.75 = 2.00$
   f) $12.05 + 4.75 = \blacksquare$

8. Benjamin entered a whole number into a calculator.
   Then he subtracted a decimal number.
   The answer was 4.75.
   a) What whole number might Benjamin have entered? Explain your reasoning.
   b) What number might Benjamin have subtracted? Explain your reasoning.

Adding and Subtracting Close to Hundreds

You can add and subtract numbers ending in 97, 98, or 99 by thinking of the nearest hundred.

To add 98 to 56, add 100 and subtract 2.

56 + 98 = ■

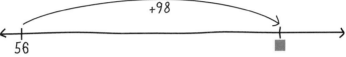

56 + 100 = 156
156 − 2 = 154

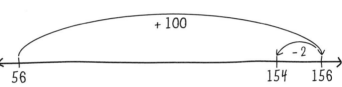

To subtract 98 from 185, subtract 100 and add 2.

185 − 98 = ■

185 − 100 = 85
85 + 2 = 87

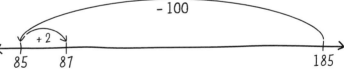

A. Why do you add 100 and subtract 2 instead of adding 98?

B. Why do you subtract 100 and add 2 instead of subtracting 98?

Try These

1. Calculate each sum.
   a) 88 + 98   b) 68 + 99   c) 199 + 58   d) 135 + 198

2. Calculate each difference.
   a) 134 − 98   b) 167 − 99   c) 335 − 199   d) 567 − 298

Skills Bank

LESSON

1 1. Use mental math to calculate each answer.
   a) 12 + 48   c) 99 + 157   e) 249 + 251   g) 4000 − 750
   b) 75 + 75   d) 250 + 751   f) 7000 − 45   h) 2456 + 3000

2. Explain how knowing 350 + 250 = 600 can help you
   to calculate each answer.
   a) 349 + 250   b) 348 + 248   c) 600 − 350   d) 600 − 249

3. A Grade 5 class is collecting pop can tabs.
   Their goal is to collect 3000 tabs in five weeks.
   Use mental math to calculate how many more
   tabs they need to collect after each week.
   a) In the first week, they collected 1000.
   b) In the second week, they collected 302.
   c) In the third week, they collected 698.
   d) In the fourth week, they collected 250 + 450.

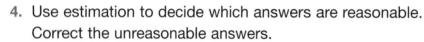

2 4. Use estimation to decide which answers are reasonable.
   Correct the unreasonable answers.
   a) 4555 + 2588 = 7143   d) 7056 − 4935 = 2121
   b) 9177 − 2989 = 7188   e) 3499 + 1257 + 3751 = 6507
   c) 1965 + 5678 = 7643   f) 185 + 650 + 203 + 498 = 1038

5. a) A plane flew 3387 km from Vancouver to
      Toronto and then flew back to Vancouver.
      How far did the plane travel altogether?
   b) Is your answer reasonable?

6. a) A crane lifts three crates
      with masses of 1249 kg,
      2758 kg, and 4496 kg.
      How many kilograms
      is the crane lifting?
   b) Is your answer reasonable?

7. a) Three schools recycled telephone books to raise money. How many telephone books did they recycle altogether?

b) Is your answer reasonable?

Telephone Books Recycled

School	Number of books
Lakeview	1259
Northside	2685
Southside	3107

8. Estimate.

a) 1457 + 2856   **b)** 4567 + 1289 + 3167   **c)** 4445 + 1287 + 2099

9. Add. Show your work.

a) 2485 + 3888 + 189   **b)** 1666 + 2345 + 1765   **c)** 6006 + 9898 + 4592

10. The chart shows the population of each age group in the towns of Harrisburg and Newton.

a) What is the total population in each town?

b) Which town has more people?

Populations of Age Groups

Ages (years)	Harrisburg	Newton
0–12	2931	5343
13–18	2876	2111
over 18	4659	3651

11. Estimate.

a) 2000 − 1775 = ■   **b)** 9999 − 6789 = ■   **c)** 7000 − 4899 = ■

12. Calculate. Show your work.

a) 9458 − 1822   **b)** 4023 − 1512   **c)** 3032 − 2643

13. The Eagles hockey team sold 7000 tickets for four home games. The chart shows the number of tickets sold for three of the games. How many tickets were sold for the fourth game?

Eagles Ticket Sales

Game	Tickets sold
Eagles vs. Ravens	1456
Eagles vs. Gulls	1389
Eagles vs. Crows	2345
Eagles vs. Hawks	

14. Estimate.

    a) 0.9 + 1.9   **b)** 3.28 + 1.80   **c)** 0.92 + 1.32   **d)** 15.75 + 2.25

15. Add. Show your work.

    a) 2.5 + 3.4   **b)** 0.01 + 2.03   **c)** 12.56 + 3.67   **d)** 12.44 + 6.55

16. Ryan bought 3.85 kg of cheddar cheese and 1.36 kg of blue cheese. How much cheese did he buy?

17. Add. Show your work.

    a) $12.56 + $8.99   **b)** $16.75 + $4.25   **c)** $12.99 + $23.98

18. Estimate.

    a) $45.45 + $42.65   **b)** $35.75 + $40.29   **c)** $15.76 + $23.35 + $28.79

19. Calculate the total cost and the amount of change for each purchase.

    a)

    c)

    b)

    d)

20. Estimate.

    a) 3.61 − 2.53   **c)** $9.85 − $0.54   **e)** $92.56 − $23.84

    b) 12.5 − 2.7   **d)** 15.75 − 4.99   **f)** 64.32 − 2.73

21. Calculate. Show your work.

    a) 9.70 − 3.25 = ■   **c)** $54.29 − $3.25 = ■   **e)** $15.68 + ■ = $50.00

    b) $3.54 − $2.86 = ■   **d)** $4.80 + ■ = 32.75   **f)** 100.00 − 43.49 = ■

Problem Bank

LESSON

1

1. The list shows some numbers that can be made by adding or subtracting only the numbers 100, 300, and 900. Complete the rest of the list from 600 to 1300.

```
100
200 = 300 − 100
300
400 = 300 + 100
500 = 900 − 300 − 100
600 =
   .
   .
   .
1300 =
```

3

2. Which three consecutive four-digit numbers have a sum of 3768? Explain your reasoning.

4

3. Which two four-digit numbers have a sum of 8000 and a difference of 500? Explain your reasoning.

7

4. a) Calculate the total.
   b) Change one digit in each price so the total cost is still the same. Look for one more solution. Show your work.

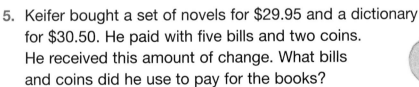

8

5. Keifer bought a set of novels for $29.95 and a dictionary for $30.50. He paid with five bills and two coins. He received this amount of change. What bills and coins did he use to pay for the books?

9

6. In a magic square, the numbers in the columns, rows, and diagonals have the same sum. Which numbers are missing from this magic square?

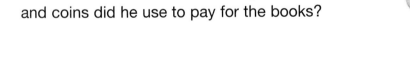

4.75		2.75
3.75	5.75	
	1.75	6.75

Chapter Review

LESSON

1

1. Use mental math to calculate each answer.
   Show your strategy for two of your answers.
   a) 75 + 125   c) 149 + 149   e) 450 + 355
   b) 500 − 198   d) 1000 − 399   f) 1500 + 2252

2. Anna is reading a book that has 760 pages.
   a) She read 199 pages in the first week.
      Use mental math to calculate the number of
      pages she has left to read.
   b) She read 175 pages in the second week
      and 125 pages in the third week.
      How many pages has she read in all?
      How many pages does she have left to read?
   c) She read the remaining pages in the fourth
      and fifth weeks. What number of pages might
      she have read in each of those two weeks?

2

3. Use estimation to decide which answers are reasonable.
   Correct the unreasonable answers.
   a) 6652 + 2345 = 8997   c) 7056 − 2935 = 4121
   b) 6099 − 1998 = 5101   d) 6754 + 300 + 1846 = 8900

4. a) Show your work for two of the estimates in Question 3.
   b) For the same two estimates, justify your choice of
      estimation strategy.

3

5. Estimate and then add. Show your work.
   a) 5329 + 2379 + 365   b) 2923 + 1079 + 3299   c) 3327 + 6938 + 1482

6. A truck can carry up to 8000 kg. Can it safely carry
   masses of 1875 kg, 2972 kg, and 3210 kg? Explain.

4

7. 9750 people attended a four-day festival.
   The chart shows the number of people who attended
   each day for the first three days.
   a) How many people attended on the fourth day?
   b) For each step, what operation did you use? Why?
   c) For each step, did you use mental math, a calculator,
      or pencil and paper? Why?

Festival Attendance

Day	Attendance
1	2154
2	2196
3	2349
4	

122

5 **8.** For each calculation, would you use pencil and paper, mental math, or a calculator? Justify your choice.
  a) 7050 + 250 + 900 + 3054
  b) 8965 − 6392
  c) 23 544 − 9089
  d) 998 + 8000 + 1002 + 6025

6 **9.** Estimate and then add. Show your work.
  a) 4.75 + 1.90
  b) 2.07 + 3.65
  c) 6.98 + 7.07
  d) 12.88 + 2.96

10. The rectangular bulletin board in Corina's class is 1.75 m wide and 0.85 m long. What is the perimeter of the bulletin board?

8 **11.** Calculate the total cost and the amount of change for each purchase.

a)

$12.89
$4.35
$16.99

b)

$24.99
$18.98

c)

$60.99
$12.75
$22.25

9 **12.** Estimate and then calculate. Show your work.
  a) 4.00 − 0.98
  b) 9.82 − 2.7
  c) 3.00 − 1.43
  d) 14.56 − 10.78

13. a) Calculate the perimeter of each triangle.
  b) How much greater is the perimeter of the larger triangle than the perimeter of the smaller triangle?

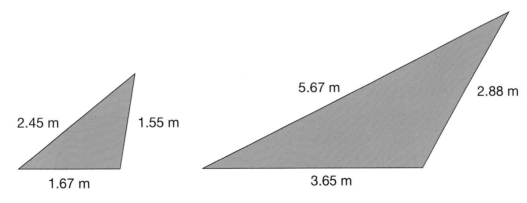

2.45 m   1.55 m
1.67 m

5.67 m   2.88 m
3.65 m

Chapter Task

Counting Calories

Nutritionists recommend that you eat food containing from 2200 to 2500 Calories each day.
Jose recorded everything he ate on Saturday and Sunday.

Jose's Food Record

	Saturday			Sunday		
	Food	Calories	Cost	Food	Calories	Cost
BREAKFAST	restaurant breakfast	710	$2.89	cereal with fruit	313	$0.76
	large orange juice	250	$1.99	350 mL orange juice	160	$0.88
SNACK	355 mL can of pop	150	$1.50	50 g cashews	50	$0.85
LUNCH	10 chicken nuggets	510	$4.29	tuna sandwich	361	$2.86
	chocolate milkshake	1150	$3.29	vanilla yogurt	165	$0.99
	french fries	610	$2.19	apple	80	$0.98
SNACK	355 mL can of pop	150	$1.50	hard-boiled egg	75	$0.17
				200 mL juice pack	95	$0.40
SUPPER	spaghetti	640	$7.99	chicken and vegetables	847	$5.94
	garlic bread	340	$4.00	250 mL whole milk	150	$0.27
	6 buffalo wings	330	$3.99	orange	65	$0.99
	large pop	397	$1.99			

? What can you conclude about what Jose ate each day?

A. Calculate the number of Calories over or under the recommended number Jose ate each day.

B. How much more did Saturday's meals cost than Sunday's meals?

C. Investigate data about Calories in foods that you like to eat. Use the data to plan three meals and snacks for one day with total Calories in the recommended range.

Task Checklist
- ✓ Did you estimate to check?
- ✓ Did you justify your choice of estimation strategy?
- ✓ Did you justify your choice of calculation method?
- ✓ Did you show all your steps?
- ✓ Did you explain your thinking?

Measuring Length and Time

Goals

You will be able to

- **estimate and measure length, perimeter, and circumference**

- **relate units of length to each other**

- **use a table to solve measurement problems**

- **measure time and relate time to distance**

- **read and write dates and times**

Measuring a basketball court

Getting Started

Skateboard Lengths

Katie has a new skateboard. She plans to put reflective tape around the edge of it.

? **How much reflective tape will Katie need to go around her skateboard?**

A. Make a paper model of the Blue Streak. Be as accurate as you can.

B. How many metres long is the Blue Streak?

C. How many metres wide is it?

D. Predict the **perimeter** of the skateboard. Then measure it. Was your prediction a good one?

E. What unit did you use to measure the perimeter? Why?

126

F. How many metres of reflective tape would Katie need for her skateboard?

G. The skateboard manufacturer says it sold about 1 km of Blue Streak skateboards this year. About how much tape would be needed to go around all of the skateboards? Explain your thinking.

Do You Remember?

1. Complete the relationships.
   a) 1 km = ■ m
   b) 1 m = ■ cm
   c) 1 m = ■ mm
   d) 1 cm = ■ mm

2. Calculate the perimeter of each shape.

   a)
   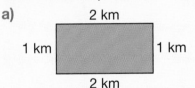
   2 km
   1 km   1 km
   2 km

   b)
   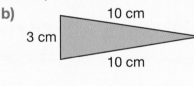
   10 cm
   3 cm
   10 cm

   c)
   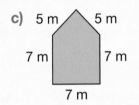
   5 m   5 m
   7 m   7 m
   7 m

3. Which shape has a perimeter of about 14 cm?

   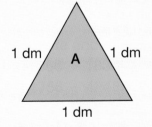
   1 dm   **A**   1 dm
   1 dm

   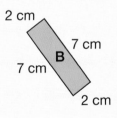
   2 cm
   7 cm
   B
   7 cm
   2 cm

   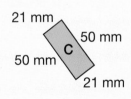
   21 mm
   50 mm
   C
   50 mm
   21 mm

4. Alain looked at the clock when he started and finished working on his computer one morning.
   a) What time was it when he started?
   b) What time was it when he finished?
   c) How much time had passed?

   start

   finish

1 Using Measurements to Describe Objects

You will need
• a ruler or a measuring tape

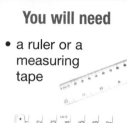

Goal Use logical reasoning to choose measurements.

Rosa made up some measurement puzzles for her friends.
Sometimes she used unusual units to make the puzzles tricky.

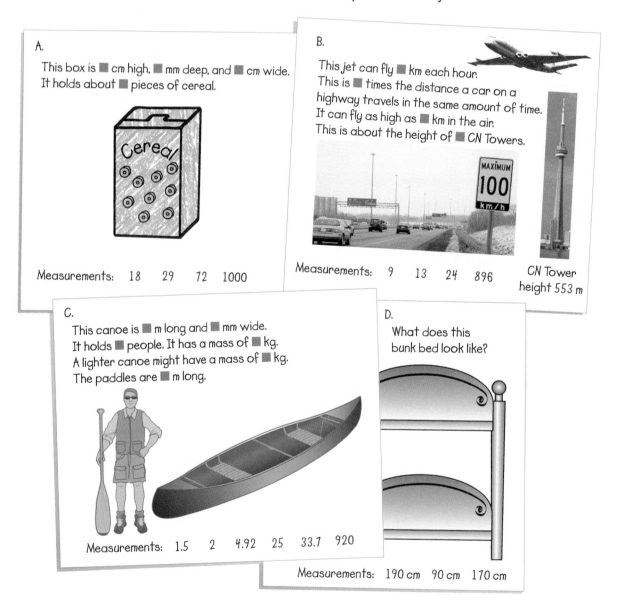

A.

This box is ■ cm high, ■ mm deep, and ■ cm wide.
It holds about ■ pieces of cereal.

Measurements: 18   29   72   1000

B.

This jet can fly ■ km each hour.
This is ■ times the distance a car on a highway travels in the same amount of time.
It can fly as high as ■ km in the air.
This is about the height of ■ CN Towers.

Measurements: 9   13   24   896

CN Tower height 553 m

C.

This canoe is ■ m long and ■ mm wide.
It holds ■ people. It has a mass of ■ kg.
A lighter canoe might have a mass of ■ kg.
The paddles are ■ m long.

Measurements: 1.5   2   4.92   25   33.7   920

D.

What does this bunk bed look like?

Measurements: 190 cm   90 cm   170 cm

? **What clues can you use to select the correct measurements?**

A. Read the information about the cereal box.
   Which measurement goes in each blank?

B. Read the information about the jet.
   Which measurement goes in each blank?

C. Read the information about the canoe.
   Which measurement goes in each blank?
   How do you know?

D. Look at the bunk bed measurements.
   a) Describe and sketch what the bed might look like.
   b) Which measurement is the length?
      How do you know?

E. Select an object in your classroom.
   Measure four or five attributes of your object.
   Make up a description of your object without the
   numbers but including the units.
   Challenge a classmate to complete the measurements.

Reflecting

1. Why are there several ways to draw the bunk bed?
   Which way do you think is the most appropriate?
   Explain you answer.

2. What clues did you use to answer Parts A, B,
   and C?

3. Look at the greatest number that you used in
   Part E. Is this number the longest measurement?
   Does it have to be?

2 Measuring Lengths

Goal Relate metric units of length to each other.

Norman and Patrick are making life-sized models of themselves. They use string to measure because they don't have a measuring tape.

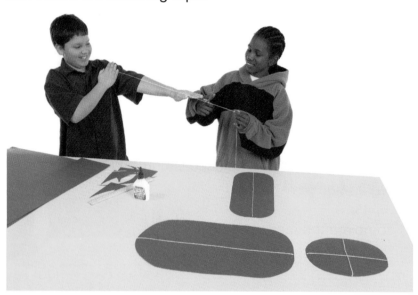

Norman's Strategy

I cut a piece of string as long as my arm.

I measured the string using a 30 cm ruler.

My left arm is 484 mm long.

? **How can you measure a 484 mm long piece of string with a 30 cm ruler?**

A. How do you know that 484 mm is longer than 30 cm?

B. About how many centimetres long is Norman's arm?

C. Is Norman's arm longer or shorter than your estimate in Part B? How do you know?

D. Use your ruler to measure and cut a piece of string 484 mm long.

Reflecting

1. How did you measure 484 mm with your ruler?

2. How is measuring 484 mm with your ruler different from measuring 284 mm with your ruler?

3. How does knowing the number of millimetres in a centimetre help you to complete the task?

Checking

4. Cut string for each measurement. Describe what you did.
   a) 75 cm   b) 642 mm   c) 0.1 m

Practising

5. Describe how to measure a 0.45 m long piece of fabric using a 30 cm ruler.

6. Draw each length.
   a) a 53 mm line segment
   b) a 1.32 m zigzag path

7. The length of Jasleen's step is about 60 cm. She wants to know the length of the room in metres, but she doesn't have a ruler. How can she use what she knows about her step to estimate the length of the room?

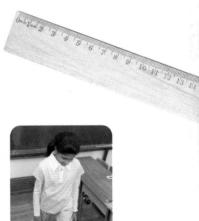

8. Tegan says she lives 90 000 cm from her grandmother.
   a) Do you think they live in the same town? Explain.
   b) What would be a better unit for describing the distance? Why?

9. How can you calculate the thickness of a piece of photocopy paper in millimetres? Use the information in the picture.

1.5 cm

Photocopy Paper

200 sheets

Close as You Can

Number of players: 2 or more
How to play: Estimate lengths of paper strips.

Step 1   Each player starts with five paper strips of different lengths. Players measure their strips and record the measurements in millimetres, centimetres, and decimetres on the back.

Step 2   Another player chooses one of your strips. Hold up the front of the strip and name a unit (millimetres, centimetres, or decimetres). The player estimates the length of the strip using the unit you named. If the estimate is within 50 mm, 5 cm, or 0.5 dm of the actual length, the other player wins the strip.

Step 3   Take turns. Name different units as you play. Play until all of the strips have been won. The person with the most strips at the end wins.

Liam's Turn

I estimate that the length of Anna's strip is 30 cm.

Anna says the measurement is 32 cm.

My estimate is within 5 cm, so I win the strip.

3 Measuring Circumference

Goal Measure around circular objects.

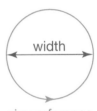

You will need
- a measuring tape
- scissors
- paper strips
- tape

? **What sizes of bracelets, armbands, and headbands would fit you?**

A. Cut a paper strip to make a circular bracelet the right size for your wrist. Tape the ends of the strip together to form a circle.

B. Measure and record the **circumference** of your bracelet. Measure and record its width.

C. Is the circumference of the bracelet closer to two times, three times, or four times its width?

D. Repeat Parts A to C to measure an armband and a headband. Complete a chart like this one.

Object	Width	Circumference
bracelet		
armband		
headband		

circumference

The distance around a circle

width

circumference

Reflecting

1. How is measuring a circumference different from measuring the length of something straight?

2. The circumference of a circle is greater than two times the width. How could you have predicted this?

3. The base of Aimee's finger is 15 mm wide. Predict the circumference of a ring that would fit her finger. Explain your prediction.

4 Measuring Perimeter

Goal Measure perimeter on a grid.

You will need
- a ruler
- centimetre grid paper

Teresa's backpack looks just like her sister's.
Teresa decides to put her initials on her backpack and
outline the letters with edging cord. Her initials are TFY.

? **How much edging
cord does Teresa
need for outlining
her initials on
her backpack?**

 Teresa's Model

I'll colour my initials on centimetre grid paper.

I'll estimate the perimeter and then measure.

Then I'll calculate the amount of cord I need.

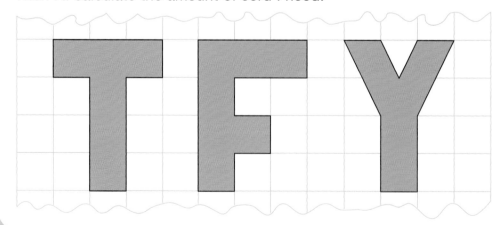

A. What would be a good way to estimate the perimeter of
the T? Use your way to estimate the perimeter.

B. Measure the perimeter of the T by counting the distance around. Do you think you made a good estimate? Explain.

C. Estimate the perimeter of the letters F and Y and then measure. Compare the measurements to your estimates.

D. How much cord does Teresa need for all three initials?

Reflecting

1. The letters T and F have the same width and height. Why does F have a greater perimeter than T?

2. Why do you need to use a ruler to measure the perimeter of Y, but not T or F?

Checking

3. Colour squares on centimetre grid paper to make these initials. Estimate the perimeter. Check by measuring.

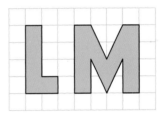

Practising

4. Determine the perimeter of each shape.

a)

b)

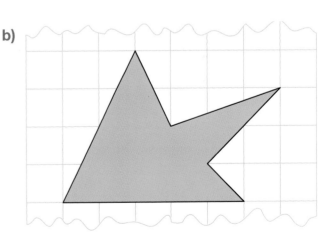

5. Draw two different shapes that each have a perimeter of 20 cm. Use centimetre grid paper. Each shape must have more than four sides.

6. Draw a shape that you think has a perimeter of 30 cm. Measure the perimeter. Was your estimate reasonable?

LESSON

Mid-Chapter Review

1 1. Complete this paragraph with the correct numbers. Explain your thinking.

The Mighty Canadian Minebuster rollercoaster is ■ m high and has a drop of ■ m. Its length is ■ km and its top speed is ■ km each hour.

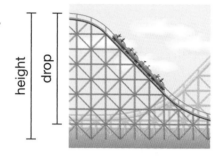

| 1.17 | 27 | 29 | 96 |

2 2. Between what two centimetre markings on a ruler would you find each length measurement? Explain.
   a) 15 mm   b) 37 mm   c) 5 mm

3 3. a) Measure the circumference of this circle in centimetres.
   b) Evan measured the circumference in millimetres. Will the number of units be greater or less than yours? Why?

4 4. Estimate and then measure the perimeter of each shape in centimetres.

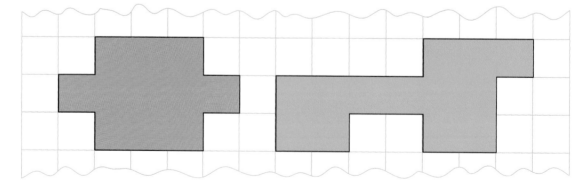

5. Draw a shape that has each perimeter. Use a centimetre grid.
   a) 16 cm   b) 200 mm

Kilometre Study Guide

Heather is creating a study guide about metric measurements.

Distance	Examples
1 km	about as far as I can walk in 15 minutes
1 km	about as far as we drive in 45 seconds on the highway
1 km	about 3400 sheets of binder paper laid end to end
1 km	almost as high as two CN Towers stacked one on top of the other

1

Distance	Examples
about 100 km	Kitchener, Ontario to London, Ontario
about 1000 km	Vancouver to Calgary
about 10 000 km	10 round trips between Toronto and Montreal
about 100 000 km	the distance that Earth travels around the Sun in an hour

2

1 Write three or four more examples for Heather's first page.
Use things that would provide good examples of 1 km.

2 Write another example for each distance on Heather's second page.

5

Measuring the Perimeter of a Rectangle

 Goal Develop and use a rule to calculate the perimeter of a rectangle.

Aaron wants to put a border around his picture. Then he wants to put trim around the border.

He has 120 cm of trim.

? **What is the greatest border size Aaron can use?**

← 20 cm →

24 cm

border size

■ cm

 Aaron's Method

Understand the Problem

The trim goes around the border.

The border with the picture inside forms a rectangle.

The perimeter of the rectangle cannot be greater than 120 cm or there won't be enough trim.

Make a Plan

I'll calculate the perimeter with a 1 cm border.

If the perimeter is less than 120 cm, I'll try a bigger border until the perimeter is 120 cm.

Carry Out the Plan

I'll sketch a 20 cm by 24 cm rectangle on newsprint. I can draw different-sized borders around it.

A. What is the length of Aaron's picture with a 1 cm border? What is the width? Record your answers in a chart.

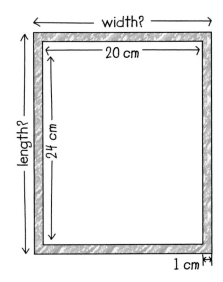

width?

20 cm

length?

24 cm

1 cm

Border size	Length	Width	Length + width	Perimeter
1 cm				
2 cm				
3 cm				

B. Calculate the sum of the length and width. Calculate the perimeter. Record your answers.

C. Sketch Aaron's picture with borders of 2 cm, 3 cm, and so on. Each time, do the calculations as in Parts A and B and record the answers in your chart. Continue until the perimeter is 120 cm.

D. How can you calculate the perimeter of a rectangle if you know the length and the width? Write your rule in words.

E. What is the greatest border size Aaron can use? Explain your thinking.

Reflecting

1. How did you know when you had the greatest possible border?

2. Why does the rule you wrote in Part D make sense? How would you change the rule to apply it to a square?

3. Why can't you use your rule from Part D to calculate the perimeter of a triangle?

Checking

4. How much trim would Aaron need if he used a 5 cm border?

5. What is the perimeter of a picture that is 10 cm wide and 15 cm long?

Practising

6. How much trim would Aaron need if he decided not to use a border?

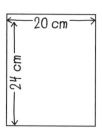

20 cm
24 cm

7. Calculate the length of fencing needed to go around each rectangular garden.

a)
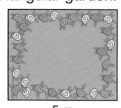
4 m
5 m

b)
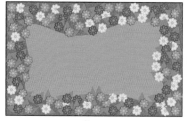
5 m
8 m

8. Juanita used a trundle wheel to measure the length of a basketball court as 22.5 m and the width as 12.8 m. What is the perimeter?

9. Which rectangle has a greater perimeter? How much greater is it? How do you know?
   A. 4.5 cm by 7.0 cm   B. 3.5 cm by 7.5 cm

10. a) How does the perimeter of this rectangle change if you add 5 m to the length?
    b) How does the perimeter change if you triple the length and the width of the rectangle?

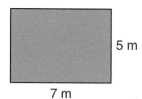
5 m
7 m

11. What is the greatest size of border you can use to frame a 22 cm by 28 cm picture if you have 1.8 m of trim?

12. To calculate the perimeter of a rectangle, Ian doubles the length and doubles the width and adds the results. Is his rule correct? Explain.

13. a) Draw three different rectangles with sides that are whole numbers of centimetres.
    b) Calculate the perimeter of each rectangle. Are the perimeters even or odd? Think about your perimeter rule and explain why.

140

Estimating Distances

Each letter on the number line represents a different distance.

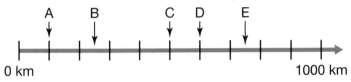

0 km   1000 km

A. Which letter represents 500 km?

B. Estimate the distance that each other letter represents.

Try These

1. Estimate the number that each letter represents.

a)

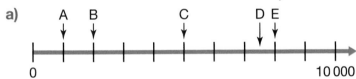

0   10 000

b)

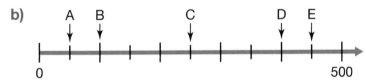

0   500

c)

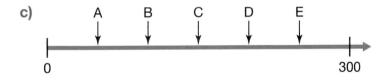

0   300

2. Place each number on a number line.

a) 15, 45, 50, 75, 99

0   100

b) 0.2, 0.4, 0.5, 0.75

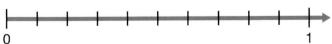

0   1

6 Solve Problems Using Tables

Goal Use tables to solve distance problems.

Akiko enjoys speed walking. She can walk 75 m each minute.

? **About how many minutes would it take Akiko to walk 5 km if she kept up her speed-walking pace?**

Akiko's Solution

Understand the Problem

I can walk 75 m each minute.

I have to figure out how long it will take to go 5 km.

I know 1 km = 1000 m, so 5 km = 5000 m.

Make a Plan

I'll make a table for distances and times.

I can go 75 m in 1 minute, so I can go 750 m in 10 minutes.

I'll skip count by 750 m with my calculator until I get close to 5000 m.

Carry Out the Plan

In 70 minutes, I will have walked past 5000 m, so it will take between 60 minutes and 70 minutes. I'll predict 65 minutes.

I multiply 65 by 75 on my calculator.

$65 \times 75 = 4875$. That's a little low.

I'll estimate 67 minutes.

My Speedwalking

Distance (m)	Time (minutes)
750	10
1500	20
2250	30
3000	40
3750	50
4500	60
5250	70

← 5 km is between 4500 m and 5250 m.

Reflecting

1. Why did Akiko estimate 67 minutes?

2. How did making a table help Akiko estimate her answer?

3. What other strategy could Akiko have used to solve the problem?

Checking

4. Extend Akiko's table to estimate how long it would take her to walk 7 km.

Practising

5. Cale's mother was driving at a speed of 4 km every 3 minutes. How long would it take them to get to Cale's grandmother's house if she lives 62 km away?

6. Tom Longboat won the Boston Marathon in 1907. He ran 40 km in about 2 hours 24 minutes.
   a) Tom Longboat once ran 8 km in about 23 minutes. If he kept up that speed, how long would it take him to run 40 km?
   b) About how much longer did it take him to run the Boston Marathon than your answer to part a)?

Tom Longboat

7. About how much farther would the Boeing 737 go than the other planes in 90 minutes?

Airplane Speeds

Airplane	Kilometres travelled in one hour
De Havilland Dash 8	306
Canadair Regional Jet	786
Boeing 737	816

8. Tamara can walk 70 m each minute. Bronwyn can walk 1 km in 12 minutes. Create two tables to find out which girl can walk farther in an hour. How much farther?

7 Measuring Time

 Goal

Estimate and measure time to the nearest second.

Each Wednesday, the students in Yoshi's class use a fluoride rinse. They swish for one minute. Yoshi looked at the clock when they started and finished.

start rinsing   finish rinsing

? **Did the class swish for one minute?**

Yoshi's Timing

The thinnest hand on the clock is the second hand.

It moves to the next small mark on the clock each second.

When we started rinsing, the clock showed that the time was 53 seconds after 8:45.

8:45:53

A. Where should the hands on the finish rinsing clock be if the class swished for one minute? Why?

B. What time does the finish rinsing clock actually show?

C. Which hand is not where you expected?

D. Did the class swish for more than or less than one minute? Explain.

144

Reflecting

1. What is the difference between the actual swishing time and one minute?

2. Would it be easier to wait until 8:46:00 to start timing the rinse? Explain your thinking.

Checking

3. Juanita was asked to brush her teeth for three minutes. Estimate and then calculate how long she brushed her teeth.
Did she brush long enough?

start brushing

finish brushing

Practising

4. Khalid wonders how long TV commercials usually are. Estimate and then calculate the time for each set of commercials.

a)   start commercial   finish commercial

b)   start commercial   finish commercial

5. A relay race begins at 7:05:42 p.m. and ends at 7:09:15 p.m. How long was the race in minutes and seconds?

6. The runner-up in a race finishes at 2:32:02 p.m.
The winner finishes at 2:31:48 p.m.
By how many seconds did the winner win?

7. Look at your classroom clock.
When the second hand reaches 12, look away.
Twiddle your thumbs for what you think is 30 seconds.
Look up when you think 30 seconds is over.
Record the time on the clock.
How close was your estimate?

8 Recording Dates and Times

Goal Write dates and times using numeric format.

Sofia noticed that the computers in the school lab show the date and time in different ways. She found out that the one using only numbers is called numeric format.

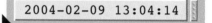

February 9, 2004, 1:04:14 p.m.   2004-02-09 13:04:14

Sofia's Dates and Times

I'll write the birth dates and times of my sisters and me using numeric format.

To write numeric dates, I write the year, then a space, then the month number, then a space.

Then I write the number of the day.

Numeric times use a **24 h clock**.

Midnight is 00:00:00. Noon is 12:00:00.

The next hour past noon is 13.

| Birth date | 1990-06-09 |
| Birth time | 04:14:12 |

| Birth date | 1997-01-11 |
| Birth time | 10:42:05 |

| Birth date | 1995-04-13 |
| Birth time | 15:20:00 |

| Birth date | 1990-06-09 |
| Birth time | 04:30:23 |

24 h clock
A method of naming the hours of the day from 0 to 23. The symbol for hour is h.

? **What is Sofia's birth date and time?**

A. Which date represents the youngest girl?
How do you know? How would you say this date?

B. Which girls were born in the morning? Which girls were born at a time when you would probably be sleeping?

C. How far apart are Sofia's two older sisters in age?

D. Sofia has one younger sister. What is Sofia's birth date? Was she born in the morning or the afternoon?

Reflecting

1. Why might some people prefer writing numeric dates rather than dates like June 4, 1998?

2. Why might airlines prefer the 24 h clock to the 12 h clock?

Checking

3. Jane was born on December 7, 1995 at 13 **min** 34 **s** after 2:00 p.m. How would she write her birth date and time in numeric format?

4. Eli was born two weeks before Jane at noon. How would Eli write his birth date and time in numeric format?

min
The symbol for minutes

s
The symbol for seconds

Practising

5. Write each birth date and time in numeric format.
   a) June 17, 1996 at 10:12 p.m.
   b) April 2, 2000 at 13 s after 8:23 a.m.

6. The stamp on Colin's parking stub reads 17:23:53. If he leaves the lot at 18:41:17, what should the charge be?

Parking
35¢ for each half hour or part of a half hour

7. a) Write your own birth date and time in numeric format.
   b) Which of your classmates was born closest to each time?
      i) midnight   ii) noon   iii) 6 p.m.

Skills Bank

LESSON

1. Complete each sentence with the appropriate number.

   a) An airplane flies ■ km in 1 hour.

   b) A car travels ■ m in 1 minute.

   c) A walker travels ■ m in 1 hour.

     | 850 | 1667 | 4000 |

2. Record the most appropriate unit to describe this stapler.

   a) 176 ■ long

   b) 3.5 ■ wide

   c) 0.5 ■ high

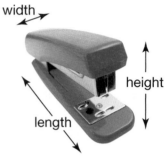

width

height

length

3. Describe how to measure each length with a 30 cm ruler.

   a) 720 mm   **b)** 1.4 m

4. Complete the relationships.

   a) 1 km = ■ m   **b)** 1 m = ■ mm   **c)** 1 km = ■ cm

5. Complete the relationships.

   a) 1 ■ = 0.1 cm   **b)** 1 dm = 0.1 ■   **c)** 1 ■ = 0.01 m

6. Estimate and then measure the circumference of each lid. Record the estimates and the measurements.

   a)

   b)

7. Determine the perimeter of each shape.

a)
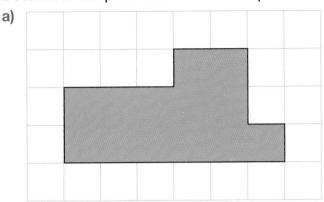

b)
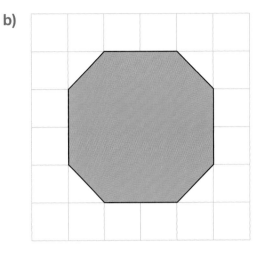

8. Calculate the perimeter of each rectangle.

a)
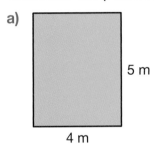

5 m

4 m

b)
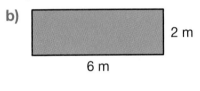

2 m

6 m

9. A train is travelling at a rate of 76 km each hour. Make a table to estimate the time it will take the train to travel 399 km.

10. Popcorn takes 2 minutes 10 seconds to cook. It is 8:42:52 p.m. now. When will the popcorn be done?

11. How much time has passed between each start clock and end clock?

a)

start   end

b)

start   end

12. A date-and-time stamp on a store receipt says 10/24/2004 17:21. Write this in numeric format.

Problem Bank

LESSON

2

1. Keely is getting measured for new clothes. The clerk measures Keely's arm length as 42.0 cm and her leg length as 538 mm. How much longer is Keely's leg than her arm?

2. A car is about 4 m long. About how many cars would have to line up end to end to stretch from one town to another town 23 km away?

3

3. Measure the circumference of a circular object. Experiment with string to see about how much wider the object would have to be to have a circumference 10 cm greater.

4. The width of a plate is about 25 cm less than its circumference. Experiment to figure out about how wide the plate is.

4

5. Use 4 cm by 4 cm grids. Draw at least four shapes with a perimeter of 12 cm that can fit on a grid.

6. Use a 4 cm by 4 cm grid. Draw a shape with only vertical and horizontal sides and a perimeter greater than 20 cm.

5

7. A rectangular garden has a length of 42 m and a width of 36 m. If fencing costs $4 each metre, how much will it cost to fence the garden?

8. A rectangle has a perimeter of 32 cm. The length is 6 cm longer than the width. What is the length?

5 9. What is the perimeter of this shape?

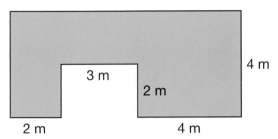

4 m

3 m

2 m

2 m

4 m

6 10. A cyclist rides 225 m each minute.
About how long does it take to ride 15 km?

11. Ian's father drives 90 km each hour.
He has to drive to a town 230 km away.
About how many minutes will the drive take?

7 12. These are the best 2003 Ottawa marathon times in hours,
minutes, and seconds. How long after the winner crossed
the finish line did the fifth-place runner cross?

Ottawa Marathon Times for 2003

1st	2nd	3rd	4th	5th
2:15:29	2:16:10	2:19:16	2:20:43	2:25:02

13. Create a problem that has an answer of 1 minute
34 seconds.

8 14. The schedule shows flights leaving North Bay each day.
The times when the flights were supposed to leave are
in the first column of the schedule.
If the next to last flight left 1 h 20 min after the time on
the schedule and the last one left 10 min early, how far
apart in time did the flights leave?

North Bay ON (YYB)

Departs	Arrives Toronto					300 km
06:20	07:25	◆	7770	X67	0	
09:45	10:50	◆	7772	Daily	0	
13:45	14:50	◆	7368	X67	0	
16:25	17:30	◆	7776	Daily	0	
19:55	21:00	◆	7778	Daily	0	

CHAPTER 5

Chapter Review

LESSON

1 1. Yasmin lives 400 m from Anton. Kevin lives 0.45 km from Anton. Jared lives 40 000 mm from Anton. Who lives closest to Anton? How do you know?

2 2. You have a 30 cm ruler. How can you measure a piece of fabric 675 mm long?

3 3. Estimate and measure each circumference.

a) b)

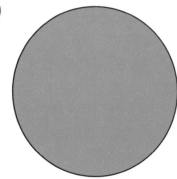

4 4. Measure the perimeter of each shape.

a) b)

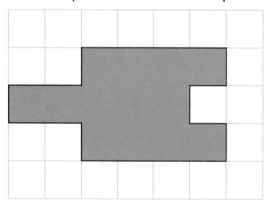 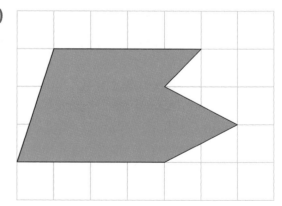

5. How many side lengths do you need to know to calculate each perimeter without measuring?

a) b)

rectangle equilateral triangle

4

6. Draw a shape on a grid that has a perimeter of 14 cm and is not a rectangle.

5

7. Describe a rule for measuring the perimeter of a rectangle.

8. Calculate the perimeter of each rectangle.
   Show your work.

   a)

   2 m
   7 m

   b)

   12 km
   15 km

9. Frank thinks the perimeter of half a sheet of paper is probably half the perimeter of the whole sheet. Is this true? Explain.

6

10. A spider walks about 19 cm each second.
    About how long would it take the spider to walk around the perimeter of a room that is 3 m wide and 4 m long?

7

11. Jeff looked at the clock when he started brushing his teeth. He looked at the clock when he finished. The dentist said that Jeff should brush for 3 minutes. Did he? Explain your answer.

    start brushing   finish brushing

12. At the 2002 Winter Olympics, Gabriella Paruzzi won the 30 km cross-country ski event with a time of 1 hour 30 minutes 57 seconds. The second-place skier took 1 hour 31 minutes 2 seconds.
    By how much time did the gold medallist win?

8

13. Prince William was born on June 21, 1982 at 9:03 p.m.
    a) Write Prince William's birth date and time in numeric format.
    b) How long before midnight was he born?

Chapter Task

Perimeter Walk

As part of his healthy-living project, Adrick is walking 10 000 steps each day. He wants to walk around one of these city parks.

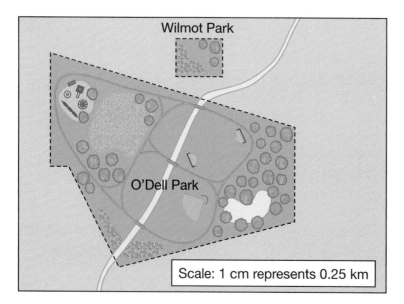

Scale: 1 cm represents 0.25 km

? **How many times will Adrick have to walk around each park to walk 10 000 steps? How long will it take him?**

A. Use the length of your step to estimate the length of Adrick's step.

B. What is the perimeter of each park?

C. How many times will Adrick have to walk around each park to walk 10 000 steps?

D. Use your own walking speed to estimate Adrick's walking speed. Show your thinking.

E. How long will it take Adrick to walk 10 000 steps around each park?

Task Checklist

☑ Were your measurements reasonably accurate?

☑ Did you show all your steps?

☑ Did you explain all your calculations?

☑ Did you find the perimeters as efficiently as you could?

Multiplication and Division

Goals

You will be able to

- solve two-step problems using tree diagrams, multiplication, and division

- estimate products and quotients

- multiply two-digit numbers

- divide three-digit and four-digit numbers by one-digit numbers

CD groups

Getting Started

Making Dreamcatchers

You will need
- base ten blocks

Anna and her grandmother are making eight dreamcatchers as gifts.
Each dreamcatcher is made with 65 cm of willow and 125 cm of string.

? **About how much string and willow are needed for everyone in your class to make a dreamcatcher?**

A. How many centimetres of willow and string do Anna and her grandmother need to make 8 dreamcatchers? Show your work.

B. How can you tell that they need between 5 m and 6 m of willow and exactly 10 m of string?

C. Did you use mental math, base ten blocks, or pencil and paper to answer Part B? Explain your choice.

D. How can you use your answers to Parts A and B to calculate the lengths of willow and string needed to make 4 dreamcatchers? 16 dreamcatchers?

E. Estimate the lengths of string and willow needed for everyone in your class to make a dreamcatcher. Explain your thinking.

Do You Remember?

1. Estimate. Show your work.
   a) 5×458
   b) $6\overline{)288}$

2. Use mental math to calculate.
   a) $6 \times 1000 = \blacksquare$
   b) $240 \div 3 = \blacksquare$

3. Use base ten blocks to calculate.
   a) 23×4
   b) $2\overline{)256}$

4. Calculate.
   a) $465 \times 3 = \blacksquare$
   b) $435 \div 6 = \blacksquare$

5. 144 students are going to the Children's Festival on 3 buses. Admission for each student is $5.00.
   a) Each bus has the same number of students. How many students are on each bus?
   b) What does admission cost for each busload of students?
   c) What does admission cost for all 144 students?

1 Multiplying Tens

You will need
- base ten blocks

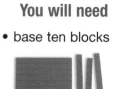

Goal Use number facts to multiply by tens.

A dragonfly flaps its wings 20 to 40 times each second.

? **What are the least and greatest numbers of times a dragonfly can flap its wings in 30 s?**

Martin's Array

I need to multiply the number of seconds by the number of flaps each second.

To calculate the least number of times the dragonfly flaps its wings in 30 s, I'll calculate 30 × 20.

I can make a 30-by-20 array with blocks. My array is 2 rows of 30 tens.

I can also make an array that is 2 rows of 3 hundreds.

A. Explain how Martin's array shows 30 × 20.

B. How many tens blocks did Martin use in his array? Complete his calculation.

C. What is the least number of times a dragonfly can flap its wings in 30 s?

D. Use an array of blocks to calculate the greatest number of times a dragonfly can flap its wings in 30 s.

Reflecting

1. a) How does thinking of a 30-by-20 array as 2 rows of 30 tens help you calculate 30 × 20?

   b) How does thinking of a 30-by-20 array as 2 rows of 3 hundreds help you calculate 30 × 20?

2. Explain how the number fact 3 × 2 = 6 can help you calculate 30 × 20.

Checking

3. a) What are the least and greatest numbers of times a dragonfly can flap its wings in 1 min? Use an array of blocks to solve the problem.

   b) How can you use the number fact 6 × 4 = 24 when you calculate 60 × 40?

Practising

4. How can you use this array to calculate 20 × 40?

5. Use an array to multiply 30 by 30.

6. Calculate the area of each shape.

a)
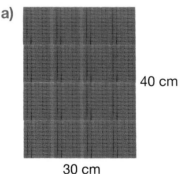
30 cm
40 cm

b)
50 cm
80 cm

c)
60 cm
60 cm

7. Calculate each product. Show your work.
   a) 10 × 10
   b) 20 × 10
   c) 30 × 50
   d) 20 × 50
   e) 50 × 80
   f) 90 × 90

2 Estimating Products

You will need
- a calculator

Goal Solve two-step problems and use estimation to check the reasonableness of a calculation.

24 students in Patrick's class are playing a Cree game of counting sticks.

One player divides a pile of 39 sticks into 2 bundles and holds 1 bundle in each hand. Another player guesses which hand contains an even number of sticks.

? **How many boxes of sticks does the class need if everyone plays at the same time?**

Patrick's Solution

Craft Sticks
150 sticks

Our class needs enough sticks for 12 pairs of students.

My calculator shows that $12 \times 39 = 468$.

I'll estimate to see if this answer is reasonable.

12×39 is close to 12×40.

$6 \times 40 = 240$, so $12 \times 40 = 480$.

480 is close to 468, so the calculator answer is reasonable.

Craft sticks come in boxes of 150. I can calculate the number of boxes needed for the class.

A. How many craft sticks are there in 2 boxes? in 3 boxes? in 4 boxes? Show your work.

B. How can you use your answers to Part A to calculate the number of boxes the class needs?

Reflecting

1. Describe another way to check that 12 × 39 = 468 is a reasonable answer.

2. Why is it a good idea for Patrick to check that his answer to the first calculation is reasonable?

Checking

3. Your class is going to play a version of the game with 19 sticks.

   a) Use a calculator to determine the number of sticks you need.

   b) Use estimation to check that the answer you calculated is reasonable. Explain your reasoning.

   c) Calculate the number of boxes of sticks needed for your class.

Practising

4. Jasleen has 60 dimes and 60 nickels. She wants to buy a book that costs $9.75. How much more money does she need to buy the book? Explain how you solved the problem.

5. Use estimation to decide if the answers are reasonable.

   a) 345 × 6 = 2070
   b) 1234 × 5 = 6170
   c) 12 × 18 = 316
   d) 15 × 19 = 285
   e) 24 × 29 = 496
   f) 39 × 39 = 1521

6. A class of 36 students is having a contest to build the strongest bridge. Each group of 4 students gets 35 straws to make its bridge.

   a) The straws come in bags of 50. Calculate the number of bags needed for the class. Show your steps.

   b) Use estimation to show that your calculation is reasonable.

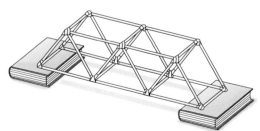

3 Solve Problems Using Tree Diagrams

Goal Use a tree diagram to solve combination problems.

Akiko is making party invitations on her computer. She wants each invitation to be different.

Font	Clip art	Colour
Arial		blue
Times New Roman		green
Lucida Handwriting		

? **How many different invitations can Akiko make using these combinations?**

Akiko's Solution

Understand

I need a way to list all the possible combinations.

I can choose one font, one clip art, and one colour for each invitation.

Make a Plan

I'll use one font at a time and combine it with each clip art.

Then I'll combine each colour with the font and clip art combinations. I'll use a tree diagram to list each combination of font and clip art.

Carry Out the Plan

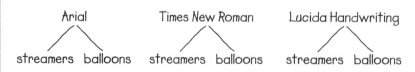

Arial   Times New Roman Lucida Handwriting

streamers balloons streamers balloons streamers balloons

You're invited to my party!

Saturday 2:00 p.m.

Lucida Handwriting balloons

There are $3 \times 2 = 6$ different invitations that can be made from three fonts and two pieces of clip art.

Now I can include the colours.

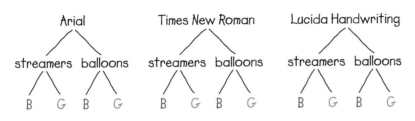

Arial
/ \
streamers balloons
/ \   / \
B   G   B   G

Times New Roman
/ \
streamers balloons
/ \   / \
B   G   B   G

Lucida Handwriting
/ \
streamers balloons
/ \   / \
B   G   B   G

I can make 6 × 2 = 12 different invitations.

You're invited to my party!

Saturday 2:00 p.m.

Lucida Handwriting
balloons
green

Reflecting

1. a) Show how Akiko's tree diagram would look if she combined font and colour before clip art.
   b) Does the order of combinations change the answer? Explain.

2. How many invitations could she make if there were four fonts to choose from? Explain your reasoning.

Checking

3. How many different invitations can you make using three fonts, three pieces of clip art, and two colours? Use a tree diagram.

Practising

4. Norman is creating a different bookmark for each of his six friends.
   He can pick from two shapes and three colours.
   Will he be able to make enough bookmarks?
   Explain your reasoning.

5. Create and solve a problem that involves combinations of items. Explain how you solved the problem.

4 Multiplying by Regrouping

Goal Use mental math to multiply two two-digit numbers.

The school board is making posters for a math fair.
12 schools will each get 12 posters.

Come to the Math Fair!

See what your kids can teach you!

Monday 4–5   Tuesday 4–6

? How many posters does the school board need to make?

Heather's Number Line

I calculated the number of posters using a number line.
I can count 10 jumps of 12 and 2 jumps of 12.

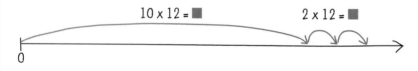

$10 \times 12 = \blacksquare$ $2 \times 12 = \blacksquare$

0

Dan's Mental Math

I used mental math to calculate 12×12.
12 twelves is the same as 10 twelves plus 2 twelves.
$12 \times 12 = 10 \times 12 + 2 \times 12$

A. Complete Heather's number sentences.
What is the total for the two jumps?

B. Complete Dan's mental math. How many posters does the school board need to make?

Reflecting

1. Show what Heather's number line would look like if she counted 12 twelves instead of counting a jump of 10 twelves and then 2 twelves.

2. How did you calculate 10 × 12?

Checking

3. Calculate the number of posters needed if 13 schools each get 14 posters.

Practising

4. Use each number line to calculate.

   a) 11 × 13 = ■

   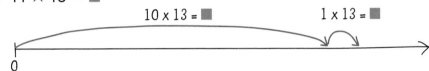

   b) 12 × 13 = ■

5. Use mental math to calculate.

   a) 11 × 14 = ■   b) 12 × 16 = ■   c) 12 × 18 = ■

6. Calculate.

   a) 11 × 11   c) 12 × 15
   b) 11 × 15   d) 12 × 25

7. How many eggs are in 11 dozen?

8. A bus holds 12 passengers. How many passengers can 17 buses hold?

9. How many months old will you be on your 14th birthday?

5 Multiplying with Arrays

Goal Multiply two-digit numbers.

Marcus is making a table to record contact information about the 22 students in his class.

Given name	Family name	E-mail address
Aaron	Ghosh	aaron@home.com
Alain	Lebeau	alain@home.com ← cell
Akiko	Sakamoto	akiko@home.com

The table has 23 rows and 19 columns.

? How many cells are in Marcus's table?

Marcus's Array

I can calculate the number of cells using base ten blocks.

Step 1 I make a 23-by-19 array using hundreds, tens, and ones blocks.

$$\begin{array}{r} 19 \\ \times 23 \\ \hline \end{array}$$

Step 2 I can break the array into four parts. I start with the 3-by-9 array and the 3-by-10 array.

$3 \times 9 = 27$
$3 \times 10 = 30$
$27 + 30 = 57$

I can write this in two steps or in one step.

3 x 10   3 x 9

$$\begin{array}{r} 19 \\ \times\,23 \\ \hline 27 \\ 30 \end{array} \qquad \begin{array}{r} {}^{2} \\ 19 \\ \times\,23 \\ \hline 57 \end{array}$$

Step 3 There is also a 20-by-9 array and a 20-by-10 array.

$20 \times 9 = 180$
$20 \times 10 = 200$
$180 + 200 = 380$

I can write this in two steps or in one step.

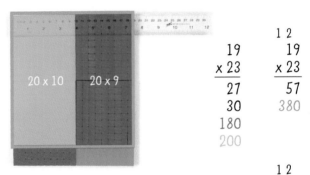

20 x 10   20 x 9

$$\begin{array}{r} 19 \\ \times\,23 \\ \hline 27 \\ 30 \\ 180 \\ 200 \end{array} \qquad \begin{array}{r} {}^{1\ 2} \\ 19 \\ \times\,23 \\ \hline 57 \\ 380 \end{array}$$

Step 4 I add. There are 437 cells in the table.

Step 5 I estimate to check that my answer is reasonable.
$20 \times 20 = 400$ is close to 19×23.
My answer of 437 is reasonable.

$$\begin{array}{r} 19 \\ \times\,23 \\ \hline 27 \\ 30 \\ 180 \\ +\,200 \\ \hline 437 \end{array} \qquad \begin{array}{r} {}^{1\ 2} \\ 19 \\ \times\,23 \\ \hline 57 \\ +\,380 \\ \hline 437 \end{array}$$

Reflecting

1. The numbers 27, 30, 180, and 200 represent the areas of the four parts of Marcus's array. Explain how the numbers 57 and 380 represent the areas of two parts of his array.

2. Explain why Marcus wrote the digit 2 above the tens column in Step 2.

Checking

3. **a)** Use base ten blocks to calculate the number of cells in a table with 15 rows and 22 columns.

   b) Show how to use paper and pencil to record your calculations in four steps and in two steps as Marcus did.

   c) Show how to use mental math, estimation, or a number line to check your answer.

Practising

4. Calculate the number of cells in each table.

   a) 12 rows and 16 columns   **b)** 22 rows and 18 columns

5. **a)** What multiplication is represented by these base ten blocks?

   b) Calculate the product.

6. Calculate the area of each rectangle.

   a) 12 cm by 12 cm   **b)** 11 cm by 22 cm

7. Calculate. Estimate to check that each answer is reasonable.

   a) $23 \times 25 = \blacksquare$ **c)** $75 \times 74 = \blacksquare$

   b) $18 \times 19 = \blacksquare$ **d)** $45 \times 69 = \blacksquare$

8. Each day in March, Winnie exercised for 45 min. How many minutes did she exercise in March? Show your work.

9. A floor has 23 rows of 45 tiles. How many tiles are on the floor?

10. How tall is a stack of 35 boxes if the height of each box is 24 cm?

11. **a)** Create a problem that can be solved by multiplying two two-digit numbers.

    b) Solve your problem.

    c) Explain how you know that your answer is reasonable.

Array Multiplication

You can multiply a pair of numbers by placing them in an array. Suppose you want to multiply 67 by 48. Begin by drawing a two-by-two array.
Write the two factors to show the place value of each digit.

$67 \times 48 = \blacksquare$

	60 + 7	
40		
+ 8		

Use multiplication to complete the rows and columns in the array.

$40 \times 60 = 2400$ $40 \times 7 = 280$

$8 \times 60 = 480$ $8 \times 7 = 56$

	60 + 7	
40	2400	280
+ 8	480	56

Add the numbers in the rows and the columns.

$2400 + 280 = 2680$ $2400 + 480 = 2880$

$480 + 56 = 536$ $280 + 56 = 336$

	60 + 7		
40	2400	280	2680
+ 8	480	56	536
	2880	336	

Add the numbers in the column beside the array. Check the answer by adding the numbers in the row below the array.

```
  2680          2880
+  536        +  336
  3216          3216
```

	60 + 7		
40	2400	280	2680
+ 8	480	56	536
	2880	336	3216

$67 \times 48 = 3216$

Use array multiplication to calculate each product.

a) $46 \times 55 = \blacksquare$ c) $65 \times 65 = \blacksquare$

b) $23 \times 59 = \blacksquare$ d) $82 \times 83 = \blacksquare$

Mid-Chapter Review

1 1. Susan's school district bought 70 CD organizers.
Each organizer holds 40 CDs.
How many CDs do they hold altogether?

2. A string of holiday lights contains 60 bulbs.
How many lights are on 30 strings?

3. Use mental math to calculate each product.
   a) 20×6 b) 10×40 c) 30×30 d) 90×80

4. Explain how to use the number fact $4 \times 5 = 20$ to
calculate each product.
   a) 40×5 b) 4×50 c) 40×50 d) 500×4

2 5. Estimate to determine which answers are reasonable.
   a) $9 \times 125 = 1125$ c) $44 \times 44 = 2936$ e) $88 \times 92 = 7096$
   b) $6 \times 2311 = 13\,866$ d) $21 \times 79 = 1659$ f) $55 \times 65 = 2575$

4 6. People blink about 15 times each minute.
About how many times will you blink in 12 min?

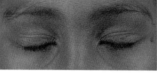

7. Each package contains 25 stickers.
Each box contains 12 packages.
How many stickers are in a box?

5 8. Calculate.
   a) $123 \times 6 = $ ■   c) $15 \times 18 = $ ■   e) $88 \times 89 = $ ■
   b) $13 \times 17 = $ ■   d) $23 \times 25 = $ ■   f) $75 \times 99 = $ ■

6 Dividing Hundreds by One-Digit Numbers

Goal Use division facts to divide hundreds.

Suppose you have 1200 mL of apple juice.
You want to pour equal amounts into Thermos bottles.

? How many millilitres of juice will be in each Thermos bottle?

A. Use hundreds blocks to model 1200 mL of juice. Divide the hundreds blocks to show the amount that would be in each of two Thermos bottles.

B. Write a division sentence to show what you did to solve the problem.

C. How can you use 12 ÷ 2 = 6 to solve the problem?

D. Use hundreds blocks to model 1200 mL of juice. Divide the hundreds blocks to show the amount that would be in each of three, four, and six Thermos bottles.

E. Explain how each model in Part D is related to a division fact.

F. 1500 mL of juice is divided equally into three Thermos bottles. Use a division fact to determine the amount of juice in each bottle. Use hundreds blocks to check.

G. Create and solve your own problem about creating equal amounts of juice.

Reflecting

1. Show how to use multiplication to check each of your answers in Part D.

2. Explain how writing 1200 as 12 hundreds can help you divide 1200 by 3.

3. Explain how to use 48 ÷ 8 = 6 to calculate 4800 ÷ 8.

7 Estimating Quotients

Goal Overestimate and underestimate when dividing.

Sofia is doing a report on extreme weather for Science class.
She discovers that, in La Réunion Island, it once rained 4653 mm in six days.
She thinks this amount of water is higher than her school! She wants to estimate the number of millimetres of rain for each day.

? About how many millimetres of rain fell each day?

Sofia's Estimates

I'll make two estimates for the number of millimetres of rain that fell each day.

First I'll underestimate, and then I'll overestimate.

The answer will be between these two estimates.

First I'll divide 4200 by 6. Then I'll divide 4800 by 6.

A. Complete Sofia's two estimates. Explain how to use mental math to divide 4200 by 6 and 4800 by 6.

B. Why do you think Sofia chose the numbers 4200 and 4800 for her two estimates?

C. When you divide 4653 by 6, do you think the answer is closer to your underestimate, closer to your overestimate, or about halfway in between? Explain your reasoning.

Reflecting

1. Why do you think Sofia said that the total amount of rain would be higher than her school?

2. How do you know that the daily amount of rain is greater than 0.5 m?

3. Imagine that 4653 mm of rain fell in five days instead of in six days. What numbers might you choose for overestimating and underestimating? Explain.

4. Why does it make more sense to estimate than to calculate the amount of rainfall each day?

Checking

5. In one eight-day period, 5286 mm of rain fell on La Réunion Island.
   a) Show how to overestimate and underestimate the amount of rain that fell each day.
   b) Explain how you can use your two estimates to make a closer estimate.

Practising

6. Estimate to solve each problem. Explain your reasoning.
   a) The total attendance at a powwow in July was 5208 people in 7 days. The total attendance at a powwow in August was 2934 in 3 days. Which powwow had the greater daily attendance?
   b) A movie store rented 3354 DVDs in 2 days and 4487 VHS tapes in 3 days. Which type of movie had the greater daily rental?
   c) The cost of 6 televisions is $5136. The cost of 5 computer monitors is $3195. Which item costs more?

7. Overestimate and underestimate each division. Show the numbers you used to estimate.
   a) 2)1512
   b) 9)6655
   c) 3)4218
   d) 8)5846
   e) 6)3355
   f) 7)5238

8 Dividing Greater Numbers

Goal Divide a four-digit number by a one-digit number.

1455 m of wire fencing was used to fence a square field. The side lengths of the square are whole numbers. There is less than 4 m left over.

? How long are the sides of the fence?

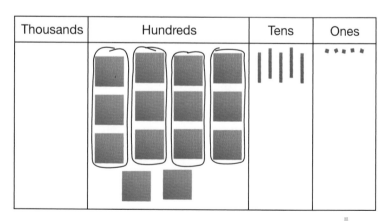

Alain's Division

A square has four equal sides.
I'll divide 1455 by 4 to calculate the length of each side.

I estimate that each side has a length between 300 m and 400 m.

Step 1 I'll show 1455 on a place value chart.

Thousands	Hundreds	Tens	Ones
▢	▢ ▢ ▢ ▢	|||||	⋯⋯

Step 2 I'll regroup the thousands block as 10 hundreds. Now I can divide 14 hundreds by 4. I have 255 left to divide.

$$
\begin{array}{r}
3 \\
4\overline{)1455} \\
-1200 \\
\hline
255
\end{array}
$$

Thousands	Hundreds	Tens	Ones
	▢▢▢ ▢▢▢ ▢▢▢ ▢▢▢ ▢ ▢	|||||	⋯⋯

Juanita's Division

Step 1 I'll use multiplication to divide.
$1455 \div 4 = \blacksquare$ means $4 \times \blacksquare = 1455$.
$4 \times 300 = 1200$, so the answer is just over 300.
I have 255 left to divide.

$$\begin{array}{r|r} 4\overline{)1455} \\ -\ 1200 & 300 \\ \hline 255 \end{array}$$

Step 2 $255 \div 4 = \blacksquare$ means $4 \times \blacksquare = 255$.
$4 \times 60 = 240$, so the answer is just over $300 + 60 = 360$.
I have 15 left to divide.

$$\begin{array}{r|r} 4\overline{)1455} \\ -\ 1200 & 300 \\ 255 \\ -\ 240 & 60 \\ \hline 15 \end{array} \Big) 360$$

A. Why did Alain place the digit 3 above the hundreds?

B. Why did Alain subtract 1200 from 1455?

C. Complete both Alain's and Juanita's divisions.
How long are the sides of the fence?
How much fencing is left over?

D. Multiply and then add the remainder to check your answers.

Reflecting

1. Explain how Alain might have estimated.

2. Why do you think Juanita multiplied by 300 instead of 400 in Step 1?

Checking

3. 2701 m of wire fencing is used to fence a square schoolyard. The side lengths are whole numbers. There is less than 4 m left over. What is the length of each side?
   a) Solve the problem using Alain's method.
   b) Check your answer using Juanita's method.
   c) Check your answer by multiplying and then adding the remainder.

Practising

4. Explain why you might estimate 6540 ÷ 7 using either 6300 ÷ 7 or 7000 ÷ 7.

5. Calculate. Estimate to check that each answer is reasonable.
   a) 3)3636
   b) 4)2855
   c) 3)2001
   d) 3)1458
   e) 9)6876
   f) 7)5508
   g) 8)6500
   h) 6)5056

6. Check one of your answers in Question 5 by multiplying and then adding the remainder.

7. An airplane is flying a distance of 3367 km from Vancouver to Toronto. It lands in Winnipeg, which is 1869 km from Vancouver. How do you know that the airplane has flown more than halfway to Toronto?

1869 km

Vancouver

Winnipeg

Toronto

8. A truck carries eight identical snowmobiles. The total mass of the truck with the snowmobiles is 4060 kg. If the mass of the truck is 2100 kg, what is the mass of each snowmobile?

9. Create and solve a problem that requires dividing a three-digit or four-digit number by a one-digit number. Check your answer by multiplying and then adding the remainder.

Rolling Products

Number of players: 2 to 4

How to play: Estimate the product of two numbers.

Step 1 A player rolls one die four times, and records each roll in a box on the game card.

Step 2 Each player estimates which of these intervals contains the product.

Interval
0 to 999
1000 to 1999
2000 to 2999
3000 to 3999
4000 to 4999

Step 3 Each player calculates the product.
If the product is within the estimated interval, the player scores one point.

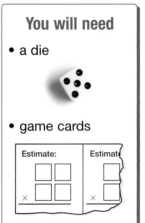

Norman's Estimate

I rolled 4, 5, 3, and 1.

I estimated that the product would be from 1000 to 1999.

I calculated the product to be 1395. I score one point.

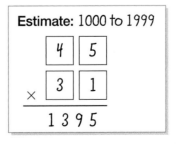

Estimate: 1000 to 1999

$$
\begin{array}{r}
4\ 5 \\
\times\ 3\ 1 \\
\hline
1\ 3\ 9\ 5
\end{array}
$$

9 Choosing Multiplication and Division Methods

Goal Choose and justify a calculation method.

? **What is the best method to multiply or divide to solve a water problem?**

Keep track of how you solve each problem.

A. How many litres of water would you use if you watered a lawn for 15 min?

B. How many bathtubs can you fill with 500 L of water?

C. How many litres of water would you use if you watered a lawn for 4 h?

D. How many days of drinking water for one person are lost by watering a lawn for 4 h?

E. Investigate other facts about using water. Use your facts or the facts on this page to create and solve multiplication and division problems.

Did you know?

• Watering a lawn uses about 35 L of water each minute.
• The average person needs about 5 L of water each day for drinking.
• A fast-dripping tap can waste about 750 L of water each week.
• A filled bathtub holds between 115 L and 190 L of water.

Reflecting

1. a) How do you decide when to multiply? How do you decide when to divide? Give examples.

   b) When do you estimate and when do you calculate? Use examples to explain.

   c) How do you decide when to use mental math, base ten blocks, pencil and paper, or a calculator? Give an example of when you used each, and justify your choice.

Doubling to Multiply by 2, 4, and 8

The dice show how you can double to multiply by 2, 4, and 8.

$2 \times 6 = 12$ $4 \times 6 = \blacksquare$ $8 \times 6 = \blacksquare$

$2 \times 6 = 12$

4 is double 2. 4×6 is double 2×6.
Double 12 is 24.

$2 \times 6 = 12$ $2 \times 6 = 12$

8 is double 4. 8×6 is double 4×6.
Double 24 is 48 .

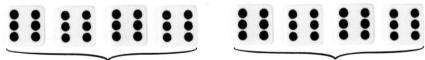

$4 \times 6 = 24$ $4 \times 6 = 24$

A. How can you use $2 \times 15 = 30$ to calculate 4×15?

B. How can you use the answer to 4×15 to calculate 8×15?

Try These

1. Calculate each product.

a) $2 \times 13 = 26$
$4 \times 13 = \blacksquare$
$8 \times 13 = \blacksquare$

b) $2 \times 25 = 50$
$4 \times 25 = \blacksquare$
$8 \times 25 = \blacksquare$

c) $2 \times 9 = 18$
$4 \times 9 = \blacksquare$
$8 \times 9 = \blacksquare$

d) $2 \times 50 = 100$
$4 \times 50 = \blacksquare$
$8 \times 50 = \blacksquare$

Skills Bank

LESSON

1

1. Calculate each product using mental math.
   a) 7×30
   b) 5×900
   c) 60×60
   d) 80×50

2. Solve each problem using mental math.
   a) A baseball field has 20 bleachers. If each bleacher can seat 30 people, how many people can be seated?
   b) A Web site gets 70 hits each minute. How many hits will the Web site get each hour?
   c) How many seconds are in one hour?

2

3. Which calculations are reasonable?
   a) $12 \times 18 = 216$
   c) $19 \times 18 = 342$
   e) $27 \times 27 = 729$
   b) $36 \times 36 = 2296$
   d) $32 \times 93 = 2976$
   f) $68 \times 18 = 2224$

4. Which products are greater than 4000? Explain your reasoning.
   a) 36×55
   b) 71×73
   c) 88×93
   d) 48×62

3

5. Calculate the number of different sandwiches you can make using three types of filling and four types of bread. Each sandwich uses one filling and one type of bread. Use a tree diagram.

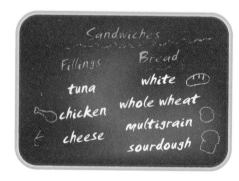

4

6. Calculate. Use a number line or mental math.
   a) 11×15
   b) 12×12

5

7. Calculate. Use base ten blocks.
   a) 12×21
   b) 15×15

8. There are 12 shelves in the library. Each shelf has 35 videos. How many videos are on the shelves?

9. a) Most NHL hockey teams have about 24 players. About how many players in total are there on the 30 teams?
   b) Each player on an NHL team uses about 40 hockey sticks in a season. How many sticks does each team use in a season?

10. Chloe trains for a race by swimming 48 lengths each day. The pool that she swims in is 25 m long. How many metres does she swim each day?

11. In Fort Langley, B.C., Aboriginal people used to trade beaver pelts for goods. The values of all other pelts were compared to the value of a beaver pelt. If 15 muskrat pelts had the same value as 1 beaver pelt, how many muskrat pelts would have the same value as 25 beaver pelts?

12. Calculate.
    a) $7 \times 175 = \blacksquare$
    b) $6 \times 1599 = \blacksquare$
    c) $18 \times 11 = \blacksquare$
    d) $67 \times 68 = \blacksquare$

13. What is the area of a 25 cm by 64 cm rectangle? Show your work.

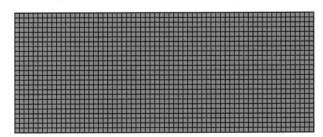

25 cm

64 cm

14. How many students can be carried by each number of buses if each bus carries 48 students? Show your work.
    a) 15 buses
    b) 25 buses
    c) 32 buses
    d) 45 buses

6 **15.** Calculate using mental math.

    a) $7\overline{)210}$ **b)** $3\overline{)1500}$ **c)** $5\overline{)4500}$ **d)** $7\overline{)4900}$

16. Multiply to check each answer in Question 15.

17. A hockey rink has 4 sections of seats.
The attendance for a game was 3600.
If each section had an equal number of fans,
how many fans were in each section?

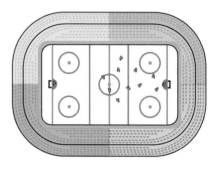

18. A 4800 mL container of juice is used to fill six glasses
equally. How much juice is in each glass?

7 **19.** Which calculations are reasonable?

    a) $3985 \div 5 = 697$ **b)** $2988 \div 9 = 332$ **c)** $\dfrac{759}{3\overline{)2577}}$ **d)** $\dfrac{868}{6\overline{)5208}}$

8 **20.** Calculate.

    a) $286 \div 7$ **d)** $9\overline{)8000}$ **g)** $9\overline{)3636}$

    b) $4\overline{)1536}$ **e)** $8709 \div 8$ **h)** $1000 \div 8$

    c) $4409 \div 5$ **f)** $7\overline{)6398}$ **i)** $6\overline{)8888}$

21. Check each answer in Question 20 by multiplying and
then adding the remainder.

22. An arena bought 3248 hot dogs to sell at a game.
There are 8 buns in a package.
How many packages of buns does the arena need to buy?

23. A square park has a perimeter of 3484 m.
What is the length of each side of the park?

24. Every 7th bottle cap shows a prize. How many prizes are
likely to be in a supermarket containing 1009 bottles?

Problem Bank

LESSON

1 1. A square field has a perimeter of 360 m.
   What is its area?

   2. A square field has an area of 900 square metres.
   What is its perimeter?

2 3. a) Estimate the number of weeks you have lived.
   b) Use your answer to estimate the number of weeks
   you have slept.

4 4. Teresa is placing chairs in 15 rows of 12 for a school
   concert. How many chairs does she need?

5 5. Determine the missing digits.

```
      4■
  ×  3 6
  -------
    2 7 0
+ 1 3 ■ ■
  -------
  ■ ■ ■ ■
```

6. Aaron is at a spot in his book where the page numbers
   of the two facing pages have a product of 1980.
   What are the two page numbers?

8 7. a) Determine the first number greater than 1001 that can
   be divided by both 2 and 5 without a remainder.
   b) Use your answer to determine the first number
   greater than 1001 that gives a remainder of 1 when
   divided by both 2 and 5.

8. The area of a strip of Metis finger weaving is 2025 cm^2.
   If the weaving is 5 cm wide, how long is the strip?

Chapter Review

LESSON

1. Use a multiplication fact to calculate each product.
   Show your work.
   a) 3×20 **b)** 5×300 **c)** 20×20 **d)** 60×90

2. The Toronto Blue Jays have 12 pitchers and 2 catchers.
   How many pitcher-catcher combinations could the team have?

3. Amaranta's class of 23 students each
   planted 25 seedlings. Arthur's class of
   32 students each planted 20 seedlings.
   Which class planted more seedlings?
   How many more did they plant?

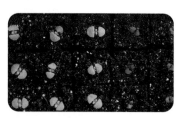

4. A school Web site gets 15 hits each night for 12 nights.
   How many hits did the Web site get during that time?
   Explain how you know your answer is reasonable.

5. Calculate the area of each rectangle.
   Explain how you know each answer is reasonable.

a)

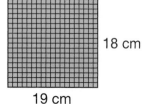

18 cm

19 cm

c)

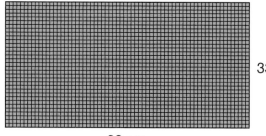

33 cm

66 cm

b)

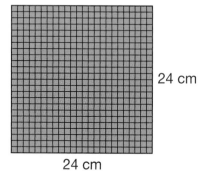

24 cm

24 cm

d)

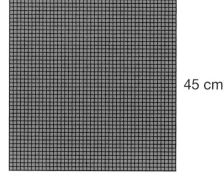

45 cm

45 cm

5 **6.** Calculate.

   a) 2400 ÷ 6   **b)** $5\overline{)2500}$ **c)** 1800 ÷ 3   **d)** $6\overline{)3600}$

8 **7.** Which answers are reasonable?
   Correct the unreasonable answers.

   a) 3986 ÷ 8 = 498 R2   **b)** $\dfrac{595}{5\overline{)2475}}$ **c)** $\dfrac{835}{6\overline{)5010}}$ **d)** 7696 ÷ 9 = 755 R1

8. a) Show that 2520 can be divided by 2, 3, 4, 5, 6, 7, 8, 9, and 10 without any remainder.

   b) What patterns do you notice?

9. What division would you write next?

   $7\overline{)1002}$ $7\overline{)1009}$ $7\overline{)1016}$ $7\overline{)1023}$

9 **10.** Keep track of how you solve each problem. Juanita's heart rate is 100 beats per minute when she runs.

   a) How many times will her heart beat in five minutes?

   b) About how many times will her heart beat each second?

   c) How many times will her heart beat in one hour?

   d) About how long will it take for her heart to beat 10 000 times?

11. For each problem you solved in Question 10, answer these questions.

   a) Did you multiply or divide? Explain your choice.

   b) Did you estimate or calculate? Explain your choice.

   c) Did you use mental math, base ten blocks, pencil and paper, or a calculator? Justify your choice.

Chapter Task

Raising Money

Drake's Boy Scout troop sold 235 boxes of hot chocolate and 256 tins of popcorn. Teresa's Girl Guide unit sold 95 carry cartons of cookies. Each carry carton contains 12 boxes of cookies.

$4.00 each box

$7.00 each box

$8.00 each tin

❓ Who raised more money?

Part 1

A. How much money did Drake's Boy Scout troop raise? Explain how you know each calculation is reasonable.

B. How much money did Teresa's Girl Guide unit raise? Explain how you know each calculation is reasonable.

C. Who raised more money? How much more?

Part 2

D. Drakes' Boy Scout troop and Teresa's Girl Guide unit each want to raise about $10 000. How many more items does each group have to sell to reach the goal? Explain how you know that each calculation is reasonable.

Task Checklist

- ☑ Did you estimate to check that each calculation is reasonable?
- ☑ Did you justify your choice of calculation method?
- ☑ Did you show all your steps?
- ☑ Did you explain your thinking?

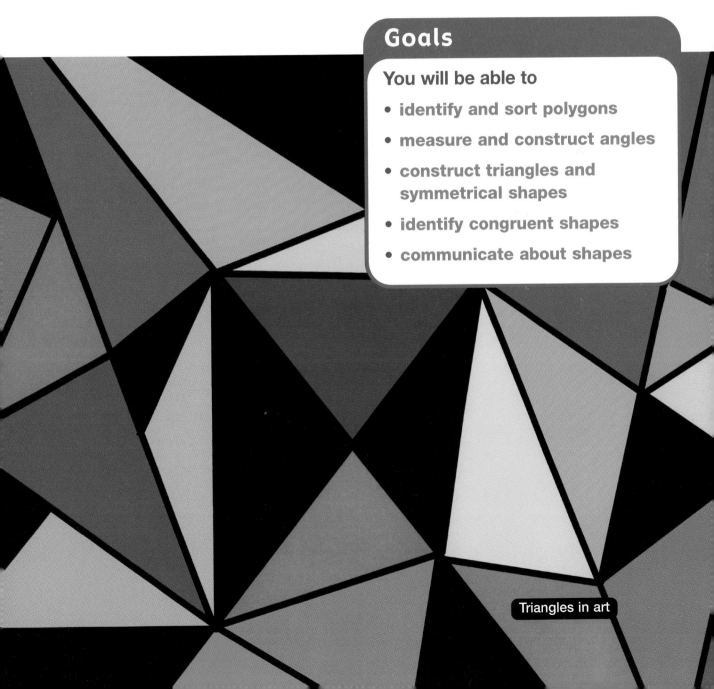

2-D Geometry

CHAPTER 7

Goals

You will be able to

- identify and sort polygons
- measure and construct angles
- construct triangles and symmetrical shapes
- identify congruent shapes
- communicate about shapes

Triangles in art

Getting Started

Shape Hunt

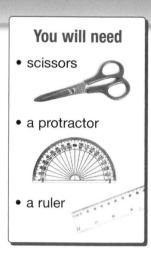

You will need
- scissors
- a protractor
- a ruler

? What two-dimensional (2-D) shapes can you find in this picture?

A. Find 2-D shapes with straight sides in the picture.
Trace them. Cut out the shapes.

B. Look at your shapes. Describe their attributes.
Which shapes have sides that are equal lengths?
Which shapes have opposite sides that are equal lengths?
Which shapes have **parallel** sides?
Which shapes have angles that are equal?
Which shapes have opposite angles that are equal?

C. Sort the shapes using a **Venn diagram**.

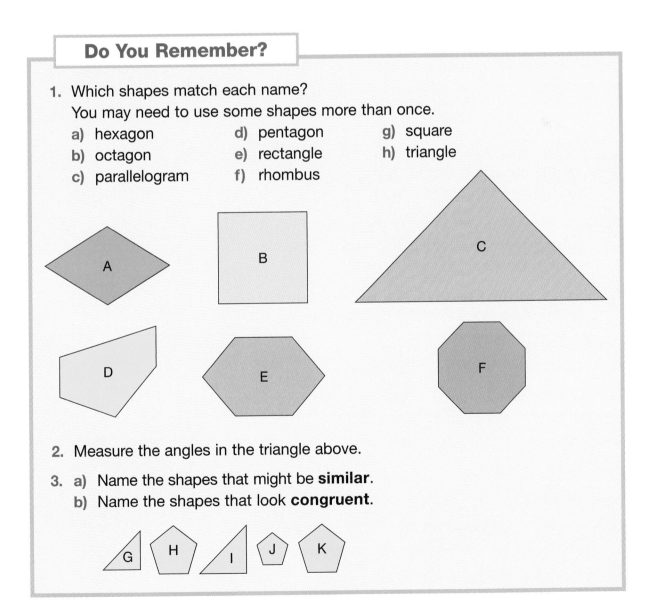

Do You Remember?

1. Which shapes match each name?
   You may need to use some shapes more than once.
   a) hexagon   d) pentagon   g) square
   b) octagon   e) rectangle   h) triangle
   c) parallelogram f) rhombus

2. Measure the angles in the triangle above.

3. a) Name the shapes that might be **similar**.
   b) Name the shapes that look **congruent**.

1 Constructing Symmetrical Shapes

Goal Construct 2-D shapes with one line of symmetry.

You will need
- grid paper

- a transparent mirror

- a ruler

- a protractor

Alain's Symmetry Puzzle

I made a puzzle by hiding the left half of a symmetrical picture.

? How can you use symmetry to complete Alain's picture?

A. Complete Alain's picture on grid paper. Use the grid to draw a matching side so that the picture is symmetrical.

B. Check for symmetry using a transparent mirror. Check again by folding the paper along the **line of symmetry**.

C. Mark a point on one half of the picture.

D. Use a transparent mirror to find the matching point on the other half of the picture.

E. Connect the two matching points.

F. Measure the distance from each point to the line of symmetry.

G. Measure angle G made by the line of symmetry and the **line segment** joining the two matching points.

H. Mark three more pairs of matching points.

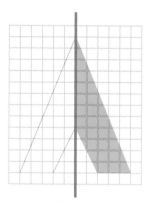

line of symmetry

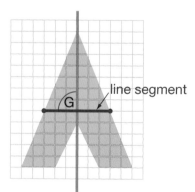

line of symmetry

190

Reflecting

1. How can you find a matching point without using a transparent mirror?

2. Norman said, "I can find a matching point for every point on a symmetrical picture." Do you agree? Explain your answer.

3. How can you complete Alain's puzzle by using matching points without a grid?

Checking

4. a) Copy this symmetry puzzle.
      Use symmetry to complete the picture.
   b) Check for symmetry using a transparent mirror and by folding the paper.
   c) Mark three pairs of matching points.

Practising

5. a) Copy this symmetry puzzle onto grid paper.
      Use symmetry to complete the picture.
   b) Check for symmetry using a transparent mirror and by folding the paper.
   c) Mark three pairs of matching points.

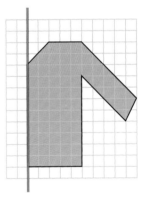

6. a) Copy this symmetry puzzle onto plain paper.

   b) Complete the picture and check for symmetry.
   c) Describe the method you used to check the symmetry.

7. a) Create your own symmetry puzzle.
   b) Ask a classmate to complete your picture.
   c) Check for symmetry.

2 Constructing Triangles

Goal Draw triangles with given side lengths and angle measures.

Heather made a model of a ramp used in stunt shows.
It includes a triangle with one side length of 6 cm.
The angles are measured in **degrees** (°).
One angle of the triangle is 105° and another is 25°.

degree (°)
A unit for measuring angles. 45 degrees can be written as 45°.

? How can you draw Heather's triangle?

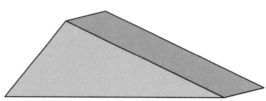

Aaron's Solution

Step 1 I started with one given side length, 6 cm.
I drew a line segment 6 cm long and labelled it.

Step 2 On one end of the line segment, I drew an angle that is 105° and labelled it.

Step 3 At the other end of the first line segment, I drew an angle that is 25° and labelled it.

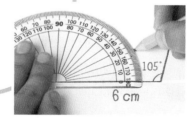

Step 4 I used a ruler to make the sides longer. I kept making them longer until they met to make a triangle. Then I erased the extra lengths.

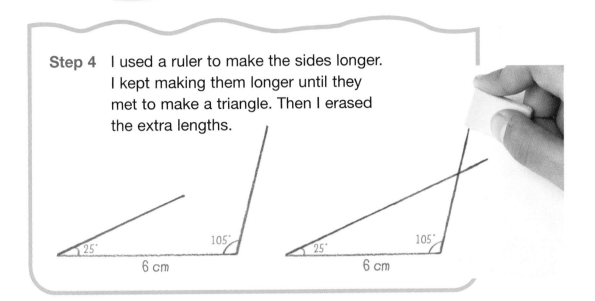

Reflecting

1. a) Where else could Aaron have drawn the 25° angle? Explain your answer.
   b) What would the new triangle look like?
   c) Would this triangle be congruent to Heather's triangle? Explain why or why not.

Checking

2. Draw two different triangles with one side length of 6 cm and an angle of 45°.

Practising

3. Draw two different triangles that have an angle of 120° and a side length of 6 cm.

4. Draw these triangles.
   a) Two of the side lengths are 4 cm and 7 cm. The angle between these sides is 100°.
   b) One side length is 8 cm and two angles are 50° and 85°.

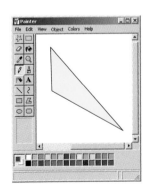

5. Compare your triangles from Question 4 with a classmate's triangles. Which triangles are congruent?

3 Classifying Triangles by Angles

You will need
• a ruler
• a protractor

 Goal Investigate angle measures in triangles.

Roofs have different shapes. Some roofs are steep so that snow slides off easily.

roof peak

? **How does the angle at the peak relate to the steepness of the roof?**

Teresa's Solution

I'll draw roof triangles with different angles at the peak.
Triangle A has a **right angle**.

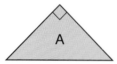
A

Triangle B has an **obtuse angle**.
It's not as steep as triangle A.

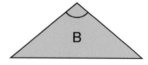
B

The angles in triangle C are all **acute angles**.
It's steeper than triangles A and B.

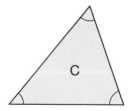
C

right angle
The angle made by a square corner. A right angle measures 90°.

90°

obtuse angle
An angle that measures greater than 90°

135°

acute angle
An angle that measures less than 90°

45°

A. Triangles can be classified as **right-angled**, **obtuse-angled**, or **acute-angled triangles**. Classify Teresa's roof triangles by the sizes of their angles.

B. Draw three roof triangles of different steepness.

C. Measure the three angles of each triangle. Label the angle measures.

D. Classify your triangles by the sizes of their angles.

E. How do the measures of the peak angles change as the roofs get steeper?

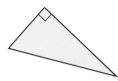

right-angled triangle

A triangle with one right angle

obtuse-angled triangle

A triangle with one obtuse angle

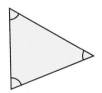

acute-angled triangle

A triangle with only acute angles

Reflecting

1. Which angle would you measure first to classify each triangle? Why?

   a)
   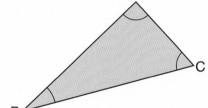

   b)
   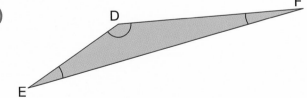

   c)
   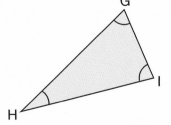

2. Do you need to measure all three angles to classify a triangle? Explain your answer.

Checking

3. **a)** What type of triangle has an angle that measures 120° and an angle that measures 30°?
   b) What type of triangle has an angle that measures 20° and an angle that measures 90°?

4. Classify the triangles by the sizes of their angles. Measure the angles if necessary.

   a)

   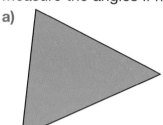

   b)

   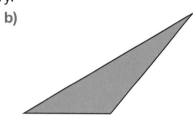

Practising

5. Kumiko's class made triangle name tags for open house. Classify the triangles.

   a)

   Erlwanger

   c)

   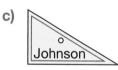
   Johnson

   b)

   Gorman

   d)

   Li

6. Look around the room. Find triangle shapes with different kinds of angles.
   a) Measure the sides and angles of the triangles.
   b) Draw the triangles. Label the angles.
   c) Classify the triangles according to their angle sizes.

7. Explain why you agree or disagree with each statement.
   a) Glynis said, "My triangle has one right angle, so it is a right-angled triangle."
   b) Martin said, "My triangle has one acute angle, so it is an acute-angled triangle."
   c) Jose said, "My triangle has one obtuse angle, so it is an obtuse-angled triangle."

Diagonal Angles

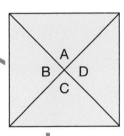

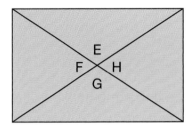

1 Measure and record the angles where the **diagonals** cross on the square and the other rectangle.

Angle Measures

Square		Rectangle	
A		E	
B		F	
C		G	
D		H	

2 a) What do you notice about the angles where the diagonals of a square cross?

b) What do you notice about the angles of the other rectangle?

3 Draw two rectangles of different sizes and measure the angles where the diagonals cross.
What conclusion can you make?

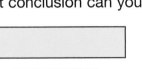

4 Measure the lengths of the diagonals in Question 1 from the **vertex** to the point where the diagonals cross. What do you notice?

4 Classifying Triangles by Side Lengths

Goal Investigate side lengths of triangles.

Camille builds model sailboats. She experiments with different sail shapes.

? How can you classify the sails by the lengths of their sides?

 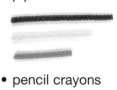
Camille's Pipe Cleaner Models

I use pipe cleaners to model and sort the sail shapes.

I can classify the sails by the lengths of their sides.

This model has three equal sides. It is an **equilateral triangle**.

This model has two equal sides. It is an **isosceles triangle**.

This model has sides of all different lengths. It is a **scalene triangle**.

equilateral
Having all sides equal in length

isosceles
Having two sides equal in length

scalene
Having no two sides equal in length

A. Make as many different triangles as you can. Use only one pipe cleaner for each side.

B. Record your triangles in colour on chart paper.

C. Identify other triangles **similar** to the blue triangle. How are these triangles similar? Look at side lengths and angle measures.

D. Identify other triangles like this two-coloured triangle. How are these triangles alike?

E. How is the three-coloured triangle different from all the others?

F. Classify your triangles by the lengths of their sides.

Reflecting

1. Describe a strategy for deciding whether a triangle is equilateral, isosceles, or scalene.

2. **a)** What do you notice about the angle measures of equilateral triangles?
   b) What do you notice about the angle measures of isosceles triangles?
   c) What do you notice about the angle measures of scalene triangles?

Checking

3. Classify these triangles by their side lengths and by their angle measures.

a)

90°

b)
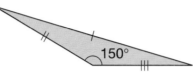
150°

c)

60°
60°   60°

4. Are these triangles classified correctly? Explain how you know.

a)
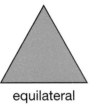
equilateral

b)
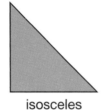
isosceles

c)
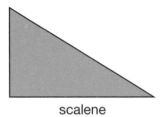
scalene

Practising

5. Classify the triangles by the lengths of their sides.

a)
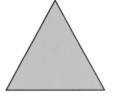

c)

e)
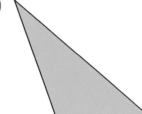

b)
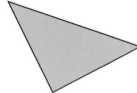

d)
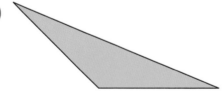

f)
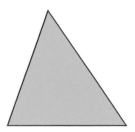

6. Use the triangles from Question 5 to complete a chart like this.

	Classification by size of angles	Number of lines of symmetry
a)		
b)		

200

Mid-Chapter Review

1 1. Use symmetry to complete these pictures.

a)

b)

2 2. Draw each triangle.

a) A side length is 4 cm and two angle measures are 60° and 80°.

b) Two side lengths are 5 cm and 6 cm and the angle between these sides is 120°.

3 3. Measure and record the angle measures of these triangles. Classify the triangles by their angle measures.

a)

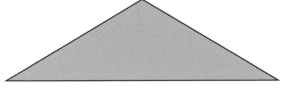

c)

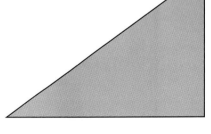

b)

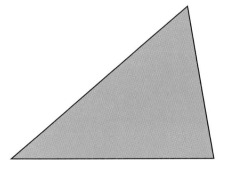

d)

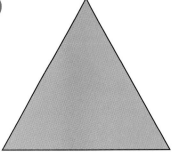

4 4. Measure and record the side lengths of the triangles in Question 3. Classify the triangles by their side lengths.

5 Measuring Angles in Polygons

Goal Identify and classify regular polygons by their angle measures.

Crackers come in different **polygon** shapes. Anna is playing a game of Mystery Cracker.

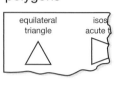
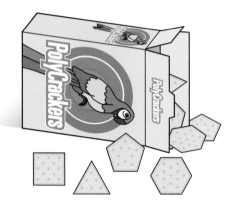

polygon

A closed 2-D shape with sides made from straight line segments

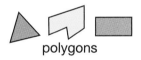
polygons

not polygons

Anna's Mystery Cracker

I'll measure the angles on a cracker shape and write a clue.

My cracker has six angles of 120°.

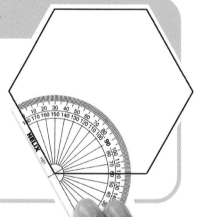

? **How can you identify a cracker by its angles?**

A. Measure the angles on a cracker drawing.

B. Write a clue about the angles of the cracker.

C. Trade clues with a classmate and solve the mystery.

Reflecting

1. What strategies did you use to identify the mystery cracker?

2. a) How does angle size change as the number of sides increases in these **regular polygons**?

   b) Predict the angle sizes in a regular octagon. Would they be greater or less than 120°? Why? Measure to check.

   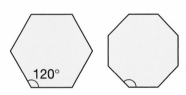

regular polygon

A polygon with all side lengths equal and all angles equal

regular polygons

not a regular polygon

Finding Shapes

1. Which of shapes A to I can you find in the square?

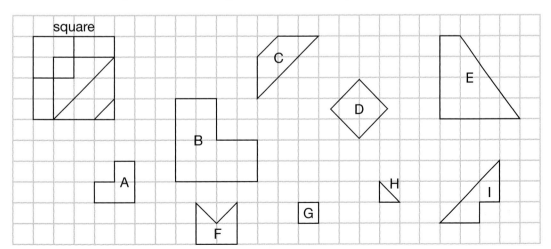

6 Properties of Polygons

Goal Investigate properties of geometric shapes.

Marcus's older brother, Geoff, is studying for his driver's licence test. He needs to learn these road signs.

yield

warning

speed limit

school crossing

stop

? **How can Marcus help Geoff recognize road signs by their shapes?**

Marcus's Shapes

It has three equal angles.
It has three lines of symmetry.
The side lengths are ———
Which sign is it?

front

yield

back

I'll make a study card for each sign. I can describe the **properties** of the polygon in each sign.

I can describe the yield sign using these properties:
- number of sides and angles
- side lengths
- angle measures
- number of parallel sides
- number of lines of symmetry

properties

The features of a shape that describe it

The properties of a square are 4 equal sides, 4 equal angles (all right angles), 2 pairs of parallel sides, and 4 lines of symmetry.

A. Finish Marcus's study card for the yield sign.

B. Make study cards for the other signs.
Use the properties of the polygons.

C. Ask a classmate to identify the signs by reading only the
front of your cards. If necessary, improve your descriptions
of the properties of the signs.

Reflecting

1. Which shapes can be identified
easily by the number of sides?

2. Which shapes can be identified
easily if you know some sides
are parallel?

3. Which shapes can be identified
easily if you know the angle sizes?

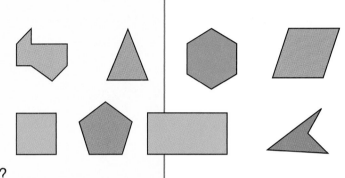

Checking

4. Name the polygon with these properties.

It has four lines of symmetry.

It has two pairs of parallel sides.

All of its angles are equal.

The opposite sides are equal.

Practising

5. Describe the properties of these polygons.

a)

b)

6. Find a polygon shape in your classroom.
Describe the properties of the shape.
Exchange your description with a classmate.
Figure out each other's shape.

7. Write a study card for a parallelogram.
Compare this study card with one for a square.

7 Sorting Polygons

Goal Sort and classify polygons by sides, angles, and vertices.

You will need
- polygons

  equilateral   isos
  triangle   acute t

- scissors

- Venn diagrams

- pattern blocks

Dan sorted polygons using a Venn diagram.
He labelled the circles but left out the last word.

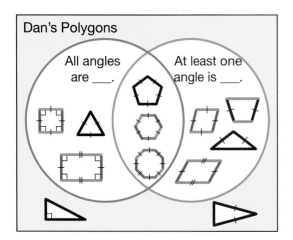

? **Can you figure out Dan's sorting rule?**

A. How are the polygons in the green circle the same?

B. How are the polygons in the red circle the same?

C. Three polygons are inside both circles.
What two things do these shapes have in common?

D. Two polygons are outside both circles.
Why are they not in either circle?

E. Work with a classmate. Sort Dan's polygons in a different
way using two properties from the list. Use a Venn diagram.

F. Figure out each other's sorting rules.

G. Sort Dan's polygons by the number of angles. Sketch the
sorting. What do you notice about the number of vertices
in each group?

H. What do you notice about the number of sides in
each group?

Properties
- number of sides
- number of angles
- number of vertices
- number of lines of
  symmetry
- number of parallel
  sides
- side lengths
- angle measures

Reflecting

1. What conclusion can you make about the number of angles, vertices, and sides in polygons?

2. Which sorting rules did you find easiest to use?

Checking

3. Do you agree with this sorting? Explain why or why not.

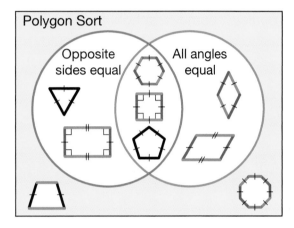

Practising

4. **a)** Sort eight of Dan's polygons using a Venn diagram. Decide on the sorting rules using the property list. Label the diagram.
   b) How are the shapes inside both circles the same?
   c) How are the shapes outside both circles the same?

5. What could be the sorting rule for this Venn diagram? Explain your thinking.

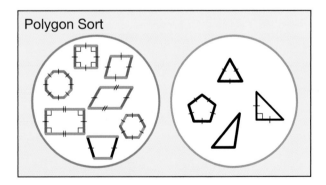

6. Sort pattern blocks using a Venn diagram.

8 Communicate About Shapes

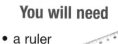

You will need
- a ruler
- a protractor

Goal Use math language to describe geometric ideas.

Monique couldn't come to school today. Sofia e-mailed directions so Monique could draw the picture they did in class.

? **How can Sofia improve her description?**

Sofia's Description

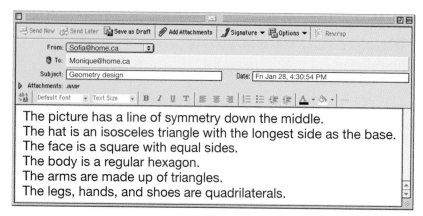

Send Now | Send Later | Save as Draft | Add Attachments | Signature ▼ | Options ▼ | Rewrap

From: Sofia@home.ca
To: Monique@home.ca
Subject: Geometry design   Date: Fri Jan 28, 4:30:54 PM
Attachments: none

Default Font | Text Size | B I U T | ≡ ≡ ≡ | ≣ ≣ ≣ ≣ | A ▼ ✎ ▼

The picture has a line of symmetry down the middle.
The hat is an isosceles triangle with the longest side as the base.
The face is a square with equal sides.
The body is a regular hexagon.
The arms are made up of triangles.
The legs, hands, and shoes are quadrilaterals.

Monique's Picture

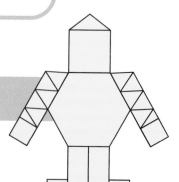

I made the picture according to Sofia's description.

A. Identify the strengths of Sofia's description.
Use the Communication Checklist.

B. Which directions probably gave Monique the most trouble?
Explain why.

Reflecting

1. What math language did Sofia use to communicate her ideas?

2. Which part do you think is easier, giving directions or following them? Why?

Checking

3. Rewrite Sofia's description so Monique's picture will be the same as the one they did in class.

Practising

4. Describe the clown face. Use math language.

5. Create your own shape picture. Work with a classmate. Take turns giving directions to draw each other's picture.

Skills Bank

1. Copy each symmetry puzzle.
   Use symmetry to complete the pictures.

   a)

   b)

2. Use symmetry to create a picture.
   How many lines of symmetry does your picture have?

3. Draw these triangles.
   a) One side length is 7 cm and one angle is 80°.
   b) One side length is 7 cm and two angles are 80° and 60°.
   c) Two side lengths are 5 cm each and the angle between them is 105°.

4. Classify the triangles by the sizes of their angles.

   a)

   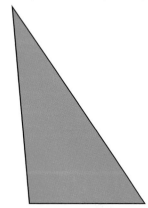

   b)

4 **5.** Draw an example of each.

   a) obtuse-angled triangle   **d)** scalene triangle
   b) acute-angled triangle   **e)** equilateral triangle
   c) right-angled triangle   **f)** isosceles triangle

5 **6. a)** Name these regular polygons in order from least to greatest angle size.
   b) Measure and record the angles to check.

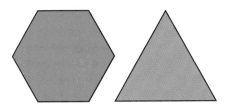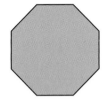

6 **7. a)** Write some properties of a parallelogram.
   b) Explain why a rectangle is a parallelogram.
   c) Explain why a square is a parallelogram.
   d) Explain why a rhombus is a parallelogram.

7 **8. a)** How are the shapes in the green circle the same?
   b) How are the shapes in the red circle the same?

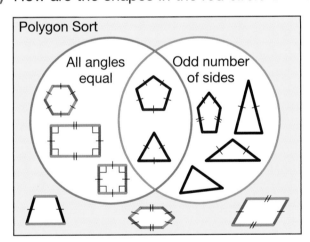

   c) Why are there three shapes outside both circles?
   d) Where do these shapes belong in the Venn diagram?

Problem Bank

LESSON

3

1. **a)** How can you cut this right-angled triangle once to get two right-angled triangles?
   b) How can you cut this right-angled triangle once to get an acute-angled triangle and an obtuse-angled triangle?

4

2. **a)** Choose a yellow card and a green card. If possible, draw a triangle that matches the words on both cards.
   b) Name all the pairs of cards for which you can draw triangles.
   c) Name a pair of cards for which it is impossible to draw a triangle. Explain why it is impossible.

scalene	equilateral	isosceles	obtuse-angled	acute-angled	right-angled

3. **a)** What type of triangle do the 12 toothpicks make?
   b) What other type of triangle can you make with 12 toothpicks?
   c) Can you use 12 toothpicks to make a scalene triangle without a right angle?

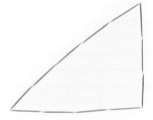

5

4. Which regular polygon in each pair has the greater angle size? Explain your answer.
   a) an equilateral triangle or a square
   b) a square or a hexagon
   c) an octagon or a pentagon

5. **a)** Use four toothpicks to make a quadrilateral with two acute angles and two obtuse angles. What is the name of the new shape?
   b) Use six toothpicks to make a regular hexagon. Show how you can change it into a hexagon with two acute angles.

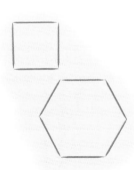

6. **What am I?** Sketch or name a shape below.

a) I have two pairs of parallel sides.
    I have two pairs of equal angles.
    Half of my angles are obtuse.

b) I have three pairs of parallel sides.
    All my sides are equal.

c) All my angles are obtuse.
    I have eight lines of symmetry.

d) All my angles are right angles.
    I have two lines of symmetry.

e) I have two parallel sides.
    I have two right angles, two acute
    angles, and one obtuse angle.

f) I have no lines of symmetry.
    I have no equal sides.

g) I have no parallel sides.
    All my angles are obtuse.

h) I have no parallel sides.
    All my angles are acute.

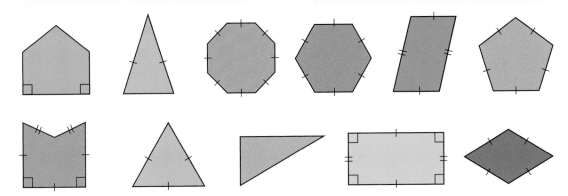

7. Which riddle in Question 6 matches each sign?

a)

b)

c) Dundas St

d)

8. One of the polygons in the Venn diagram is misplaced.
   a) Label the Venn diagram.
   b) Identify the misplaced polygon. Where should it be?

Polygon Sort

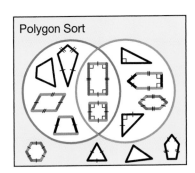

Chapter Review

LESSON

1 1. Copy this symmetry puzzle.
Use symmetry to complete the puzzle.
Describe two ways to check for symmetry.

2 2. a) Draw two different triangles, each with angle
measures of 100° and 20° and a side length of 4 cm.
   b) Measure and label the angles in your triangle.
   c) Name the angles as obtuse, acute, or right.

3 3. a) Name these regular polygons in order from least to
greatest angle size.
   b) Measure the angles to check your order.
Was it correct?

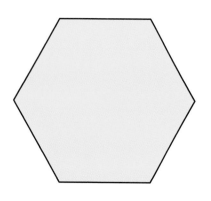
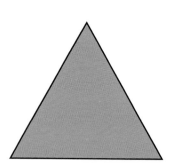
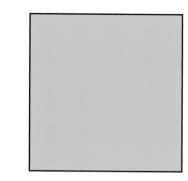

4 4. Classify these triangles by their angle measures and by their
side lengths.

a)

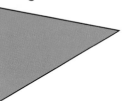

c)

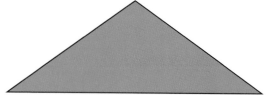

b)

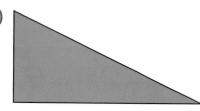

d)

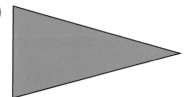

6

5. a) Sketch each polygon.

b) In your sketches, use colour to mark pairs of parallel sides.

c) Use colour to identify equal angles.

d) Draw the lines of symmetry for each polygon.

e) List three properties of each polygon.

Properties
- number of sides
- number of angles
- number of vertices
- number of lines of symmetry
- number of parallel sides
- side lengths
- angle measures

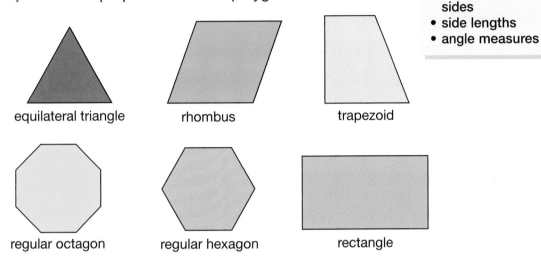

equilateral triangle   rhombus   trapezoid

regular octagon   regular hexagon   rectangle

7

6. Sort the polygons from Question 5 using lines of symmetry and angle properties. Use a Venn diagram.

8

7. Write directions so someone can draw this picture without seeing it.

Chapter Task

Design a Logo

A logo design contest is open to all Grade 5 students.

Logo Requirements
- one line of symmetry
- one right angle, one obtuse angle, and one acute angle
- seven different polygons (including an equilateral triangle, an isosceles triangle, and a scalene triangle)

? **How can you design a logo for the contest?**

A. Choose a product that you like.

B. Design a logo for the product.

C. Sketch your design according to the requirements.

D. Explain how your design meets each requirement.

Task Checklist

☑ Did you use measurements to check that your logo meets the requirements?

☑ Is your explanation clear?

☑ Did you use math language?

Cumulative Review

Cross-Strand Multiple Choice

1. Nadia bicycled 5.50 km from her home, then turned around and bicycled back 2.85 km. How far is she from her home?

   A. 8.35 km   **B.** 2.75 km   **C.** 2.65 km   **D.** 3.35 km

2. Yoshi measured the border of a rectangular sign to be 15.6 m. What might be the side lengths of the border?

   A. 8.4 m by 7.2 m   **C.** 3.2 m by 5.3 m
   B. 4.5 m by 3.3 m   **D.** 5.1 m by 10.5 m

3. 38 students each sold 16 tickets. How many tickets did they sell altogether?

   A. 608   **B.** 584   **C.** 266   **D.** 684

4. Sofia is sorting 2780 baseball cards into a book with 8 cards on each page. How can you describe the setup of the pages?

   A. 34 pages of cards, 6 cards left over
   B. 347 pages of cards, 4 cards left over
   C. 347 pages of cards, 5 cards left over
   D. 347 pages of cards, 6 cards left over

5. Which terms describe this triangle?

   A. isosceles, right-angled
   B. scalene, acute-angled
   C. scalene, obtuse-angled
   D. isosceles, obtuse-angled

   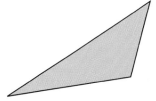

6. Petra described how regular hexagons and regular octagons are the same and how they are different.
   Which description is not correct?

   A. Both shapes have an even number of sides.
   B. Both shapes have sides of equal length.
   C. Both shapes have all angles equal.
   D. Both shapes have an odd number of vertices.

Cross-Strand Investigation

Sports Day

7. Patrick's school is having an indoor sports day.

   a) The sports day is planned for three days after January 10. Write the date for the sports day in numeric format. Use this year.

   b) Patrick's school has 281 students and 18 of them are helping to organize the sports day. The others are arranged in 9 teams that are as equal as possible. List the number of students on each team.

   c) Each student is making a triangle name tag. Each name tag has to be acute-angled and scalene, with one side length of 7 cm. Draw a name tag. Measure and label the side lengths and angles.

   d) What unit would you use to measure the perimeter of the gym? Explain your choice.

8. a) Liam sketched this shape as a logo for sports day. He wants to use beading for the outline. Estimate the length of beading he will need.

   b) Name the polygon shown on the grid.

   c) Anna's team earned these points in a game: 1.43, 4.78, and 2.50. How many points have they earned so far?
   How many more points does Anna's team need to win a banner?

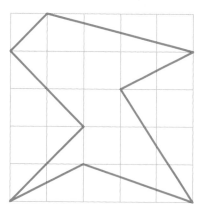

The side length of each square is 1 m.

Win a Banner!
10.00 points

   d) For Pattern Hop, each team makes a number pattern by hopping. The first person hops two times. The second person hops five times. How many times might the third person hop? Extend your pattern for a team of eight people. Describe your number pattern.

Area and Grids

Goals

You will be able to

- **estimate and measure areas of 2-D shapes**

- **explore relationships between perimeter and area**

- **develop and use a rule for calculating areas of rectangles**

- **solve area problems by solving simpler problems**

- **use coordinate systems on grids to describe locations**

Old Fort William in Thunder Bay

Getting Started

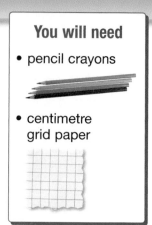
Measuring Area

Akiko made this coaster with ceramic tiles.
Each tile is one square centimetre.

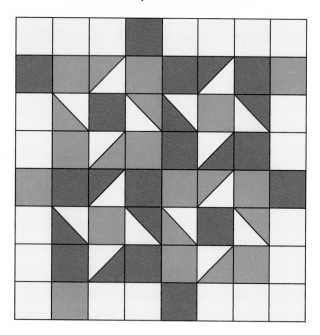

? **How can you design a coaster so that one colour covers twice as much area as each of the other two colours?**

A. Measure the area of the coaster in square centimetres.

B. Estimate the area of the coaster that is red in square centimetres.

C. Measure the area covered by each colour in square centimetres.

D. What do you notice about the sum of the areas covered by the three colours? Explain your observations.

E. What is the perimeter of the coaster?

F. Design your own coaster with three colours. One colour should cover twice as much area as each of the other two colours. Use square tiles to model your design. Draw your design on grid paper.

Do You Remember?

1. Name three things that you would measure using each area unit.
   a) square metres
   b) square centimetres

2. Draw a different rectangle that has the same area as this rectangle.

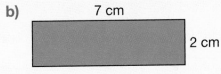

3. Create a model of each rectangle. Then calculate its area.

a)

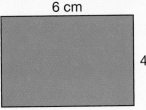

6 cm

4 cm

b)

7 cm

2 cm

4. Use coordinates to describe the location of each town or city.
   a) Welland
   b) Sault Ste Marie
   c) Windsor
   d) Pembroke

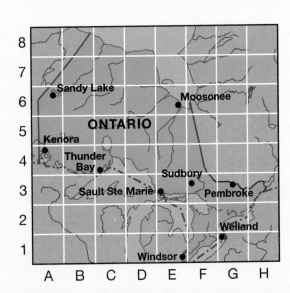

1 Areas of Polygons

Goal Estimate and measure the area of polygons.

Juanita wants to know how much fabric paint she will need to make baseball hat logos for summer camp. She used a geoboard to design the logos. She recorded her designs on dot paper.

? Which logo will need more fabric paint?

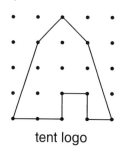
tent logo

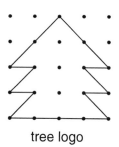
tree logo

Juanita's Estimate

I know one square has an area of one square unit.

The tent logo covers five whole squares and parts of eight other squares.

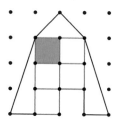

If I put together the parts, they make about three squares.

I estimate the area is about eight square units.

Juanita's Measurement

The tent logo can be divided into squares and **right-angled triangles**.

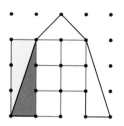 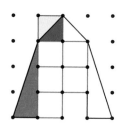

The area of the red triangle is half the area of the red rectangle. Now I know the area of the triangle, too.

I can use the rectangles and right-angled triangles to measure the area.

A. Finish calculating the area of the tent logo.

B. Model the tree logo on a geoboard.
Record it on dot paper.

C. Estimate the area of the tree logo.

D. Use Juanita's method to measure the area of the tree logo in square units. Describe how you measured the area.

E. Which logo will need more fabric paint?

Reflecting

1. Explain how you estimated the area of the tree logo.

2. Can you measure the area of this triangle using Juanita's method? Explain your answer.

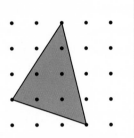

Checking

3. Martin designed this logo for the baseball hats.
   a) Estimate its area in square units.
   b) Measure its area in square units.

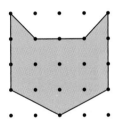

Practising

4. Estimate and then measure the area of each polygon in square units.

a)  b) 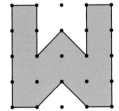 c)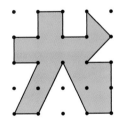

5. a) Use a geoboard to design your own logo.
   Record it on dot paper.
   b) Estimate the area of your logo in square units.
   c) Measure the area of your logo in square units.
   Describe how you measured the area.

2 Areas of Irregular 2-D Shapes

Goal Develop methods to measure the areas of irregular 2-D shapes.

Liam traced oak leaves from trees of different ages. He wants to know if the surface area of a leaf changes with the age of the tree.

? **How can you measure the area of a leaf?**

A. Cover the oak leaf with one layer of gravel. Move the gravel to centimetre grid paper. How many squares does the gravel cover? Use this method to measure the area of the leaf to the **nearest square centimetre**.

B. Place a centimetre grid transparency on top of the oak leaf. Count the whole squares inside the leaf and the whole squares you can make by putting together the part squares. Use this method to measure the area of the leaf to the nearest square centimetre.

C. Place a centimetre grid transparency on top of the oak leaf. Count the whole squares inside the leaf and the squares that are half filled or more. Use this method to measure the area of the leaf to the nearest square centimetre.

Reflecting

1. Did you get the same answer with each method? Explain why or why not.

2. Which method do you think works best for the leaf? Explain your choice.

3. Suggest how you could improve one of the methods to make your measurements more precise.

You will need

- centimetre grid paper

- aquarium gravel

- a centimetre grid transparency

- oak leaf tracing

nearest square centimetre

A rounded measure

If less than half a square remains, round down.

If more than half a square remains, round up.

Pushing Corners

1 Make a four-by-four square on a geoboard. Record it on dot paper. What is the area of the shape? What is the perimeter?

You will need
- a geoboard

- elastics

- dot paper

2 Push in one corner. Record the shape on dot paper. What is the area of the shape? What is the perimeter?

3 Continue to push in corners and record the shapes on dot paper. What is the area of each shape? What is the perimeter?

4 As you push in corners, how does the perimeter change? How does the area change?

3 Relating Perimeter and Area of Rectangles

Goal Explore relationships among side lengths, perimeter, and area of rectangles.

Camille is making a tabletop from 1 **cm²** tiles for her collection of tiny dolls. She wants the tabletop to have a perimeter of 24 cm.

? **What are the side lengths of the tabletop with the greatest area?**

A. Use tiles to make a rectangle that has a perimeter of 24 units. Draw the rectangle on centimetre grid paper. Label its side lengths.

B. Use string to model the perimeter of your rectangle. Adjust the string to fit tightly around the tiles. Cut the string.

C. Use the piece of string to make a new rectangle. Fill the rectangle with tiles. Draw the rectangle on grid paper. Label its side lengths.

D. Repeat Part C to make all of the possible rectangles.

E. Cut out the rectangle drawings and order them from least to greatest area.

F. Use an organized list to find relationships between how the rectangle looks and its area.

cm²
The symbol for the area unit square centimetre. 4 cm² is read "four square centimetres."

Rectangles with a Perimeter of 24 cm

Sketch of rectangle shape	Side 1 (cm)	Side 2 (cm)	Area (cm²)

G. What are the side lengths of the rectangular tabletop with the greatest area?

Reflecting

1. Suppose the perimeter of a rectangle stays the same while the length increases. What happens to the width?

2. a) What did you discover about how the shape of the rectangle and its area are related?
   b) If you wanted to make a rectangle with the greatest area, what type of rectangle would you make?

3. If you know the area and perimeter of a rectangle, can you be sure of its side lengths? Explain.

Dividing Areas

You will need
• dot paper

This hexagon has an area of 12 cm².

A. How can you divide the hexagon into four pieces of equal area?

B. What is the area of each piece?

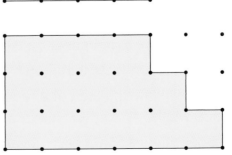

Try This

1. Show two different ways to divide this octagon into five pieces of equal area.

4 Area Rule for Rectangles

You will need
- centimetre grid paper
- a 30 cm ruler
- advertisements

Goal Develop and explain a rule for calculating the area of a rectangle.

Jose designed four different newspaper advertisements for the school book fair. The newspaper charges by the square centimetre for advertising space, so Jose wants to calculate the area of each design.

? **How can you calculate the cost of an advertisement if you know its length and width?**

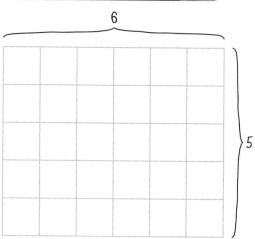

Jose's Calculation

I measure the length and width of the smallest design.
I draw it on centimetre grid paper.

The rectangle is made up of five rows of six squares or six columns of five squares. This is like a multiplication array.

5 x 6 = 30

A. Measure the length and width of each advertisement.

B. Draw each rectangle on grid paper.

C. Write the multiplication facts that match each rectangle.

D. How can you calculate the area of a rectangle if you know its length and width? Write your rule in words.

E. The newspaper charges $5 for each square centimetre of an advertisement. Which advertisement will cost about $200?

Reflecting

1. Will the area rule in Part D work for calculating the area of all rectangles? Explain why or why not.

2. If you wanted to calculate the area of a full-page advertisement, would you use a grid or the area rule? Explain your choice.

3. Jose says he cannot use the rule to calculate the area of this shape. Do you agree? Explain.

Checking

4. Jose designed two more advertisements for the book fair. Measure the length and width of each advertisement. Calculate each area. Use the rule for the area of a rectangle. Show your work.

a)

Book Fair

b)

Book Fair

Practising

5. Calculate the area of each rectangle. Use the rule for the area of a rectangle. Show your work.

a) 13 cm

15 cm

b) 30 cm

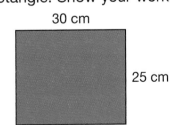

25 cm

6. a) Three different rectangles each have an area of 30 cm^2. Predict the side lengths. Use the rule for the area of a rectangle.

b) Do the rectangles all have the same perimeter? Explain.

Mid-Chapter Review

1 1. Estimate and then measure the area of each polygon in square units.

a)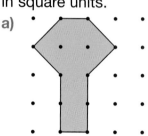

b)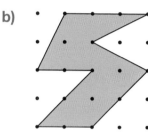

2 2. Measure the area of the muskrat track to the nearest square centimetre. Describe your method.

3 3. Mario made a rectangle with 1 cm² square tiles. It has a perimeter of 18 cm.

   a) Create a table to show the possible lengths and widths of the rectangle.

   b) Calculate the area of each rectangle in the table.

   c) What are the length and width of the rectangle with an area of 18 cm²?

4 4. Calculate each area. Use the rule for the area of a rectangle. Show your work.

a)
64 cm

36 cm

b)
75 cm

12 cm

Stretching and Shrinking Rectangles

Is each statement true?
Use square tiles to model rectangles to check.

1 Doubling the length and the width of a rectangle will double the area.

2 Doubling the length of a rectangle and not changing the width will double the area.

3 Halving the width of a rectangle and not changing the length will halve the area.

4 Halving the width and the length of a rectangle will halve the area.

5 Solve Problems by Solving Simpler Problems

Goal Solve problems by breaking them into smaller parts.

Alain's school is planting a wildflower lawn.
Each package of seeds covers 4 **m²** of ground.

3 m

8 m

5 m

3 m

? How many packages of seeds are needed?

m²
The symbol for the area unit square metre.
4 m² is read "four square metres."

Alain's Solution

Understand
I have to figure out how many packages of seeds are needed to cover the area of the lawn.

Make a Plan
The lawn shape can be divided into two rectangles: 5 m by 3 m and 8 m by 3 m.

I'll multiply the length by the width to calculate the area of each rectangle.

I'll add the two areas. Then I'll divide by 4 because each package covers 4 m².

3 m

8 m

5 m   area 1

area 2

3 m

Carry Out the Plan
area 1: 5 m x 3 m = 15 m²
area 2: 8 m x 3 m = 24 m²
area total: 15 m² + 24 m² = 39 m²

39 ÷ 4 is almost 10.

We need 10 packages of seeds.

1. Why was solving two simpler problems a good strategy for Alain's area problem?

2. Yoshi says he can calculate the area of the lawn by calculating the area of an 11 m by 5 m rectangle and subtracting the area of an 8 m by 2 m rectangle. Would you get the same answer using Yoshi's method? Explain why or why not.

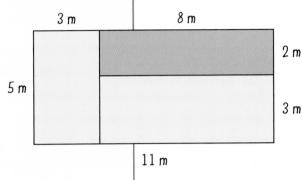

Checking

3. Heather says she found another way to divide the school's lawn into rectangles.
   a) Calculate the area of the lawn using a different set of rectangles than Alain or Yoshi.
   b) Did you get the same answer as Alain? Explain why or why not.

Practising

4. Emma is making initials to put on her backpack. Calculate the area of each letter in square centimetres. Show your work.

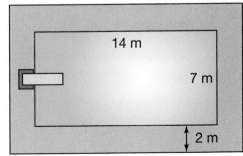

5. Ray swims in a pool that is 7 m wide and 14 m long. The pool deck is 2 m wide on all sides of the pool. What is the area of the pool deck in square metres? Show your work.

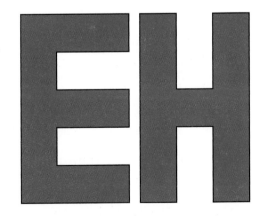

6 Modelling Area

Goal Model area using an appropriate scale.

Jasleen's school is holding a craft fair in the school playground. The playground is a rectangle with a length of 40 m and a width of 28 m.

? **How can you use a model of the playground to decide the sizes and locations of the booths?**

Jasleen's Model

I'll model the craft fair.

Metres are too big to draw on paper, so I'll make a **scale model**.

I want the model to fit on centimetre grid paper, so I'll use this **scale**: 1 cm represents 2 m.

scale model
A model that is larger or smaller than the real object, but is the same shape. A scale model is similar to the real object.

scale
The size of a model compared to what it represents. If you use this scale, 1 cm represents 1 m, a real object that is 1 m tall will be 1 cm tall in your model.

A. What are the length and width of Jasleen's model?

B. Model the playground. Include the scale of the model.

C. How much real area does an area of 1 cm² on the model represent? Why?

D. Jasleen draws a booth for selling jewellery on the model that is 1 cm by 2 cm. Add this booth to your model.

E. What is the area of the jewellery booth on the model? Include an appropriate unit.

F. What is the area of the real jewellery booth? Include an appropriate unit.

G. Add another booth to your model. Calculate the area of the real booth it represents.

Reflecting

1. Did Jasleen's scale, 1 cm represents 2 m, make sense?

2. Why did you use a different unit to describe the area of the booth on the model and the area of the real booth?

3. What are some of the advantages of using a scale model instead of a sketch that does not include units?

Checking

4. Jasleen is volunteering at an archeological dig site. The dig site is an 18 m by 14 m rectangle. She wants to make a scale model of the site on grid paper.
   a) Choose a scale. Explain why you chose that scale.
   b) Model the dig site. Include the scale of your model.
   c) What is the area of the real dig site?
   d) What is the area of the model of the dig site?
   e) If a region of the real dig site has an area of 10 m², what will be the area of the region on your model?

Practising

5. Would you measure each area in square kilometres, square metres, square centimetres, or square millimetres?
   a) number key on a cell phone   b) city

6. Jason is in charge of the pool at a community centre. He wants to make a model of the pool so he can plan roped-off areas for public swims. The pool is 50 m by 24 m.
   a) What is the area of the pool?
   b) Draw a model of the pool. Include the scale.
   c) What is the area of your model?
   d) If a region of 240 m² is roped off in the pool, what will be the area of the roped-off region on your model?

7 Coordinate Grids

You will need

• coordinate grid paper

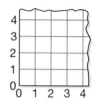

Goal Use coordinate pairs to identify and describe locations on a grid.

Glynis designed this logo for her summer camp. She wants to e-mail it to Martin, but she doesn't have a scanner.

? How can you use coordinate pairs to describe the logo?

Glynis's Solution

I'll draw the logo on a **coordinate grid**.

Then I'll use **coordinate pairs** to name points on the logo.

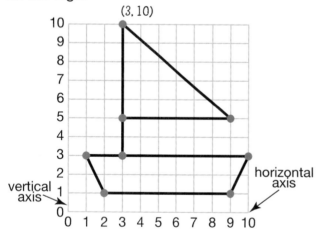

coordinate grid
A grid with each horizontal and vertical line numbered in order

coordinate pair
A pair of numbers that describes a point where a vertical and a horizontal line meet on a coordinate grid. The coordinate from the horizontal axis is always written first.

The top of Glynis's sail is at (3, 10).

A. What is the coordinate pair for the blue point at the bottom of the sail?

B. What are the coordinate pairs for the green points on the logo?

C. What instructions should Glynis include so that Martin can re-create this logo on a coordinate grid?

236

Reflecting

1. What is the difference between locating something on a map grid and locating something on a coordinate grid?

2. In a coordinate pair, the order of the numbers is important. What if Glynis said the top of the sail is at (10, 3) instead of (3, 10)?

3. Why were the coordinate pairs of only some points on the design needed?

Checking

4. Martin had another idea for a logo.
   a) What points on the logo can you use to describe it?
   b) Write the instructions to draw the logo from these points.

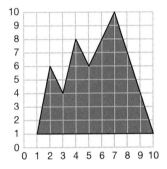

Practising

5. Michael started a drawing of his first initial on a coordinate grid.
   a) Name the coordinate pairs for the points he has drawn so far.
   b) Write the other coordinate pairs he needs to finish the M.

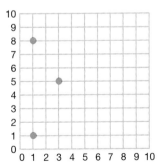

6. Draw each shape so that the vertices can be named with coordinate pairs.
   a) a right-angled triangle   b) an isosceles triangle

7. Draw a design. Use coordinate pairs to explain how to draw your design. Exchange your instructions with a classmate.

Skills Bank

LESSON

1 1. Estimate and then measure the area of each polygon in square units.

a)

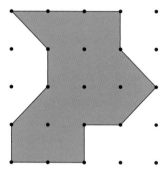

b)

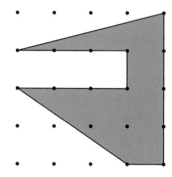

2 2. Measure the area of each shape to the nearest square centimetre.

a)

b)

3 3. Complete each table.

a) **Rectangles with a Perimeter of 28 cm**

Side 1 (cm)	Side 2 (cm)	Area (cm²)
1	13	13
7	7	49

b) **Rectangles with a Perimeter of 32 cm**

Side 1 (cm)	Side 2 (cm)	Area (cm²)
1	15	15
8	8	64

4. Calculate the area of each rectangle. Show your work.

a)

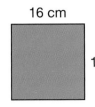

16 cm

16 cm

b)

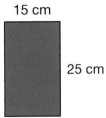

15 cm

25 cm

5. Calculate the area of each shape. Show your work.

a)

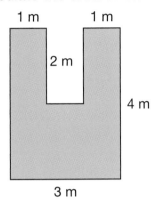

1 m   1 m

2 m

4 m

3 m

b)

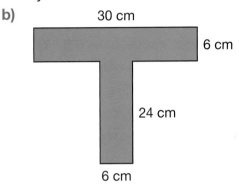

30 cm

6 cm

24 cm

6 cm

6. Would you measure each area in square kilometres, square metres, square centimetres, or square millimetres?

a) area of a stamp   c) area of a province   e) area of a stop sign
b) area of a pond   d) area of a barn door   f) area of a fingernail

7. What scale would you use to model each area on centimetre grid paper?

a) school parking lot that is 85 m long and 20 m wide
b) park that is 600 m long and 500 m wide
c) town that is 17 km long and 45 km wide

8. Write the coordinate pair for each point.

a) red   c) purple
b) blue   d) pink

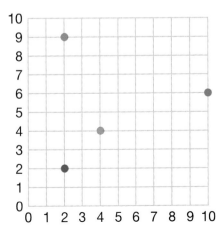

Problem Bank

1

1. Use a geoboard to design a polygon that is not a rectangle and has an area of eight square units. Record your design on dot paper.

2. Can you use grid paper to measure the area of an **obtuse-angled triangle**? Draw obtuse-angled triangles on grid paper to try to find a way to do it. Describe what you discovered.

2

3. Which province has a greater area: Alberta or Saskatchewan?

3

4. a) Draw a rectangle on centimetre grid paper. Make the number of area units the same as the number of perimeter units.

   b) Draw a rectangle on centimetre grid paper. Make the number of area units one less than the number of perimeter units.

4

5. Kaylee is making a wall hanging by gluing square sequins on 1 m² of fabric. Each sequin has an area of 1 cm². How many sequins will she need?

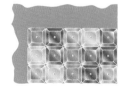

240

6. This room is being carpeted.
No carpet is needed under the wall unit.
The carpet comes in a roll 4 m wide.
   a) What length of carpet is needed?
   b) How much carpet will be left over?

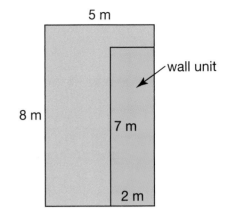

5 m

wall unit

8 m

7 m

2 m

7. Jerome made a patio on three sides
of a fish pond. Is the area of the
pond greater than or less than the
area of the patio?

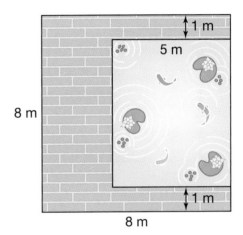

1 m

5 m

8 m

1 m

8 m

8. Louise made a scale model of this letter L.
The model had an area of 36 square units.
What scale did she use?

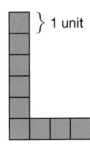

} 1 unit

9. Frances and Gary each have a gerbil in a cage. One cage
is 40 cm by 40 cm and the other cage is 50 cm by 30 cm.
They have the cages on a table that is 2 m by 1 m.
They want to build a play area on the table between the
two cages. What are the length and width of the greatest
rectangular play area they can make? Use a model.

Chapter Review

LESSON

1

1. Estimate and then measure the area of each polygon in square units.

   a)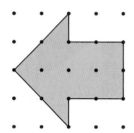

   b)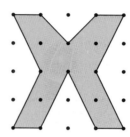

2

2. Measure the area of each shape to the nearest square centimetre. Describe the strategy you used.

   a)

   b)

3

3. Sebastian made a rectangle with 1 cm^2 square tiles. The rectangle has a perimeter of 40 cm.

   a) Create a table to show the possible lengths and widths of the rectangle.

   b) Calculate the area of each rectangle.

   c) What are the length and the width of the rectangle with an area of 96 cm^2?

4. Calculate each area. Use the rule for the area of a rectangle. Show your work.

a)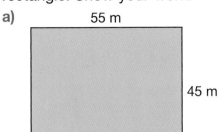

55 m

45 m

b)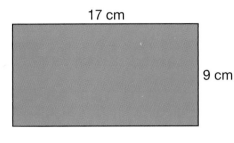

17 cm

9 cm

5. Calculate the area of each shape. Show your work.

a)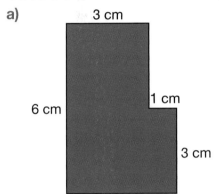

3 cm

1 cm

6 cm

3 cm

b)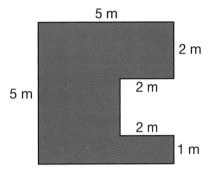

5 m

2 m

2 m

5 m

2 m

1 m

6. A park with mountain-bike trails is a rectangle with a length of 22 km and a width of 15 km.
  a) What is the area of the park?
  b) Draw a model of the park using this scale:
    1 cm represents 1 km.
  c) What is the area of your model?

7. Give the coordinate pairs and instructions needed to describe this rocket shape.

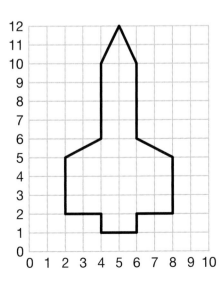

Chapter Task

Model a Han Dynasty Home

In ancient China, during the Han Dynasty (about 200 B.C.E. to 220 C.E.), people designed their homes. The homes of wealthy families often included a central courtyard, private gardens with ponds and trees, a watchtower, a waiting area, animal pens, and a vegetable garden. There was often a wall enclosing the entire home.

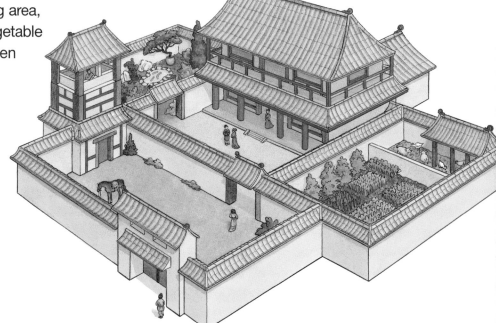

? How can you design a Han Dynasty home?

A. Make a model of a Han Dynasty home on a coordinate grid. Make at least one L-shaped courtyard and one U-shaped garden. Use this scale: 1 cm represents 1 m.

B. Use the grid to describe the location of the garden.

C. Calculate the area of each part of your model. Calculate the total area of your model.

D. If your home were built, what would be the area of each part of the home? What would be the total area of the home?

Task Checklist

- ☑ Did you label your model?
- ☑ Did you show all the work for your calculations?
- ☑ Did you include appropriate units?

Multiplying Decimals

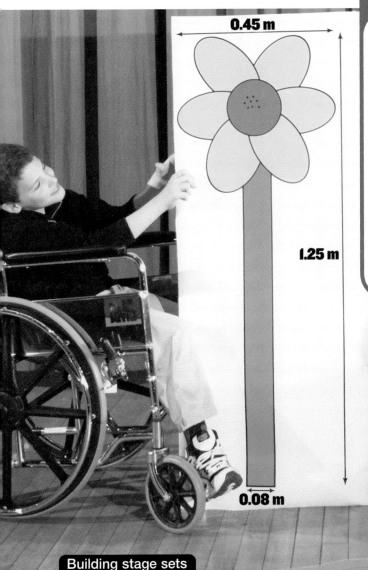

0.45 m

1.25 m

0.08 m

Building stage sets

Goals

You will be able to

- estimate products involving decimals and explain your strategies

- multiply decimals by 10 and 100

- multiply tenths and hundredths by whole numbers using models, drawings, and symbols

- select an appropriate multiplication method

CHAPTER 9

Getting Started

Trip Distances and Times

Aaron rode the school bus 4 km each way every school day last year. He went to school on 187 days.

? **If you took a trip that is either the total distance or the total time that Aaron was on the bus last year, where could you go?**

A. Estimate the total distance Aaron travelled on the school bus last year. Write an equation to show how you estimated.

B. Model 187 with base ten blocks or a sketch. Use your model to calculate the total distance Aaron travelled on the bus last year. Record the total distance.

100   10   1

C. Use the total distance from Part B. If you took a trip that distance, where could you go? Explain your answer.

D. Each 4 km bus trip took about 10 min. How many days would it be before Aaron had been on the bus one full hour? About how many hours would Aaron have been on the bus in 187 days?

E. Use the total time Aaron was on the bus last year. About how far could you go in that amount of time if you travelled 80 km each hour? Explain your estimation strategy.

F. Compare your answers to Parts B and E. Which distance is greater? Why do you think that distance is so much greater?

G. Create and solve your own problem about Aaron's bus travel.

Do You Remember?

1. Calculate.
   a) 4×23
   b) 5×37
   c) 8×46
   d) 10×51
   e) 472×100
   f) 100×36

2. Estimate each product.
   a) 6×58
   b) 23×34
   c) 9×237

3. Calculate.
   a) 5×219
   b) 4×129
   c) 8×215
   d) 22×16
   e) 41×24
   f) 37×27

4. Model each decimal with base ten blocks. Use the flat to represent 1. Sketch the model.
   a) 0.4
   b) 1.6
   c) 0.23
   d) 2.38

1   0.1 0.01

1 Estimating Products

You will need
• a calculator

 Goal Estimate products of decimal numbers using whole numbers.

All 24 Grade 3 students will be wearing bee costumes for the school concert. Three costumes can be made with a piece of fabric that is 1.2 m long.

? **About how much will it cost to make bee costumes for the 24 students?**

Glynis's Estimate

$24 \div 3 = 8$

It will take 8 pieces of fabric 1.2 m long to make all 24 costumes.

I'll round 1.2 to 1 to estimate the amount of fabric. Then I'll add a little extra later.

I'll round and multiply to estimate the cost.

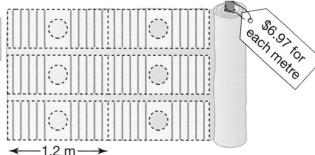

←——1.2 m——→

$6.97 for each metre

A. Estimate the number of metres of fabric needed for all 24 costumes.

B. Estimate the total cost of the fabric in dollars. Write an equation to show how you estimated.

C. Estimate the number of metres of black tape needed for 24 costumes. Explain your thinking.

D. Estimate the total cost of the black tape in dollars. Write an equation to show how you estimated.

E. About how much will all 24 costumes cost? Check your estimate by calculating the exact amount. Use a calculator.

Bee Costume

fabric: 1.2 m long

black tape for stripes: 3.8 m

$0.59 for each metre

Reflecting

1. Compare your answer to Part A with those of your classmates. Why might there be different reasonable answers?

2. Describe some strategies for estimating the cost of black tape for one costume.

3. a) Would it be better to overestimate or underestimate the amount of fabric and tape needed? Why?
   b) Would it be better to overestimate or underestimate the cost of the fabric and tape? Why?

Checking

4. It takes about 2.7 m of fabric to make 3 cat costumes. The fabric costs $4.29 for each metre.
   a) Estimate the number of metres for 26 cat costumes.
   b) Estimate the total cost of the fabric.
   c) Calculate the cost using a calculator. Was your estimate greater or less than the actual cost? Explain why.

Practising

5. Wire costs $1.29 for each metre. About how much will 12.8 m of wire cost?

6. Estimate each product using whole numbers. Explain your strategy for one of your estimates.
   a) 5 × 3.4   b) 3.2 × 1.7   c) 3.4 × $5.28

7. What estimation strategy would you use for each situation? Explain your thinking.
   a) Drake said that he is as tall as a row of 75 pennies. About how tall is Drake?
   b) Anna said that she is as tall as a row of 51 loonies. About how tall is Anna?

1.8 cm   2.6 cm

8. Create your own problem that you can solve by estimating a product of decimals. Solve the problem.

2 Multiplying by 10 or 100

Goal Multiply decimal tenths and hundredths by 10 and 100.

Drake's Measures

I wonder how long the picture of my arm would be if I were the model on the billboard.

My arm is 46.7 cm long.

If my billboard arm were 10 times as long, I could measure it in centimetres or decimetres.

? **How long would your arms and legs be if they were 10 or 100 times as long?**

A. Draw a 2 cm **line segment**. Then draw a line segment 10 times as long.

B. How many centimetres long is your new line segment? How many decimetres long is your new line segment?

C. Repeat Parts A and B with a 4 cm line segment.

D. If Drake's billboard arm were 10 times the length of his real arm, how many centimetres long would his billboard arm be? How many decimetres long would his billboard arm be?

E. How many centimetres long would Drake's billboard arm be if it were 100 times his real arm's length? How many metres long would his billboard arm be?

F. Measure your arm to the nearest tenth of a centimetre. How many decimetres long would your arm be if it were 10 times as long? How many centimetres long would it be?

G. How many metres long would your arm be if it were 100 times as long? How many centimetres long would it be?

H. Measure your leg, thumb, and total height to the nearest hundredth of a metre. Repeat Part F for these body parts.

Reflecting

1. When multiplying a decimal number by 10, why does the digit in the tenths place move to the ones place? What happens to the digit in the ones place?

2. An object is 25.7 cm long. How can you report a measurement that is 10 times as long? 100 times?

3. When multiplying a whole number by 10, you place a zero on the end: $543 \times 10 = 5430$. Why can't the same rule be used when multiplying 54.3×10?

4. Describe a rule for multiplying a decimal number by 10 or 100.

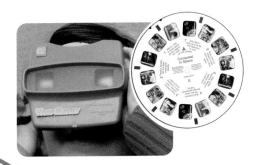

Curious Math

View-Masters

Images on round reels are enlarged when you use a View-Master.

1 This View-Master enlarges an image to 5.5 times its actual size. An image is 10 mm wide on the reel. How wide will it appear on this View-Master?

2 Suppose another View-Master enlarges an image to 10 times its actual size. An image appears 8.5 cm wide on this View-Master. How wide is it on the reel?

3 Multiplying Tenths by Whole Numbers

Goal Multiply decimal tenths by whole numbers using models, drawings, and symbols.

You will need

- base ten blocks

- a decimal place value chart

Tens	Ones	Tenths	Hundredths

- a ruler

Each puppy has a mass of about 0.4 kg.

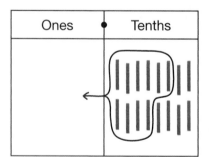

? **What is the total mass of each litter of puppies?**

 Sofia's Method

First I'll multiply to figure out the mass of the smaller litter.

I'll use base ten blocks to represent these amounts.

1   0.1

4×0.4 is 4 groups of 4 tenths, or 16 tenths.

I can regroup 10 tenths as 1 one.

Ones	Tenths

$$\begin{array}{cc} 0.4 & 4 \text{ tenths} \\ \underline{\times 4} & \underline{\times 4} \\ & 16 \text{ tenths} \end{array}$$

Ones	Tenths

$$\begin{array}{c} \overset{1}{}0.4 \\ \underline{\times 4} \\ 1.6 \end{array}$$

A. How could you have estimated that 4×0.4 would be less than 2?

B. Calculate the mass of the litter of seven puppies. Use base ten blocks.

C. A one-month-old Irish wolfhound puppy has a mass of about 3.4 kg. What is the total mass of five one-month-old Irish wolfhound puppies? Use base ten blocks and sketch your models.

Reflecting

1. Why is the product of 4×0.4 less than 4?

2. Why is there one decimal place in each product you calculated?

3. How is multiplying decimals like multiplying whole numbers? How is it different?

Checking

4. Each puppy in a litter of dalmations has a mass of about 0.3 kg. There are nine puppies in the litter. What is the total mass? Use Sofia's method.

Practising

5. Cahil's father ordered four 3.5 m long shelves for a library. How many metres did he order altogether?

6. Bianca lined up six pennies. How long was her line of pennies?

1.8 cm

7. Calculate using base ten blocks. Sketch your model.
   a) 8×0.4 b) 5×3.9 c) 7×2.2

8. Sook's cup holds 0.3 L. She drinks six cups of water every day. How many litres of water does she drink in a week?

9. Measure the length of a pencil to the nearest tenth of a centimetre. How long would a line of seven of these pencils make if they were put together end to end?

Mid-Chapter Review

LESSON

1

1. Estimate the cost for each.
   a) 5 boxes of cereal

   $2.39

   b) 2.8 m of trim

   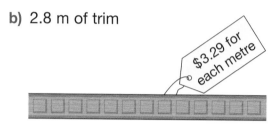
   $3.29 for each metre

2. Estimate each product as a whole number.
   Explain your strategy for each estimate.
   Do you think your estimate is high or low? Why?
   a) 2.4×3 b) 3.2×5.2 c) 9.7×3.74

2

3. Timo made a scale model of an insect for his science project. The insect is 1.3 cm long.

   a) The model is 10 times as long as the actual insect. How long is the model?
   b) Would a model 100 times as long be appropriate? Explain your answer.

4. How do you know that 10×67.3 is 673, not 6730?

5. Calculate.
   a) 4.2×10
   b) 28.6×10
   c) 10×37.52
   d) 100×5.4
   e) 100×42.23
   f) 100×0.75

3

6. Use base ten blocks to model each product.
   Sketch your model and complete each equation.
   a) $5 \times 3.2 = \blacksquare$ b) $3 \times 0.9 = \blacksquare$ c) $4 \times 2.7 = \blacksquare$

7. A track is 0.3 km long. Molly runs around the track eight times.
   She says she has gone 0.24 km. Do you agree?
   Explain why or why not.

Front-End Multiplication

You can multiply by using the digits at the left (front end) of the numbers first.

Jose's Method

To calculate 6 × 45,
I regroup 45 as 40 + 5.
I calculate 6 × 40 first.
Then I add 6 × 5.

$6 \times 45 = \underbrace{6 \times 40}_{} + \underbrace{6 \times 5}_{}$
$ = 240 + 30$
$ = 270$

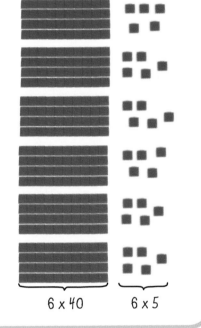

6 × 40   6 × 5

A. How can you calculate 6 × 40 by thinking of 6 × 4 = 24?

B. Why did Jose add 6 × 5 to 240 instead of just adding 5?

Try These

1. Complete each equation using Jose's method.
   a) 3 × 45 = ■
   b) 2 × 95 = ■
   c) 4 × 53 = ■
   d) 6 × 55 = ■
   e) 5 × 35 = ■
   f) 4 × 125 = ■
   g) 8 × 105 = ■
   h) 9 × 53 = ■

2. Determine the missing digit in each equation.
   a) 4 × ■5 = 200 + 20
   b) 9 × ■05 = 900 + 45

4 Multiplying Hundredths by Whole Numbers

Goal Multiply decimal hundredths by whole numbers using models, drawings, and symbols.

You will need
- base ten blocks

- play coins
- a decimal place value chart

Tens	Ones	Tenths	Hundredths

Karin is ordering three books that cost $3.35 each.

? **What is the cost of Karin's book order before taxes and shipping?**

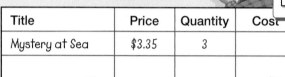

Mysterious Book Club
Order Form

Title	Price	Quantity	Cost
Mystery at Sea	$3.35	3	

Karin's Method

I'll model three sets of 3.35 with base ten blocks.

Ones	Tenths	Hundredths

```
    3.35
  x    3
```

I can regroup 10 hundredths as 1 tenth.

I can regroup 10 tenths as 1 one.

There are 10 ones, 0 tenths, and 5 hundredths.

The three books cost $10.05.

Ones	Tenths	Hundredths

```
   1 1
   3.35
 x    3
 10.05
```

Reflecting

1. How can you model the problem using loonies, dimes, and pennies? How is this like Karin's model?

2. How is multiplying 3 by 3.35 like multiplying 3 by 335? How is it different?

3. Why did Karin record two zeros in the product?

4. What do the two decimal places in the product represent?

Checking

5. Karin also ordered two books that cost $2.79 each.
   Use a model to calculate the total cost for the two books before taxes and shipping.
   Write an equation to show your work.

Practising

6. Martin ordered five books. Each book costs $2.28.
   a) Use coins to model and calculate the total cost. Sketch the coins.
   b) Use base ten blocks to model the total cost. Sketch the blocks.
   c) How could you have predicted that the total cost would be a little less than $12.00?

7. Calculate. Estimate to check.
   a) 2×0.57 b) $6 \times \$3.65$ c) 3×2.37

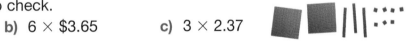

8. Nadia rode 2.46 km on her horse.
   Evan rode four times as far.
   a) How do you know that Evan rode less than 10 km?
   b) How far did Evan ride? Use base ten blocks.
   c) How could you have predicted that the distance Evan rode would have two decimal places?

9. A long narrow tablecloth is folded in half twice.
   The final folded measurement is 0.45 m.
   How long is the tablecloth when it is unfolded?

0.45 m

5 Communicate About Estimation Strategies

Goal Explain estimation strategies to determine if a solution is reasonable.

Marcus's family bought some items online from an American store. On that day, $1.00 US was worth $1.32 Canadian. Marcus calculated that the total cost was $20.18 Canadian.

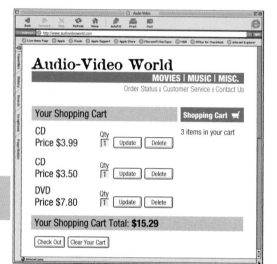

? **How can Marcus estimate to decide if his calculation is reasonable?**

Marcus's Explanation

The order was for $15.29 US.

I know that $1.00 US was worth $1.32 Canadian.

 =

That means $2.00 US is worth $2.64 and $3.00 US is worth $3.96. That's about $4.

So the order will cost about $20 Canadian.

$20.18 seems reasonable.

A. How can you improve Marcus's explanation? Use the Communication Checklist.

B. Write your improved explanation.

Communication Checklist

- ✓ Did you show all your steps?
- ✓ Did you use a model?
- ✓ Did you explain your thinking?

Reflecting

1. What part of Marcus's explanation was the clearest?

2. Why is it important not to leave out steps in an explanation?

3. How can using a model improve the explanation?

Checking

4. a) Identify at least one strength in Anna's explanation. Use the Communication Checklist.

   b) Improve Anna's explanation.

Anna's Explanation

I'll estimate to see if Marcus's calculation is reasonable.
I'll find out how much a $10 US order will cost and
then how much a $20 US order will cost.
Then I'll use the number in the middle.

Practising

5. One euro (€1) was worth $1.67 Canadian when Teresa bought a sweatshirt for €25.
   How can you estimate to decide if a cost of $41.75 Canadian makes sense? Explain your strategy.

6. Timothy, who lives in Oregon, ordered gloves online from a Canadian store. The cost was $29.53 Canadian. Each Canadian dollar was worth $0.76 US.
   He said the cost was $22.44 US. Explain how to estimate to check the US price.

6 Choosing a Multiplication Method

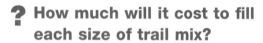

Goal Justify the choice of a multiplication method.

You are making bags of trail mix.
You are asked to use equal masses of all
four ingredients for each size of the trail mix.

? **How much will it cost to fill
each size of trail mix?**

A. How many grams are in a kilogram?

B. Each bag contains four ingredients
to make up the total mass.
How much of each ingredient
would you need for the small bag?
the medium bag? the large bag?

C. Calculate the cost of each ingredient
for each size of bag.

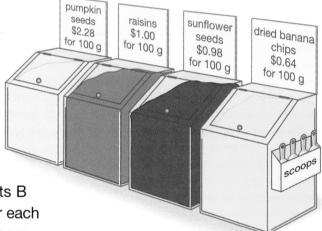

D. Look at the calculations you did in Parts B
and C. Which method would be best for each
calculation: mental math, pencil and paper,
base ten blocks, or a calculator?

E. How much will it cost to fill each size of bag?

Reflecting

1. If you know the price for 100 g, how can you
calculate the price for 1000 g?

2. If you know the price to fill the small bag, how can
you calculate the price to fill the large bag?

3. Why is it sometimes faster to do a calculation
mentally than with a calculator? Give an example.

Up to 100

Number of players: 2 or more
How to play: Estimate and multiply to get as close as possible to 100 without going over.

Step 1 Roll a die three times. Use the numbers that you rolled to make a decimal. Use the first roll for the ones digit, the second roll for the tenths digit, and the third roll for the hundredths digit. Players enter the number into their calculators.

Step 2 Each player chooses a number to multiply by to get as close as possible to 100 without going over. Multiply on your calculator to check.

Step 3 The player with the closest estimate gets a point.

The first person with 10 points wins.

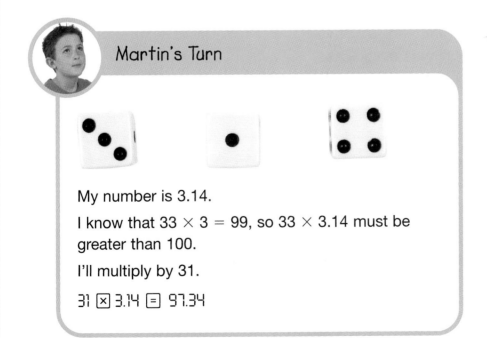

Martin's Turn

My number is 3.14.

I know that $33 \times 3 = 99$, so 33×3.14 must be greater than 100.

I'll multiply by 31.

$31 \boxed{\times} 3.14 \boxed{=} 97.34$

Skills Bank

1

1. Which products are close to 25? Estimate.
   A. 6.2×4 C. 13×2.87 E. 19×4.95 G. 15×1.7
   B. 7.7×3 D. 5×5.12 F. 8.6×4 H. 3.73×4

2. Estimate each product as a whole number.
   a) 3.1×5.7 c) 2.99×3.2 e) 9.42×3.49 g) 4.3×4.07
   b) 2.2×8.7 d) $3.7 \times \$6.79$ f) $5.8 \times \$8.25$ h) $\$7.58 \times 6.61$

3. Estimate to check which answers are reasonable.
   a) $3.4 \times 1.2 = 4.08$ b) $12 \times 19.97 = 23.94$ c) $18 \times 6.7 = 120.6$

2

4. Each length is stretched to 10 times as long.
   Record the new length in centimetres and in decimetres.
   a) 2.7 cm   b) 32.1 cm   c) 2.5 cm   d) 86.4 cm

5. Each length is stretched to 100 times as long.
   Record the new length in centimetres and in metres.
   a) 2.7 cm   b) 3.1 cm   c) 15.02 cm   d) 91.53 cm

6. Calculate each product.
   a) $10 \times 32.1 = \blacksquare$ c) $100 \times 12.6 = \blacksquare$ e) $10 \times 4.7 = \blacksquare$
   b) $10 \times 4.02 = \blacksquare$ d) $100 \times 0.45 = \blacksquare$ f) $100 \times 1.11 = \blacksquare$

3

7. Calculate. Model with base ten blocks.
   a) 6×0.7 c) 7×1.3 e) 4×5.3 g) 2×4.6
   b) 3×2.9 d) 5×3.4 f) 8×1.8 h) 9×0.5

8. Calculate the total length.
   a)

   2.8 m   2.8 m   2.8 m   2.8 m

   b)

   8.2 m   8.2 m   8.2 m

   c)

   2.3 cm   2.3 cm   2.3 cm   2.3 cm   2.3 cm   2.3 cm

3   **9.** Which product is greater? How much greater?

     a) 6 × 2.9 or 5 × 1.7   **b)** 8 × 7.4 or 9 × 2.8

4   **10.** Calculate each product. Use base ten blocks or coins as a model. Sketch any three models.

     a) 6 × 2.03 = ■   **c)** 8 × 1.23 = ■   **e)** 5 × 3.92 = ■

     b) 3 × 0.14 = ■   **d)** 5 × 0.73 = ■   **f)** 4 × 1.88 = ■

11. Calculate the total cost.

     a)

     b)

     c)

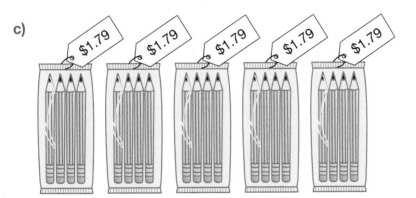

6   **12.** Which calculations can you do mentally?
Record the product for each of those.

     A. 7 × 0.3   **C.** 8 × 0.05   **E.** 8 × 5.13   **G.** 0.08 × 40

     B. 10 × 0.45   **D.** 12 × 1.27   **F.** 20 × 2.52   **H.** 2.74 × 2.09

13. Which calculations from Question 12 would you do with pencil and paper? Record the product for each of those.

Problem Bank

LESSON

1 1. Kristine bought 3.7 m of fabric. The total cost of the fabric was $16.98. Estimate the cost for each metre. Explain your strategy.

2. a) About how much less is 8.9 × 4.2 than 4.9 × 8.2?
   b) Create two decimal multiplication sentences where the difference is about 8 when you switch the whole number parts.

2 3. The distance around the hamster wheel is 35.9 cm.
   a) If Helen Hamster spins the wheel 100 times, what distance will she travel around the wheel?
   b) About how many times would she have to cross a 3.1 m room to get the same amount of exercise?

4. Mason has a 0.05 m length of modelling clay. He puts it in the machine, then he takes the piece that comes out and puts it back in the machine. How long is the final length of modelling clay?

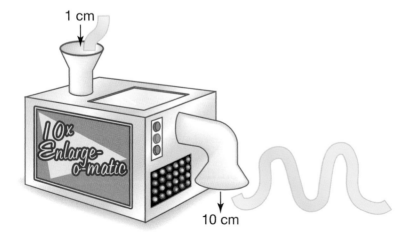

1 cm

10 cm

2 **5.** On a map, 1 cm represents 11 km. Two towns are 3.8 cm apart on the map. How far apart are they really?

3 **6.** Create two numbers that result in the greatest possible product. Use one decimal point and each of the digits 3, 4, 5, and 6 once.

7. The side length of a square is 12.4 cm. What is its perimeter?

8. A rectangle has a width of 5.8 cm. It is twice as long as it is wide. What is its perimeter?

9. A granola bar has 7.7 g of protein. How many grams of protein are in three bars?

4 **10.** Chen spent exactly $7.51 on pens and notebooks. How many pens did he buy?

11. Use each of the digits from 0 to 5 once to make these products true.

$$\begin{array}{r} 5.0\blacksquare \\ \times \quad 6 \\ \hline \blacksquare 0.1\,2 \end{array} \qquad \begin{array}{r} 3.2\blacksquare \\ \times \quad \blacksquare \\ \hline \blacksquare 6.2\blacksquare \end{array}$$

12. How much more would three T-shirts cost than five books?

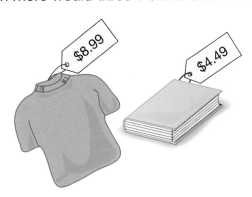

Chapter Review

LESSON

1 1. Estimate each product using whole numbers.
Explain your strategy for one of your estimates.
a) 3 × $12.46   b) 9.3 × $2.12   c) 6.4 × $8.25

2. Estimate the cost of each length of ribbon.
a) 2.3 m   b) 5 m

$0.79 for each metre

$1.39 for each metre

3. Estimate the cost for each. Predict whether your
estimate is high or low. Use a calculator to check.
a) 3.1 m of moulding   b) 5.5 m of cable

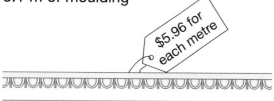
$5.96 for each metre

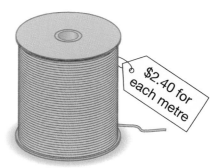
$2.40 for each metre

2 4. You multiply a decimal by 10 and the result is 32.
What was the decimal number? How do you know?

5. A 4.8 cm long object is stretched to 100 times as long.
Describe the stretched length in two different ways.

3 6. Calculate each product using base ten blocks.
Sketch your model.
a) 6 × 1.8 = ■   b) 4 × 2.6 = ■   c) 9 × 3.2 = ■

7. a) Use models to show that 6 × 2.5 = 3 × 5.0.
b) Explain your thinking.
c) How is this equation useful?

266

3 8. Calculate the perimeter of each regular polygon.

a)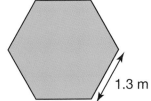
1.3 m

b)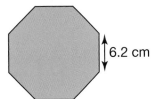
6.2 cm

4 9. A snail travels about 0.13 cm in one minute.

a) How far would it travel in 7 min if it keeps up the same speed?

b) About how long would it take to go 3 m?

10. a) How much would Jenn pay for two packs of paper and two packs of pens?

b) How do you know that nine packs of paper cost less than $40?

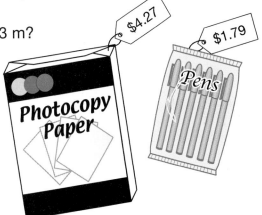
$4.27
$1.79
Photocopy Paper
Pens

5 11. Kurt exchanged $32 in Canadian money for US money. Each Canadian dollar was worth $0.76 US. Explain how you would estimate how much the money is worth in US dollars.

6 12. Use each of the digits 2, 5, 1, 0, and 6 once to complete each statement.

a) ■■ × ■.■■ is a product you would calculate mentally.

b) ■ × ■■.■■ is a product you would calculate with pencil and paper.

c) ■■ × ■.■■ is a product you would calculate using a calculator.

13. When you want to multiply a number by 10, would you use a calculator, pencil and paper, or mental math? Explain your choice.

Chapter Task

Body Proportions

This picture shows predicted body measurements using the height and width of the head.

? **How close to the predicted body measurements are your measurements?**

Part 1

A. Measure the height and width of your head in hundredths of a metre.

B. Use the measurements from Part A to estimate each of these measurements in metres.
- your height
- your width from shoulder to shoulder
- the distance from your waist to your toes
- the distance from your shoulder to your fingertips

Write equations to describe your estimates.

C. Work with a classmate to measure each length in Part B. Compare your estimates in Part B to your actual measurements.

Part 2

D. Compare your results from Part C with the results of a classmate.

E. Do the predicted body measurements in the picture seem reasonable? Explain.

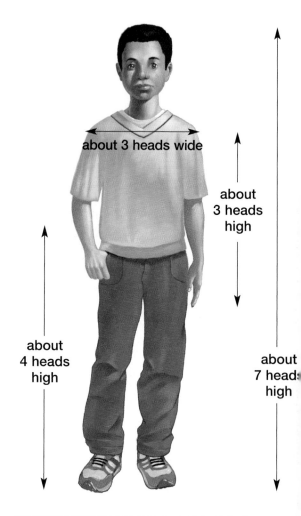

about 3 heads wide

about 3 heads high

about 4 heads high

about 7 heads high

Task Checklist

☑ Did you use appropriate strategies to estimate?

☑ Did you predict and then measure all four measurements?

☑ Did you organize your work so it is easy to follow?

☑ Did you explain your thinking?

☑ Did you use math language?

Dividing Decimals

Goals

You will be able to

- **estimate the quotient when dividing a decimal number**

- **divide whole numbers and decimals by whole numbers up to 10**

- **use division and other operations to solve problems**

- **solve problems by working backward**

Dividing a track

Getting Started

Opening Ceremony

A school district is holding a track and field event with 880 athletes. A coach suggests that the athletes should enter the field in several lines.

? **How can the athletes be arranged into equal lines with no athletes left over?**

A. Calculate the number of athletes in each line if they are arranged in two lines. Record your answer and the remainder in a table.

Number of lines	Number of athletes in each line	Remainder
2		
3		
4		
5		
6		
7		
8		
9		

B. What operation did you use in Part A? Explain your choice.

C. Complete the table for different numbers of lines.

D. For each calculation, did you use mental math or paper and pencil? **Justify** your choice.

E. Multiply to check your answers when the athletes are arranged in two, three, and four lines.

F. Which numbers of lines have an equal number of athletes with no athletes left over?

Do You Remember?

1. What would you do with the remainder in each situation?
   a) 4 friends share $13.
   b) 4 friends share 13 licorice sticks.
   c) 4 friends share 13 movie passes.
   d) 13 friends go on an amusement park ride that holds 4 people in each car.

2. Calculate.
   a) $240 \div 6$ **b)** $720 \div 6$ **c)** $8\overline{)760}$

3. Estimate the quotient.
   a) $119 \div 6$ **b)** $7\overline{)500}$ **c)** $9\overline{)269}$

4. Use multiplication to check each answer. Correct the incorrect answers.

   a) $\dfrac{80}{7\overline{)560}}$ **b)** $\dfrac{50 \text{ R1}}{2\overline{)101}}$ **c)** $\dfrac{150 \text{ R3}}{4\overline{)503}}$

1 Estimating Quotients

You will need

* a measuring tape

* string

Goal Estimate quotients when dividing decimal numbers.

Simon, a Coast Salish carver, has been asked to carve a 6.75 m Westcoast totem pole. He plans to carve it over a number of months.

❓ What length of the pole does he need to carve each month?

A. If he completes the pole in two months, about what length does he need to carve each month?

B. Estimate the length he needs to carve each month if he completes the pole in each of three, four, five, and six months.

C. Use a 6.75 m piece of string to model the totem pole. How can you use the string to check your estimates in Parts A and B? Check each estimate.

D. Simon is planning to carve a pole as a gift to his community. Choose a length for the pole and repeat Parts A to C. Use a length measured in hundredths of a metre that is between 1.00 m and 10.00 m.

Reflecting

1. What estimation strategies did you use for Parts A and B? Explain your choices.

2. Did you use the same estimation strategies for the second pole as you did for the first pole? Why or why not?

3. You estimated the length of pole that would be carved each month for three months. How can you use that estimate to help you estimate the length of pole carved each month for six months?

Estimate the Quotient

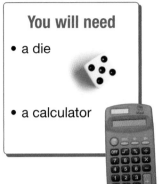

You will need
- a die
- a calculator

Number of players: 2 to 4

How to play: Estimate the quotient when dividing a decimal number by a one-digit number.

Step 1   Roll the die four times to make a **dividend**.
Use the first roll for the tens digit, the second roll for the ones digit, the third roll for the tenths digit, and the fourth roll for the hundredths digit.

■■.■■

Step 2   Roll the die to make a one-digit **divisor**.

■■.■■ ÷ ■

Step 3   All players estimate the quotient.
Record your estimates.

Step 4   Calculate the quotient. Use a calculator.

Step 5   If your estimate is within one of the calculated quotient, you score one point.

Continue estimating and dividing until one player reaches five points.

Karin's Turn

We rolled 43.32 for the dividend and 3 for the divisor.

I estimate 15 because $43.32 \div 3$ is close to $45 \div 3 = 15$.

The answer is 14.44, so I get 1 point for this turn.

2 Dividing by 10

Goal Use regrouping to divide decimal numbers by 10.

Camille's pedometer showed that she walked 1000 steps.
She needs to enter the length of her step into the pedometer to calculate the total distance she walked.
She measured 10 steps and found that she walked 11.3 m.

? How far did Camille walk in 1000 steps?

You will need

• a decimal place value chart

Tens	Ones	Tenths	Hundredths

• a measuring tape

• base ten blocks

• a calculator

Camille's Calculation

First I need to calculate 11.3 ÷ 10 to determine the length of one step.

I'll use blocks to represent these amounts.

10	1	0.1	0.01

Step 1 I model 11.3.

Tens	Ones	• Tenths	Hundredths
		|||	

Step 2 To divide by 10, I need to get numbers in each place value that can be divided by 10. I regroup 1 ten as 10 ones. I regroup 1 one as 10 tenths. I regroup 3 tenths as 30 hundredths.

Step 3 Next I divide each number by 10.
When I divide 10 ones by 10, I get 1 one.

Tens	Ones	●	Tenths	Hundredths

A. Continue to divide the number in each place value by 10. Sketch the model of the quotient.

B. What is the length of one of Camille's steps?

C. Show how to use multiplication to check your answer in Part B.

D. How far did Camille walk in 1000 steps? Use your answer from Part B and a calculator.

Reflecting

1. How did you use regrouping of each place value to divide by 10?

2. Compare the model of the dividend with the model of the quotient. How are the numbers the same? How are they different?

3. How could you have predicted the quotient before doing the regrouping?

Checking

4. Camille's classmates are also using pedometers.

   a) Use base ten blocks and a decimal place value chart to calculate the length of each student's step. Sketch models of the dividend and quotient.

   b) Use multiplication to check each quotient.

Distance Walked in 10 Steps

Student	Distance
Norman	13.1 m
Monique	12.0 m
Liam	10.5 m
Sofia	9.2 m

Practising

5. a) Measure the distance that you walk in 10 steps. Use that distance to calculate the length of your step.

   b) Your pedometer shows 1000 steps. What distance have you walked?

6. A swimming pool has 10 lanes. The width of the pool is 25 m. What is the width of each lane?

7. Calculate.

   a) $14 \div 10$ c) $72.1 \div 10$ e) $145.6 \div 10$

   b) $10\overline{)12.3}$ d) $10\overline{)55.5}$ f) $10\overline{)3219}$

8. Multiply by 10 to check each answer in Question 7.

Mental Math

Dividing in Parts

You can simplify division by breaking a number into easily divided parts.

To divide 135 by 3, think $135 = 120 + 15$.

A. What is another way to break 135 into parts that are easier to divide by 3?

$$135 \div 3 = \underbrace{120 \div 3} + \underbrace{15 \div 3}$$
$$= \quad 40 \quad + \quad 5$$
$$= 45$$

Try These

1. Calculate by breaking into parts. Show your strategy.

   a) $76 \div 4$ c) $64 \div 4$ e) $180 \div 5$ g) $760 \div 8$

   b) $8\overline{)120}$ d) $7\overline{)91}$ f) $6\overline{)450}$ h) $9\overline{)297}$

Exploring Patterns in Decimal Quotients

You will need

• a calculator

When you use a calculator to divide a whole number by a one-digit number, you often see many digits after the decimal point. These digits may follow a pattern.

1

a) Enter 101 into a calculator. Divide this number by 2. Record the quotient.

b) Try dividing other whole number dividends by 2. What digits are possible after the decimal point when the divisor is 2?

2 Repeat Question 1 using 3 as the divisor. What digits are possible after the decimal point when the divisor is 3?

3 Repeat Question 1 using another number as a divisor. What digits are possible after the decimal point with this divisor?

Calculating a Decimal Quotient

Goal Express quotients as decimal numbers to tenths or hundredths.

You will need
- base ten blocks

- a decimal place value chart

Tens	Ones	Tenths	Hundr

Juanita is volunteering at the organic food co-op. She wants to divide 5.00 kg of basmati rice into four plastic bags. Her scale measures mass to hundredths of a kilogram.

? **What number should the scale read for each bag of rice?**

Juanita's Division

I estimate that the mass of each bag will be more than 1 kg.

I need to calculate 5.00 ÷ 4 to two decimal places to match the **precision** of the scale.

I'll use blocks to represent these amounts.

1   0.1   0.01

Step 1 I model 5.00.

Ones	•	Tenths	Hundredths

Step 2 I divide 5 into four equal groups with a remainder of 1 one.

$$\begin{array}{r} 1 \\ 4\overline{)5.00} \\ -4 \\ \hline 1 \end{array}$$

$-4 \longleftarrow$ I subtract $4 \times 1 = 4$ from 5.

$1 \longleftarrow$ 1 one remainder

Each bag could have a mass of 1 kg with a remainder of 1 kg.

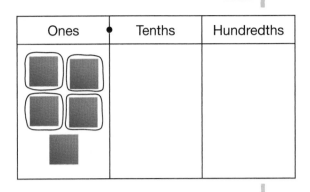

Ones		Tenths	Hundredths

Step 3 I regroup the 1 one remainder as 10 tenths.

$$\begin{array}{r} 1 \\ 4\overline{)5.00} \\ -4 \\ \hline 1.0 \end{array}$$

$1.0 \longleftarrow$ $1.0 = 10$ tenths

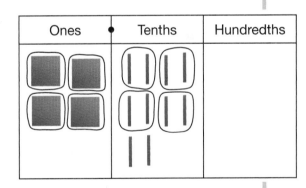

Ones		Tenths	Hundredths

Step 4 I divide 10 tenths into four equal groups of 2 tenths with 2 tenths remainder.

$$\begin{array}{r} 1.2 \\ 4\overline{)5.00} \\ -4 \\ \hline 1.0 \\ -0.8 \\ \hline 0.2 \end{array}$$

I subtract $4 \times 0.2 = 0.8$,

$-0.8 \longleftarrow$ or 8 tenths, from 1.

$0.2 \longleftarrow$ 2 tenths remainder

Each bag could have a mass of 1.2 kg with a remainder of 0.2 kg.

Ones		Tenths	Hundredths

Step 5 I regroup the 2 tenths remainder as 20 hundredths.

$$\begin{array}{r} 1.2 \\ 4\overline{)5.00} \\ -4 \\ \hline 1.0 \\ -0.8 \\ \hline 0.20 \end{array}$$ ⟵ 0.20 = 20 hundredths

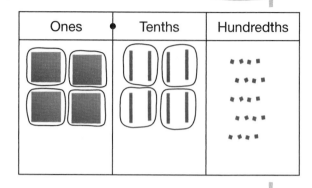

Step 6 I divide 20 hundredths into four equal groups of 5 hundredths with no remainder.

$$\begin{array}{r} 1.25 \\ 4\overline{)5.00} \\ -4 \\ \hline 1.0 \\ -0.8 \\ \hline 0.20 \\ -0.20 \\ \hline 0.00 \end{array}$$

I subtract 4 × 0.05 = 0.20, or 20 hundredths, from 20 hundredths.

0 hundredths remainder

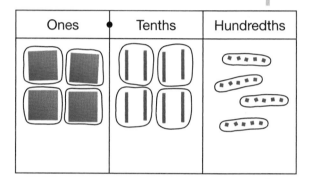

Each bag of rice will have a mass of 1.25 kg.

Reflecting

1. If Juanita's scale only measured to tenths of a kilogram, what would be her answer to the problem?

2. a) In Step 4, why do you think Juanita calculated the product of 4 and 0.2?
   b) In Step 5, why do you think Juanita regrouped 2 tenths as 20 hundredths?

3. Juanita also wants to divide 14.00 kg of rice into 5 bags. When she calculated 14.00 ÷ 5, she got 2.8 kg. However, her scale measures to hundredths. What can she do to calculate the mass to 2 decimal places?

Checking

4. Juanita has 4.00 kg of shelled peas. She wants to divide the peas into five plastic bags. Calculate the mass of each bag to two decimal places. Show your work.

Practising

5. What will be the mass of each bag? The scale measures to tenths of a kilogram.
   a) 9.0 kg divided into two bags
   b) 3.0 kg divided into six bags

6. Calculate to two decimal places.
   a) $18.00 \div 8$
   b) $4\overline{)3.00}$
   c) $6.00 \div 5$
   d) $5\overline{)2.00}$

7. Marvin wants to cut 9.00 m of ribbon into four equal pieces.
   Calculate the length of each piece to two decimal places.

8. How much less is $4.44 \div 8$ than $8.88 \div 4$?

9. What could the divisor and dividend be?

$$\begin{array}{r} 1\,2\,.\,4\,5 \\ \blacksquare\overline{)\blacksquare\blacksquare.\blacksquare\blacksquare} \end{array}$$

10. Create and solve a problem where you divide a whole number dividend by a one-digit divisor and the quotient is a decimal.

4 Dividing Decimals by Whole Numbers

You will need
- base ten blocks

- a decimal place value chart

Tens	Ones	Tenths	Hundredths

- a calculator

Goal Divide a decimal by a one-digit whole number using models and symbols.

Drake divided a garden into six equal sections to test fertilizers. He needs to know the area of each section to determine the amount of fertilizer to use.

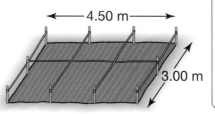

← 4.50 m →

3.00 m

? **What is the area of each section of the garden?**

Drake's Division

First I calculate the area of the garden. The area is 13.50 m².

I estimate the area of each section to be between 2 m² and 3 m².
Next I calculate 13.50 ÷ 6 to two decimal places.

I'll use blocks to represent these amounts.

10   1   0.1   0.01

Step 1   I model 13.50.

Tens	Ones	•	Tenths	Hundredths
■	■ ■ ■	•	| | | | |	

Step 2   I regroup the ten as 10 ones.

A. Complete Drake's division. Sketch your models.
What is the area of each section of the garden?

B. Describe how Drake might have estimated. Use his estimate to determine if your answer is reasonable.

Reflecting

1. Show how Drake might have calculated the total area.

2. Why did regrouping the ten as 10 ones help with this division?

3. Drake says he could also find the area of each section by regrouping 13.50 as 1350 hundredths and then dividing by six. Do you agree or disagree? Explain.

Checking

4. Nikki has a garden that is 6.00 m by 3.75 m. She divided it into five equal sections.
   a) Estimate the area of each section. Show your work.
   b) Calculate the area of each section to two decimal places. Show your work.

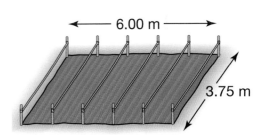

Practising

5. Calculate to two decimal places.
   a) $9.45 \div 5 = \blacksquare$ c) $1.36 \div 2 = \blacksquare$
   b) $15.28 \div 4 = \blacksquare$ d) $8.40 \div 3 = \blacksquare$

6. Nora's class is painting a mural about the four seasons that is 8.00 m by 5.44 m. Each season gets the same area. Calculate the area for spring to two decimal places.

	8.00 m	
	spring	summer
	fall	winter

5.44 m

7. Derrick walked his bike and found that it travelled 14.35 m when the front wheel turned seven complete turns.
   a) Estimate the **circumference** of the front wheel.
   b) Calculate the circumference of the wheel to hundredths of a metre.
   c) What distance will the bike travel in three complete turns of the wheel?

Mid-Chapter Review

LESSON

1
1. Estimate. Show your work.
   a) 15.75 ÷ 3 b) 9.65 ÷ 5 c) 8)18.45 d) 7)63.95

2
2. Calculate.
   a) 12.5 ÷ 10 b) 1.8 ÷ 10 c) 10)15 d) 10)5.5

3. 4.8 L of pasta sauce is poured equally into 10 freezer bags. How many litres of sauce will be in each bag?

3
4. Calculate to one decimal place.
   a) 4)14.0   b) 2)5.0

5. Calculate to two decimal places.
   a) 11.00 ÷ 4 = ■   c) 3.00 ÷ 2 = ■
   b) 6.00 ÷ 8 = ■   d) 3.00 ÷ 5 = ■

6. 2.00 L of orange juice is poured equally into eight glasses. Calculate the amount of orange juice in each glass to two decimal places.

4
7. A farmer supplies blueberries to three fruit stands. Each day, he divides his harvest into three equal quantities. What mass of blueberries will each fruit stand receive? Calculate to hundredths of a kilogram.
   a) 16.89 kg b) 78.90 kg c) 2.82 kg d) 1.20 kg

8. A sandcastle competition is being held on a 9.12 m by 5.00 m area of beach. The beach area is divided into six equal sections.
   a) Estimate the area of each section. Show your work.
   b) Calculate the area of each section to two decimal places. Show your work.

5 Choosing a Calculation Method

You will need
• a calculator

Goal Justify your choice of calculation method.

Pencils are made from a piece of wood 7.2 cm wide. The piece is eight pencils wide and 17.8 cm long, which is the length of each pencil before the eraser is added. Liam made a set of problems about pencils for a game.

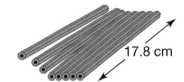

17.8 cm

Question 1
How wide is each pencil?

Question 2
How wide is each pencil to a tenth of a centimetre?

Question 3
What length would each pencil be to a tenth of a centimetre if you divided a pencil into two equal lengths?

Question 4
If 10 pencils were made from the piece of wood, what would be the width of each pencil?

? **Which calculation method would you use to solve each problem?**

A. Solve each problem. Show your work.

B. To solve each problem, did you use estimation, mental math, pencil and paper, or a calculator? Justify your choice.

C. For each problem, how did you determine that your answer was reasonable?

D. Create and solve your own problem about pencils involving division. Justify your choice of calculation method.

Question 5
The longest pencil in the world was about 624 cm long. How many pencils 17.8 cm long could have been made from it?

Reflecting

1. How do you decide when to use each method? Include examples in your explanations.
   a) mental math   c) estimation
   b) pencil and paper   d) calculator

6 Dividing to Compare

Goal Use division and other operations to solve problems about money.

Heather, her mother, and her grandmother, who is a senior citizen, take at least five return trips by transit a month to shop or to see a movie.

Rider	Single-fare tickets	Book of 5 tickets
adult	$2.25	$9.50
senior (over 65) student (over 12)	$1.50	$6.50
child (12 and under)	50¢	$2.25

? **How much money will each person save if she uses an entire book of tickets instead of single-fare tickets?**

Heather's Solution

Understand

I need to figure out the difference between the cost of each ticket in a book and the cost of a single-fare ticket for each person.

Make a Plan

I'll calculate the total cost of 2 books of 5 tickets needed for 5 return trips for each person.

To calculate the cost of each of the 10 tickets, I'll divide the prices by 10. Then I'll calculate the difference between the cost of each ticket in a book and the cost of a single-fare ticket.

A. Carry out Heather's plan and solve the problem. Show your work.

B. Solve the problem using a different set of steps. Explain your solution.

Reflecting

1. For each calculation in Part A, did you use mental math, play money, pencil and paper, or a calculator? Justify your choices.

2. Show how to use multiplication to check each division calculation in Part A.

Checking

3. Heather and her mother are visiting relatives in another city. During their stay, they expect to take five return trips by transit to tourist attractions.

   a) How much would each person save if she bought a book of 10 tickets instead of 10 single-fare tickets? Show your work.

   b) For each calculation in part a), did you use mental math, play money, pencil and paper, or a calculator? Justify your choices.

Rider	Single-fare tickets	Book of 10 tickets
adult	$1.75	$16.50
student	$1.50	$14.00

Practising

4. Vasco needs 15 DVD cases. A 3-pack of DVD cases costs $5.67 and a 5-pack of DVD cases costs $9.10.
   a) What is the cost of one case in each pack? Explain.
   b) How much money will Vasco save if he buys the less expensive packs?

5. Use the transit fares in Question 3 or fares of your choice to create and solve a problem about a group of people buying tickets.

7 Calculating the Mean

Goal Use division to calculate the mean.

Dan (icy hot pad) and Norman (smush) competed on different teams in an online game called Soccer Shootout. They want to compare the teams using the **mean** scores.

? **How can you use the mean to determine which team did better?**

Dan's Method

I'll use blocks to model the Team Sinclair scores.

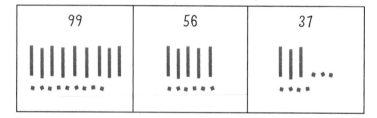

99	56	37

To calculate the mean score, I'll move blocks from one group to another and regroup if I have to until each group has about the same number of blocks.

Team Sinclair

Name	Score
wheelersdum	99
will streety	56
icy hot pad	37

Team Beckham

Name	Score
BOO	105
conr is da best	80
smush	60
Anonymous	20
goo goo	15
Magooberwood 2006	11

Norman's Method

I'll place the Team Sinclair scores on a number line.

To calculate the mean score, I'll divide the total length into three equal lengths.

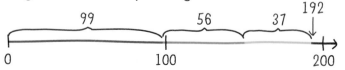

A. Calculate the mean score for Team Sinclair. Use Dan's method.

B. Calculate the mean score for Team Sinclair. Use Norman's method.

C. Calculate the mean score for Team Beckham.

D. Which team did better at the game? Explain your reasoning.

Reflecting

1. Would it be fair to use each team's total score to determine which team did better? Explain your answer.

2. Write a division sentence to represent how Norman calculated the mean length on his number line.

Checking

3. Team Sinclair and Team Beckham agree not to count the lowest score when they compare.
   a) Describe how you think the teams' mean scores will change. Explain your reasoning.
   b) Calculate the mean score of each team without the lowest score.
   c) After removing the lowest score, which team did better?

Practising

4. Calculate the mean of each set of numbers.
   a) 5, 5, 7, 9, 10
   b) 4, 3, 8, 9, 12, 6
   c) 150, 180, 375, 362
   d) 1.5, 2.7, 9.3
   e) 12.5, 9.3, 11.4, 7.8
   f) 1.75, 1.75, 3.50, 4.60

5. A scientist studying the birth rate of polar bears observed two female bears. The table shows the number of cubs each bear gave birth to each year. Which bear had a greater mean number of cubs?

Bear	Number of cubs
Darna	1, 3, 2, 2, 4
Juno	2, 2, 0, 1, 1, 3, 0, 1

8

Solve Problems by Working Backward

Goal Use a working backward strategy to solve problems.

Aaron is making a wire sculpture.
He cut a wire into four equal pieces.
Then he cut 0.50 m from each piece.
The final length of each piece was 1.25 m.

? **How long was the wire before Aaron began cutting it?**

Sofia's Solution

Understand

I need to determine the length of the wire before Aaron did any cutting.

Make a Plan

Cutting a wire into four equal pieces is like dividing by 4.
Cutting off 0.50 m is like subtracting 0.50.

I'll make a diagram to show what was done at each step.

| Length of wire? | → | Divide by 4. | → | Subtract 0.50 m. | → | Each piece is 1.25 m. |

I can work backward to calculate the original length of the wire.

I'll make a new diagram to show the calculations I'll do to solve the problem.

| Length of wire? | ← | Multiply by 4. | ← | Add 0.50 m. | ← | Each piece is 1.25 m. |

Carry Out the Plan

$1.25 + 0.50 = 1.75$

Each piece of wire was 1.75 m before the second set of cuts.

$1.75 \times 4 = 7.00$

The length of the wire was 7.00 m before the first set of cuts.

Reflecting

1. How did Sofia use her first diagram to make the second diagram?

2. How can you use Sofia's first diagram to check her answer?

Checking

3. Aaron cut 0.50 m from a length of wire. He then cut the remaining length into four equal pieces. The final length of each piece was 1.25 m. What was the length of the wire before he began cutting?
   a) Draw a diagram to represent what Aaron did.
   b) Draw a diagram to show how to solve the problem.
   c) Solve the problem.
   d) How is this problem different from Sofia's problem?

Practising

4. Melanie has a bank account. Her grandfather doubled the amount in her account and her grandmother added $50 more so Melanie had $99.50 in the bank. How much money did she have before her grandparents added money to her account? Show your work.

5. Students sold art cards to raise funds for a school trip. They sold half of the cards on a Saturday. The next Saturday they sold 20 more. They have 32 cards left to sell. How many cards did they have originally?

6. Create your own working backward problem. Give your problem to another student to solve.

LESSON

Skills Bank

1

1. Estimate. For one of the answers, explain how you estimated.
   a) 12.75 ÷ 3   b) 9.65 ÷ 2   c) 8)‾28.45   d) 7)‾6.95

2. The width of nine cereal boxes on a shelf is 55.45 cm. About how many centimetres wide is each box?

2

3. Calculate.
   a) 8.5 ÷ 10   b) 2.8 ÷ 10   c) 10)‾22.00   d) 10)‾75.5

4. Ten bags of party balloons cost $19.50. What is the cost of one bag of balloons?

5. Ten identical boards stacked on top of each other have a height of 35.5 cm. What is the thickness of each board?

6. Measure and record the length of this line to tenths of a centimetre. How long would each part be if you divided the line into 10 equal parts?

7. 10 balls placed side to side cover a distance of 95 cm. What is the width of each ball?

width

3

8. Calculate to one decimal place.
   a) 7 ÷ 2   c) 8)‾100   e) 27 ÷ 2   g) 5)‾29
   b) 18 ÷ 4   d) 5)‾19   f) 38 ÷ 4   h) 57 ÷ 6

9. Calculate to two decimal places.
   a) 17 ÷ 2   c) 8)‾20   e) 27 ÷ 6   g) 5)‾101
   b) 27 ÷ 4   d) 5)‾99   f) 51 ÷ 4   h) 97 ÷ 4

3 10. 7.00 kg of raspberries are divided equally into four plastic containers. Calculate the mass of raspberries in each container to two decimal places.

4 11. Calculate to one decimal place.
a) 24.2 ÷ 2   c) 10.8 ÷ 3   e) 33.6 ÷ 7   g) 27.6 ÷ 4
b) 8)4.8   d) 6)17.4   f) 9)59.4   h) 5)27.5

12. Calculate to two decimal places.
a) 64.20 ÷ 2   c) 10.95 ÷ 3   e) 7.04 ÷ 4   g) 34.93 ÷ 7
b) 8)5.20   d) 6)24.36   f) 9)51.12   h) 5)127.50

13. What is the length of each side of the regular octagon to hundredths of a metre?
a) The perimeter is 82.00 m.
b) The perimeter is 38.00 m.
c) The perimeter is 12.00 m.
d) The perimeter is 106.00 m.

6 14. Stephan and his father take a car on at least 10 ferry trips to and from Buckley Bay and Denman Island each month.

Ferry Fares

Riders	Single-fare return tickets	Books of return tickets
adult	$5.25	book of 10: $23.70
child (5 to 11)	$2.75	
car	$12.75	book of 5: $33.45 book of 10: $58.80

How much will they save on each return trip if they buy these books of tickets?
a) a book of 10 adult tickets
b) a book of 5 car tickets
c) a book of 10 car tickets

6 **15.** What case should you buy if you want to pay the least amount for each container of ketchup?

16. Which pieces of rope are longer: 15 m of rope in 6 equal pieces or 12 m of rope in 5 equal pieces?

7 **17.** Calculate the mean of each set of numbers.
a) 12, 18, 12
b) 1.5, 1.6, 1.8, 1.9, 2.5
c) 1.55, 3.65, 2.84
d) 2.4, 2.4, 2.4, 3.4, 4.8, 2.2, 2.0
e) 7.30, 7.90, 7.60, 7.00
f) 7.18, 10.08, 9.59, 8.86, 8.99, 9.84

18. Students in a Grade 5 class used this scale to rate a recent movie. Their ratings are reported in the chart. Did the boys or the girls give the movie a higher mean ranking?

1	Must see!
2	Good movie.
3	O.K. movie.
4	Don't go!

Student	Movie rating
boys	1, 2, 1, 3, 1, 1, 2, 3
girls	3, 3, 1, 1, 4

8 **19.** A number is doubled and then 0.5 is added to that number. The answer is 3.5. Use a working backward strategy to determine the original number.

20. Nellie the elephant ate half of a basket of apples on Sunday. On Monday, Nellie ate half of the remaining apples. She ate five apples on Tuesday, leaving only two apples for Wednesday. How many apples were in the basket on Sunday morning?

Problem Bank

LESSON

1 1. When you divide a decimal number by 6, the quotient is between 1 and 2. What are three possible dividends?

2 2. The height of a stack of 10 math books is 26.5 cm.
   a) What is the thickness of each book in centimetres?
   b) What is the thickness of each book in millimetres?
   c) Estimate the number of books in a stack 1 m high. Explain your reasoning.

3. A child can be expected to use 730 crayons by his or her tenth birthday.
   a) How many crayons does a child use each year?
   b) Show how to use the answer to part a) to calculate the number of crayons a Grade 5 student has used.

4 4. Use each of the digits 2, 4, and 5 in this division:
   ■.■ ÷ ■
   a) What is the greatest possible quotient?
   b) What is the least possible quotient?

7 5. a) Form a two-by-two square on a calendar month. Calculate the mean of the four numbers in the square.
   b) Repeat part a) using the four numbers in other squares on a calendar.
   c) What is the relationship between the mean and the numbers in each square?

S	M	T	W	T	F	S
		1	2	3	4	5
6	7	8	9	10	11	12
13	14	15	16	17	18	19
20	21	22	23	24	25	26
27	28	29	30	31		

6. Scientists are studying how far polar bears travel. They fit a collar with a satellite transmitter on each bear to track the bear's movements over several years. Which bear travelled the greatest mean annual distance?

Travelling Bears

	Distance (km)		
Year	Ursula	Nanuk	Artio
2001	2098	2205	2045
2002	2053	2897	2450
2003	3361		3015
2004			2076

CHAPTER 10

Chapter Review

LESSON

1

1. Estimate. For one answer, explain how you estimated.
   a) $12.75 \div 2$ b) $19.65 \div 2$ c) $9\overline{)35.45}$ d) $6\overline{)16.95}$

2

2. Calculate.
   a) $22.5 \div 10 = \blacksquare$ b) $49.2 \div 10 = \blacksquare$ c) $6 \div 10 = \blacksquare$ d) $0.9 \div 10 = \blacksquare$

3. Ten $2 coins are placed side by side in a line. The line is 280 mm long.

   a) What is the width of a $2 coin?
   b) How long would a line of $100 worth of $2 coins be?

4. A flea travelled 3.3 m in 10 equal jumps. How far did it travel in each jump?

3

5. Calculate the mass of each bag to two decimal places.
   a) 15.00 kg divided into four bags
   b) 1.00 kg divided into four bags
   c) 14.00 kg divided into eight bags
   d) 6.00 kg divided into four bags

6. Calculate to one decimal place.
   a) $10.0 \div 4 = \blacksquare$ b) $2.0 \div 4 = \blacksquare$ c) $12.0 \div 8 = \blacksquare$ d) $3.0 \div 5 = \blacksquare$

7. A 2.00 L can of paint was used to paint five equal walls. How many litres are needed to paint seven equal walls?

4

8. Three students are planning to grow vegetables in a community garden. Several plots are available. If they divide a plot into three equal sections, what will be the area of each section? Give your answer to hundredths of a metre.
   a) 4.00 m by 8.55 m   c) 6.00 m by 4.50 m
   b) 3.00 m by 9.25 m   d) 5.25 m by 4.00 m

9. Solve each problem. For each problem, did you use estimation, mental math, pencil and paper, or a calculator? Justify your choice.
  a) 2.2 m of wood is divided into four pieces. About how long is each piece?
  b) 1.89 m of wood is divided into three pieces. Calculate the length of each piece to two decimal places.
  c) A 12.50 m property line is fenced with 10 equal sections. What is the length of each section?
  d) 1.92 m of wood is divided into pieces that are 0.32 m long. How many 0.32 m pieces are there?

10. James and a group of friends are going to an amusement park. James plans to use 16 tickets. How much money will he save if he uses tickets bought in books of 8 instead of books of 4?

Ride Tickets

Books	Cost
4 rides	$13.00
8 rides	$22.00

11. Calculate the mean of each set.
  a) 10, 8, 11, 15
  b) 40, 37, 22, 18
  c) 220, 430, 189, 654
  d) 1.7, 2.3, 1.9, 4.2, 3.6, 2.8, 5.2, 1.1, 4.3, 2.7
  e) 1.7, 2.8, 3.4, 2.1, 3.4
  f) 2.73, 5.92, 9.31, 6.84

12. Which statements are not reasonable? Correct the unreasonable statements.
  a) The mean of 2, 4, 6, 8 is 9.
  b) The mean of 1, 1, 1, 4, 5 is 2.4.
  c) The mean of 1.5, 1.6, 1.7, 1.8, 1.9 is 1.55.

13. Shevaun planted a package of tomato seeds. One half of the seeds sprouted into seedlings. She gave 42 seedlings away and had 58 seedlings left. How many seeds did she plant?

14. In January, a farmer sold apples by the kilogram. In June, the price had gone down by half. In September, the price had gone up by $1.11 for each kilogram, and she was selling her apples for $3.34 for each kilogram. What was the price in January?

Chapter Task

Comparing the Cost of Batteries

Toys, music players, and many other devices use single-use or rechargeable batteries. Rechargeable batteries are more expensive, but they can be used over and over.

? **How many batteries do you have to use before rechargeable batteries become less expensive than single-use batteries?**

A. Survey the class to make a list of devices that use batteries. Identify the number and type of batteries each device uses. Battery types are identified by letters, such as AAA, C, and D.

B. Investigate the prices of various packages of batteries for one type of battery found in your survey. Calculate the price for each battery in a package.

C. Explain how you know each calculation is reasonable.

D. Which package has the least expensive batteries?

E. Investigate the total cost of rechargeable batteries and a battery charger. About how many packages of single-use batteries would you have to buy to equal the cost of the rechargeable batteries and the charger? Explain.

Task Checklist

- ☑ Did you estimate to check your answer?
- ☑ Did you explain how you calculated?
- ☑ Did you show all your steps?
- ☑ Did you explain your thinking?

CHAPTER 11

3-D Geometry and 3-D Measurement

Goals

You will be able to

- draw, build, and describe three-dimensional (3-D) shapes

- relate 3-D shapes to nets

- estimate, measure, and compare the capacity, volume, and mass of 3-D shapes

Recycling boxes

Getting Started

Building Shapes

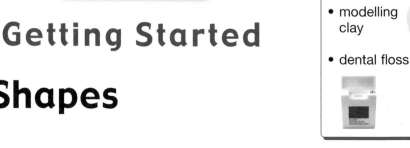

You will need

- modelling clay
- dental floss

? **How can you describe and make 3-D shapes?**

A. Name as many 3-D shapes in the picture as you can.
Use some of these words.
Name the object in the picture for each shape.

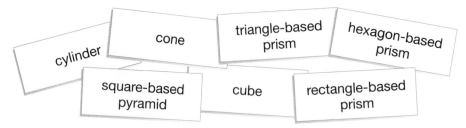

cylinder

cone

triangle-based prism

hexagon-based prism

square-based pyramid

cube

rectangle-based prism

B. Choose a prism or pyramid and build it with modelling clay.

C. Describe your shape.
- How many faces does it have?
- What are the shapes of the faces?
- Are there congruent faces?
- Are there parallel edges on the faces?
- Are there perpendicular edges on the faces?

D. Cut through your shape with dental floss to make two different 3-D shapes. Describe your new shapes.

Do You Remember?

1. What is the **volume** of each prism? Give your answer as a number of cubes.

   a)

   b)

   c)

2. Which shape in Question 1 has the same volume as this shape?

3. Which units would you use to measure the **capacity** of each container: litres or millilitres?

   a)

   b)

   c)

4. Which units would you use to measure the **mass** of each item: grams or kilograms?

   a)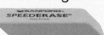

   b)

   c)

1 Making 3-D Shapes

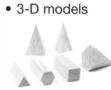
Goal Draw and build 3-D shapes.

Yoshi's class decided to make 3-D models of shelters to display for parent night.

? How can you make 3-D models?

Yoshi's Tent

I'll find a model that looks like the tent.

I'll sketch all the faces of the model.

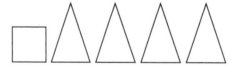

I'll use modelling clay to make the shape.
I'll make a square base first and four triangle faces joining at the top vertex.

I'll draw the model, starting with the base.
The base is a square.
I'll draw the top vertex. When I join the top vertex to the four vertices of the base, I'll be able to see the four faces.

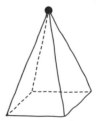

A. What shape is Yoshi's tent?

B. Choose a different shape for a shelter.
Build and draw it.

Reflecting

1. **a)** Which faces on Yoshi's tent are congruent?
   b) How can you show which faces are congruent on the clay model?

2. What attributes of a shape do you focus on first when you build and draw it?

Checking

3. **a)** What shapes are the faces of the tent? Sketch all the faces.
   b) What shape is the tent?
   c) Build the shape with modelling clay. Draw the shape.

Practising

4. **a)** Sketch the faces of each shape.
   b) How are the faces of the two shapes alike' How are they different?
   c) Build each shape using modelling clay.
   d) Draw and name each 3-D shape.

5. Build and draw each shape.
   a) a pentagon-based prism   **b)** a cone

2 Making Nets

You will need
- 3-D models

- stickers

- scissors

- tape

Goal Make nets for 3-D shapes.

Camille's recycling bin cannot
take bulky boxes.
She took apart two identical
boxes and noticed that the
two **nets** were not congruent.

? **How can you make different
nets from the same box?**

net
A 2-D shape that
can be folded into
a 3-D shape

Camille's Nets

I'll make different nets from a triangle-
based prism. This is how to make a net.

Step 1 Trace one face of the prism.

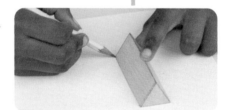

Step 2 Roll the prism over an edge
without lifting it from the paper.

Step 3 Put a sticker on the first face
that was traced.

Step 4 Trace the new face.

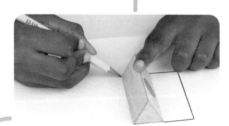

Step 5 Keep rolling and tracing until all the faces are drawn. You might have to roll back over some traced faces.

Step 6 Cut out the net. Check it by folding and taping to make the 3-D shape.

Next I follow the steps to make another net. I start with a different face and trace the faces in a different order this time.

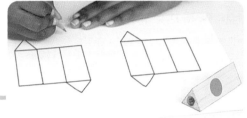

Reflecting

1. **a)** Why is it important to roll on the edge of the prism and not lift it from the paper?
   b) Why is it important to keep track of the faces that have been traced?

2. Would tracing a different face first always produce a different net?

Checking

3. This is a net for a triangle-based pyramid.
   a) Make two different nets for the same shape using a model.
   b) Cut and fold the nets to check if they make the same shape.
   c) Compare the nets. How are they the same? How are they different?

Practising

4. **a)** Make two different nets for a square-based pyramid.
   b) Fold each net to check.

5. **a)** These are nets for a pentagon-based prism. Sketch another net for this shape.
   b) What is the relationship between the number of sides of the base and the number of rectangles in the net?

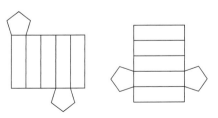

3 Identifying Nets

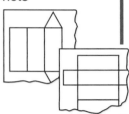
Goal Match 3-D shapes with their nets.

Dan's class made nets for a display of 3-D shapes.
The nets got all mixed up.

? **What clues can you use to match the nets with the 3-D shapes?**

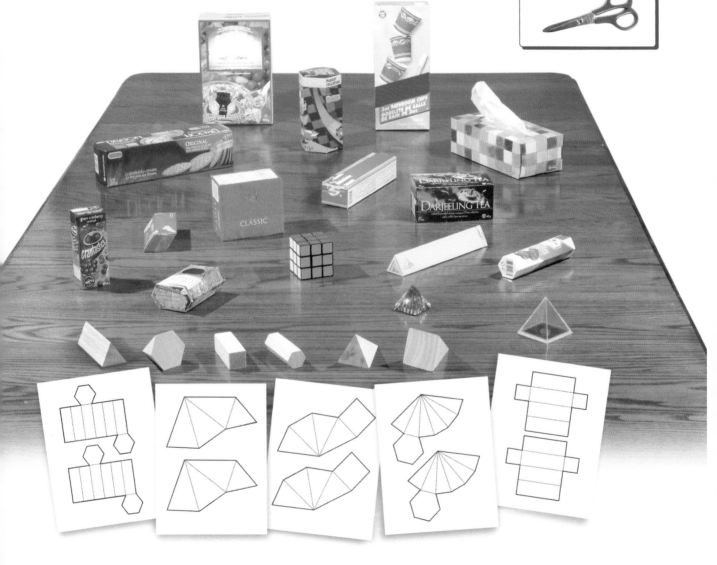

A. Compare the faces of the 3-D shape to the faces in the net.
Do the net and the 3-D shape match?
How do you know?

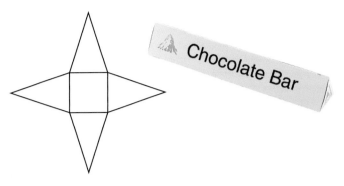

B. Match the nets and the 3-D shapes in the picture.
Record the clues you used to match each pair.

C. Cut out the nets, fold them, and check your answers.

D. Identify the 3-D shapes in the picture that don't have matching nets.

Reflecting

1. **a)** What clues can you use to match a net and a 3-D shape?
   b) Which clues are the most useful?

2. How are an object and its net the same?
   How are they different? Explain your thinking.

3. Which net would make a box for each object?
   Explain your choices.
   a) a toy car
   b) a baseball bat
   c) picture frame

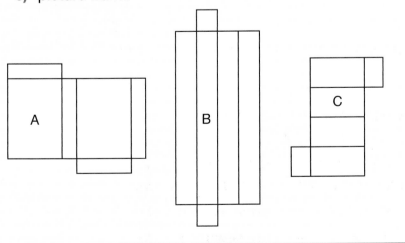

4 Communicate About Building a Model

Goal Write clear instructions for building a model from a picture.

Aaron wrote instructions for making a 3-D creature.

Aaron's Instructions

You will need 32 cubes.

Step 1 Make the body with a volume of 8 cubes. It is a square-based prism.

Step 2 Make a head with a volume of 3 cubes.

Step 3 Make 4 legs. Each leg has a volume of 4 cubes.

Step 4 Make 2 horns with a volume of 1 cube each. The horns are on the head.

Step 5 Make a tail with a volume of 3 cubes. The tail is on the body.

? How can you improve Aaron's instructions for building a 3-D model?

A. Make a creature by following Aaron's instructions.

B. Compare your creature with those of your classmates.

C. Identify the strengths of Aaron's instructions. Use the Communication Checklist.

D. How can you improve Aaron's instructions?

Communication Checklist

☑ Did you show all the steps?

☑ Did you use the right amount of detail?

☑ Did you use math language?

1. a) You compared the creatures made from Aaron's instructions. How are the creatures different?
   b) Why are they different?

2. a) When giving instructions, why is it important to give details about what to do in each step?
   b) Why is the order of the steps important?

3. Why is it a good idea to give your instructions to someone else to test?

Checking

4. a) Rewrite Aaron's instructions so that the creatures made by following his steps will be more alike.
   b) Trade the instructions you wrote with a classmate. Make a creature using your classmate's instructions.
   c) How are your creature and your classmate's creature the same? How are they different?

5. Build this creature. Describe the steps you took.

Practising

6. a) Make your own 3-D creature.
   b) Write instructions for making it.
   c) Work with a classmate to test each other's instructions.
   d) Identify the strengths of your instructions.
   e) How can you improve your instructions?

7. When would you need to describe a shape by giving instructions instead of showing a picture?

Mid–Chapter Review

LESSON

1
1. Build each shape with modelling clay. Then draw it.

a)

b)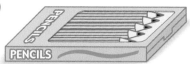

c)

2
2. Use a model for each shape.
Make a net for each. Fold each net to check.
a) triangle-based pyramid
b) rectangle-based prism
c) hexagon-based prism

3
3. Match the nets and the shapes. Explain your choices.

A.

B.

C.

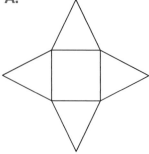

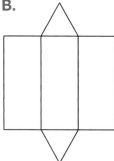

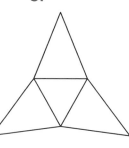

square-based
pyramid

triangle-based
pyramid

triangle-based
prism

4. Choose a 3-D shape from Question 3.
Make two different nets for it.
Cut and fold to check your nets.

Cross-Sections

Jose's Experiment

I want to see what happens when I cut 3-D shapes.

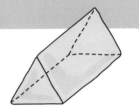

I predict that after I cut a triangle-based prism, the two shapes that are formed will have triangle faces at the cut.

I'll check my prediction by cutting a triangle-based prism with dental floss.

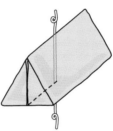

The new faces aren't what I predicted—they're rectangles.
The cut made two triangle-based prisms.
Each new prism is half the volume of the original.

1 How can you cut the triangle-based prism so that the new faces of the two halves are triangles as Jose predicted?

2 Experiment with cutting a triangle-based prism in different places. Predict the shapes of the new faces for each cut. Describe the new 3-D shapes.

5 Measuring and Comparing Capacity

Goal Estimate, measure, and compare capacities, and determine relationships among units.

Heather wants to order juice. She can choose a regular-sized cup with one free refill or a large-sized cup with no refills for the same price. Heather experiments with the cups using water.

? **Which choice would give Heather more juice? How much more?**

A. Use two cups of different sizes. Estimate the number of millilitres of water each cup holds. Measure to check your estimate.

B. Estimate the number of cups of each size that will fill 1 L. Measure to check your estimate.

C. Complete a chart like this one.

Size of cup	Estimate of capacity in millilitres	Actual capacity in millilitres	Estimate of number of cups to fill 1 L	Actual number of cups to fill 1 L
R				
L				

D. How many millilitres are in two regular-sized cups?

E. Which choice would give Heather more juice: two regular-sized cups or one large-sized cup? How do you know?

1. Why did you compare the capacity of two regular-sized cups with the capacity of one large-sized cup to answer the question?

2. How can you estimate the capacity of the cups in litres?

3. How can you compare the capacities of the cups using a different method?

Counting Faces, Vertices, and Edges

You can see only one triangle face and one rectangle face in this triangle-based prism. The other faces are hidden. You can also see six edges and five vertices.

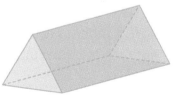

If you draw or imagine the hidden edges, you can count the faces, edges, and vertices. There are three rectangle faces and two triangle faces for a total of five faces.

A. Imagine the hidden edges and count the edges and vertices.

Try These

1. Draw or imagine the hidden edges. Count the faces, vertices, and edges.
   a) hexagon-based prism

   b) hexagon-based pyramid

6 Measuring and Comparing Volume

Goal Estimate, measure, and compare volumes using cubic centimetres.

Jasleen and Alain made cube creatures using centimetre linking cubes.
They cannot tell which creature has a greater volume by looking at them.

? **How can you compare the volumes of the creatures?**

Jasleen's creature   Alain's creature

Jasleen's Creature

I think my creature has a greater volume.

If I look at my creature from above, I see two rows, each with six columns.

I can count the cubes in each column.

I'll record my work in a chart. The number in each square tells the number of cubes in that column.

1	4	5	5	4	1
1	1	4	4	1	1

Alain's Creature

I think my creature has a greater volume. I can count the cubes in each body part.

Body part	Number of cubes
head	4
body	12
4 legs	8 (2 in each leg)
tail	6

cubic centimetre (cm³)

A unit of measurement for volume

1 cm³

A. How many cubes did it take to build Jasleen's creature? How many did it take to build Alain's creature?

B. What is the volume of each creature in **cubic centimetres (cm³)**?

C. Which creature has a greater volume?

Reflecting

1. How can two different shapes have the same volume?

2. How can you use symmetry to measure the volume of Jasleen's creature?

3. Which method of determining volume do you like? Why?

Checking

4. a) What is the volume of the flat?
   b) What is the volume of the cube?

5. a) Estimate the volume of each creature. Which creature do you think has a greater volume?
   b) Determine the volume of each creature in cubic centimetres. Use Jasleen's counting method for one creature and Alain's counting method for the other. Were your estimates close? Why or why not?

Practising

6. a) Make your own cube creature.
   b) Estimate and then determine the volume of your creature in cubic centimetres.
   c) Describe the method you used.

7. Martin made a model of a loaf of bread using base ten blocks. Estimate the volume of this loaf of bread in cubic centimetres. Explain how you made your estimate.

7 Relating Capacity Units to Volume

Goal Identify the relationship between capacity units and volume units.

Akiko is studying water displacement in science class.

? **How is the amount of water displaced by a shape related to its volume?**

Akiko's Shape

My shape has a volume of 100 cm³.

I can put my shape under water and measure the amount of water displaced.

When I put the shape in the beaker, the water rises. The difference in water levels is the amount of water displaced.

The water level rose from 600 mL to 700 mL when I put the shape in. The amount of water displaced is 100 mL.

Shape	Volume (cm³)	Amount of water displaced (mL)
1	100	100
2		

A. Use cubes to make a shape for each volume: 125 cm³, 90 cm³, and 200 cm³.

You will need

- centimetre linking cubes

- measuring cups

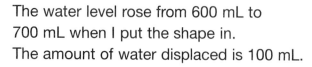

- water
- small objects that sink

B. Repeat Akiko's experiment with your shapes. Make sure the water is always at 600 mL before you sink each shape.

C. Record the amount of water displaced by each shape.

D. What do you notice about the values in your chart? Describe the relationship between cubic centimetres and millilitres.

Reflecting

1. Why is it important to record the water level before you put the shapes in the water?

2. Why is it important to make sure the shape is completely under water?

Checking

3. **a)** Measure the volume of an object by water displacement. Record the amount of water displaced.
   b) Record the volume of the object in cubic centimetres.

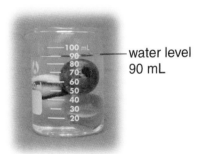

Practising

4. The water level was 60 mL before the three marbles were put in. What is the volume of each marble?

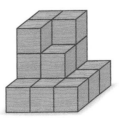

water level 90 mL

5. The two shapes are identical in size and shape, but the one built with wooden cubes is heavier.
   a) Would the two shapes displace the same amount of water? Why or why not?
   b) Conduct the experiment.
   c) Does the result agree with your prediction? Explain.

8 Measuring and Comparing Mass

Goal Estimate, measure, and compare the masses of objects using appropriate units.

Marcus's class is organizing a Play Ball Day for the school. Each student has to carry balls and equipment for setup.

This is heavy!

Equipment for Play Ball Day	
volleyballs	10
footballs	10
soccer balls	5
baseball bats	15
softballs	15
table-tennis balls	20
table-tennis paddles	40

? **What sports equipment can each student carry?**

Marcus's Measuring

I'll decide on a unit of measure for each object.
Then I'll measure the mass with balance scales.

I'll use either **grams** or **kilograms**.

1000 g = 1 kg

A. Measure the mass of each object.
Record your measurements in a chart.

Ball or equipment	Mass of each object	Number of objects needed	Total mass of objects
table-tennis ball		20	
softball		15	

B. Which object has the greatest mass? the least mass?

C. Order the equipment from least to greatest mass.

D. Calculate the total mass for each group of objects.
Record the calculations in your chart.

E. A reasonable mass for a student to carry is 5 kg.
Combine the equipment to make groups of up to
5 kg in mass.

F. List some combinations of balls and equipment for a
student to carry.

Reflecting

1. How can you decide which unit to use to measure
the mass of an object?

2. **a)** Which mass unit is greater: 1 kg or 1 g?
   b) If grams and kilograms are used to describe the
   mass of the same object, would you use more
   grams or more kilograms? Explain.

9 Using Tonnes

Goal Relate tonnes to kilograms.

A library is being built on soft ground.
An engineer has warned that if the books in the library have a
mass greater than 10 **tonnes** (10 **t**), the library will be unsafe.

? How many books can the library safely hold?

A. Measure the mass of your math book. Record the mass in a chart.

Object	Mass (g or kg)	Estimated number of books in a tonne
math book		

tonne (t)

A unit of measurement for mass
1 t = 1000 kg
1 kg = 1000 g

B. Measure the mass of several other books in the classroom. Record each mass in your chart.

C. Estimate the number of books that would make a tonne.

D. What would you recommend as a safe number of books for the library?

Reflecting

1. **a)** How did you estimate a safe number of books for the library?
   b) How would you estimate a safe number of DVDs for the library?

2. Karin said, "The greater the mass of an object, the more we need to make a tonne. The less the mass of the object, the fewer we need to make a tonne." Do you agree? Why or why not?

3. **a)** Which has a greater mass: a tonne of feathers or a tonne of rocks?
   b) Which has a greater volume: a tonne of feathers or a tonne of rocks? Explain your answer.

Skills Bank

2

1. Choose a 3-D shape.
   a) Draw the faces and the shape.
   b) Make a net by tracing the faces.
   c) Cut out the net and make the shape.
   d) Compare your shape with the 3-D shape you chose. Are they the same?

3

2. a) Is this the net of a pyramid or a prism? How do you know?
   b) Name the 3-D shape.

5

3. a) Choose two different glasses. Estimate and measure the capacity of each glass.
   b) Predict the number of each glass needed to fill 1 L.
   c) Measure with water and record your results.

6

4. a) Make a shape using centimetre linking cubes.
   b) What is the volume of the shape?
   c) How did you determine the volume of the shape?

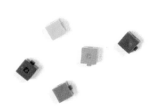

7

5. Use the shape you made in Question 4.
   a) Predict the amount of water the shape will displace in millilitres.
   b) Measure to check your prediction.

322

6. a) Before the golf ball was put in the water, the water level was 140 mL. What is the volume of the ball in cubic centimetres?

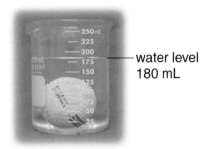

water level
180 mL

b) What is the volume of the toy frog in cubic centimetres? How do you know?

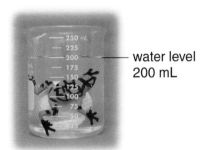

water level
200 mL

7. Which mass estimates are reasonable? Measure to check estimates that you think are unreasonable.

    a) pencil: 10 kg   **c)** hardcover book: 2 g   **e)** lunch: 70 kg

    b) glue: 50 g   **d)** eraser: 30 g   **f)** full water bottle: 20 g

8. What is the most appropriate unit for measuring each mass?

a)

d)

b)

e)

c)

f)

Problem Bank

1 1. Match these clues to the 3-D shapes they describe.

a) I have 6 rectangular faces, 12 edges, and 3 different sets of congruent faces. What am I?

c) I have 2 triangular faces and 3 rectangular faces. What am I?

b) I have 6 rectangular faces, 12 edges, and 2 different sets of congruent faces. What am I?

d) I have only one face that has right angles and parallel sides. What am I?

A B C D E F

3 2. Monique wrote descriptions for nets of pyramids and prisms. Name a pyramid or prism that matches each description.

a) Each face is congruent to at least one other face.

c) All the faces are rectangles.

b) There are no rectangles.

d) All the faces are congruent.

3. Which net would make a box for each object? Explain your reasoning.
a) a hockey stick
b) a pair of shoes
c) a CD

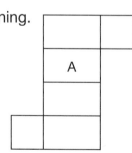 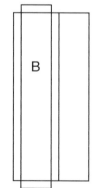 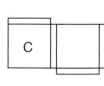

A B C

6 **4. a)** What is the volume of this creature in cubic centimetres?

    b) How can you check the volume using a different method?

    c) Build a different cube creature with the same volume and grid design as the one in the picture, but with different numbers in the squares of the grid.

1	1	5	4	5	1	1
1	0	1	0	1	0	1

7 **5.** The water level was 195 mL after the objects were put in. Each marble displaced 10 mL of water.

    a) What is the total amount of water displaced by the three marbles and the pyramid?

    b) How much water did the pyramid displace?

    c) What is the volume of the pyramid?

water level 125 mL

9 **6.** The mass labels for these pictures are mixed up. Match the labels with the pictures.

  2 kg   75 g   30 kg   300 g   1 t   5000 t

7. A zoo needs to transport a herd of 10 elephants on a boat.
Each elephant has a mass of 2 t.
The boat can hold a maximum mass of 15 t of elephants.

    a) What is the mass of the herd in tonnes?

    b) How many trips must the boat take to transport the herd? How many elephants are on each trip?

Chapter Review

LESSON

2 1. a) Choose a shape and draw it.
   b) Draw its net.
   c) Build the shape with modelling clay.
   d) Cut out the net and make the shape from the net.
   e) Does the shape match the one you chose?

3 2. a) Predict the shapes from their nets. Explain your thinking.
   b) Trace the nets, cut them out, and make the shapes. Were your predictions correct?

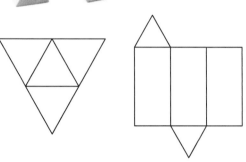

4 3. a) Make a shape using 30 linking cubes.
   b) Write instructions for making your shape.
   c) Give the instructions to a classmate to make the shape.
   d) How can you improve your instructions?

5 4. Freya wants to choose the bowl with the greater capacity for her cereal. Describe two ways she can figure out which bowl to choose.

A   B

6 5. Use up to 50 centimetre linking cubes to make a cube creature. Determine the volume of your creature.

6. a) Predict the amount of water that will be displaced when you sink the cube creature from Question 5 in water.
   b) Carry out the experiment.
   c) Was your prediction correct?

7. Estimate and measure the volume of four common objects by water displacement.

8. a) Select two common objects whose mass you would measure in grams and two whose mass you would measure in kilograms.
   b) Estimate, measure, and record the masses.
   c) Compare each measure to your estimate.

9. Choose an appropriate unit of measure for the mass of each object. Explain your choice.

a)

c)

e)

b)

d)

f)

10. Match each mass to an object in Question 9.
    a) 80 g   c) 4 kg   e) 2 t
    b) 500 g   d) 12 kg   f) 20 t

Chapter Task

Food Drive

The students are baking bread for a food drive.

crate: 1 kg

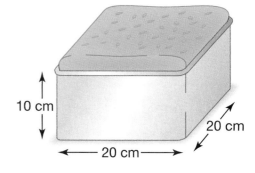

10 cm

20 cm

20 cm

? **How many loaves of bread can the truck deliver on one trip?**

A. What is the volume of one loaf of bread in cubic centimetres? Round to the nearest thousand cubic centimetres.

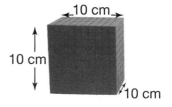

10 cm

10 cm

10 cm

B. 1000 cm³ of bread has a mass of 100 g. What is the mass of one loaf of bread?

C. A truck has a mass limit of 2 t and a capacity limit of 500 crates. Four loaves of bread fit in a crate. How many loaves of bread can the truck deliver in one trip? Explain your reasoning.

Task Checklist

☑ Did you use appropriate equipment?

☑ Did you use a model?

☑ Did you explain your thinking?

☑ Did you use math language?

Cumulative Review

Cross-Strand Multiple Choice

1. A rectangular poster is 24 cm wide. The length is double the width. What is the area of the poster?
   A. 576 cm²   **B.** 1152 cm²   **C.** 144 cm²   **D.** 864 cm²

2. What are the coordinates of the vertices of the triangle?
   A. (3, 2), (1, 8), (9, 4)
   B. (2, 3), (1, 7), (4, 9)
   C. (2, 3), (8, 1), (4, 8)
   D. (2, 3), (8, 1), (4, 9)

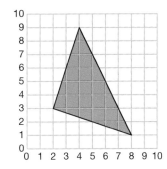

3. What is the product of 7 × 4.9?
   A. 343   **B.** 0.34   **C.** 34.3   **D.** 3.43

4. What is the quotient of 44 ÷ 8?
   A. 5.5   **B.** 5.7   **C.** 5.52   **D.** 57

5. What is the quotient of 7.8 ÷ 10?
   A. 78   **B.** 0.78   **C.** 0.8   **D.** 7

6. What shape can be made with this net?
   A. octagon-based pyramid   **C.** hexagon-based prism
   B. pentagon-based pyramid   **D.** hexagon-based pyramid

7. How many 10 kg masses have the same mass as 1 t?
   A. 1000   **B.** 100   **C.** 10 000   **D.** 10

8. Dan used 31 centimetre linking cubes to build a statue. When the statue was put underwater, the water level rose to 225 mL. What was the water level before the statue was put in?
   A. 31 mL   **B.** 194 mL   **C.** 256 mL   **D.** 231 mL

Cross-Strand Investigation

Camping Trip

9. Jasleen's family is planning a
camping trip with some friends.
   a) What is the area of the
   campground?
   b) Sketch a different campground
   with the same area.
   Explain how you know the
   campgrounds have the
   same area.
   c) Seven campers are sharing the cost of a bag
   of marshmallows equally. Estimate the cost
   for each camper. Explain your thinking.
   Justify your estimation strategy.
   d) Jasleen bought veggie dogs to cook at
   the campfire. How much do eight packages
   of veggie dogs cost?
   e) What is the cost for one veggie dog
   with a bun?
   f) Jasleen needs a new tent. Use a 3-D shape
   to create a net for a tent. Then fold your net
   to make the tent. Sketch your tent.
   What 3-D shape did you use?
   Explain why you chose this shape.

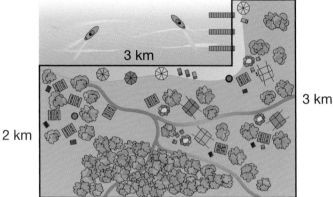

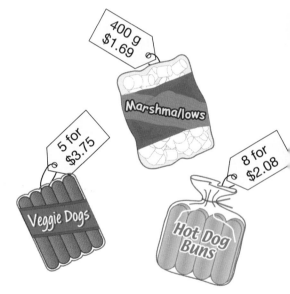

10. a) Renting a canoe costs $8 for each hour. Monique
    has a coupon to save $2.50 off the total rental cost.
    How much would she pay to rent a canoe for 3 h?
    Explain your thinking.
   b) The campground operators surveyed people
   to find out which parts of the campground
   they prefer.
   Draw a graph to show the data from the chart.
   Describe what your graph shows.
   Explain how you chose your scale.

Favourite Campground Spots

Campground spot	Number who chose this spot
beach	326
campsite	253
boating area	37
forest trails	127

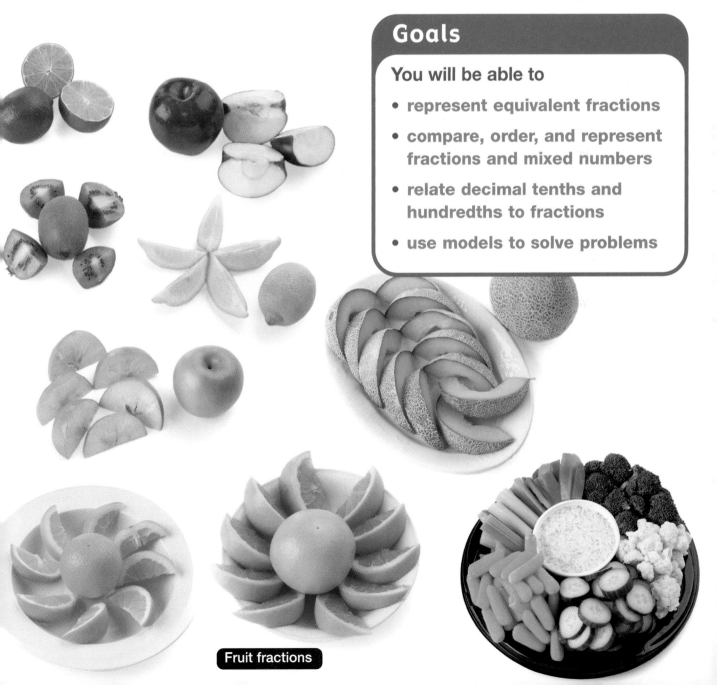

Fractions

Goals

You will be able to

- **represent equivalent fractions**
- **compare, order, and represent fractions and mixed numbers**
- **relate decimal tenths and hundredths to fractions**
- **use models to solve problems**

Fruit fractions

Getting Started

Zoomobiles and Riders

You will need
- counters

- pencil crayons

- zoo cars

- pattern blocks

Zoomobiles carry visitors around a zoo.
Two cars joined together make a zoomobile.
Each car has four benches. A bench holds three visitors.

? **What fractions can you use to describe the zoomobile cars?**

A. 15 visitors will ride in the zoomobile. How can you arrange the visitors in the two cars without filling all the seats in either car? Use one colour of counter to represent children and the other colour to represent adults.

B. Write a fraction for each car to represent the number of filled seats. Which fraction is greater?

C. Write a fraction for each car to represent the number of seats filled by children.

D. Write a fraction for each car to represent the number of seats filled by adults.

E. Order your four fractions in Parts C and D from least to greatest.

F. Model a car that fits this description:
$\frac{7}{12}$ of the seats are filled. Children fill $\frac{4}{12}$ of the seats.

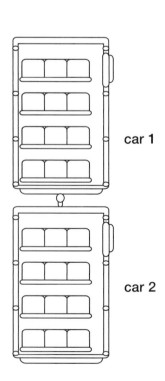

car 1

car 2

G. Model a car with $\frac{1}{4}$ of the seats filled.
Write a different fraction to describe how full it is.
Write two fractions to represent the empty seats.

H. Fill 18 seats in empty cars. Fill each car before using the next one. Write a **mixed number** to represent the number of cars filled.

Do You Remember?

1. The 10-by-10 grid shows how the zoo uses the space in the African Savannah. Write a fraction for each area.

   ☐ gorillas
   ☐ walking paths
   ☐ giraffes
   ☐ elephants
   ☐ lions
   ☐ other

   a) gorillas   d) giraffes
   b) lions   e) other
   c) elephants   f) walking paths

2. Use the fractions you wrote for Question 1.
   a) Which is the greatest fraction?
   b) Identify two animals that have equal fractions of area.

3. Think of the hexagon pattern block as the whole. Write a fraction of the hexagon for each.
   a) one triangle   c) two triangles
   b) one rhombus   d) three rhombuses

4. Identify the models that show $\frac{3}{4}$ blue. Explain how you know.
   a)

   c)

   b)

   marbles

   d)

Fraction Puzzles

You will need

- square tiles

- pencil crayons

- grid paper

Goal Use patterns to represent the same fraction in different ways.

? How can you use different numbers of tiles to model the same fraction?

A. Write fractions to represent the fraction of red tiles for each rectangle.

B. Why can you describe both rectangles as $\frac{1}{2}$ red?

C. Show how to use other numbers of tiles to model rectangles that are $\frac{1}{2}$ red. Complete a table to display your models.

Number of red tiles	Total number of tiles in rectangle	Fraction of red tiles in rectangle	Picture
3	6	$\frac{3}{6}$	
4	8	$\frac{4}{8}$	

D. How do you know the rectangles are $\frac{1}{2}$ red?

E. Make a rectangle that is $\frac{2}{5}$ red and $\frac{3}{5}$ blue. How many red tiles did you use? How many tiles did you use in total?

F. Use a different number of tiles to model a rectangle that is $\frac{2}{5}$ red and $\frac{3}{5}$ blue.

G. Use three other numbers of tiles to show models that are $\frac{2}{5}$ red. Make a table like the one in Part C to record your models.

H. Choose your own fraction. Use three different numbers of tiles to form rectangles where that fraction is red. Record your work.

Reflecting

1. Is it possible to use square tiles to make a three-by-five rectangle that is $\frac{1}{2}$ **red**? Explain.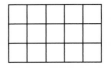

2. How did you use **denominators** and **numerators** to answer Parts C, F, and H?

3. Is there a fraction you can't model in at least two ways with red and blue tiles? Explain.

4. Look at the Fraction of **red** tiles column in Part C. Describe the pattern in the numerators and denominators for any fraction related to $\frac{1}{2}$.

Mental Math

Multiply by Doubling

You can think of 6 when you want to multiply by 12.

$12 \times 5 =$ double 6×5 6×5 30

$6 \times 5 = 30$ $+ \ 6 \times 5$ $+ \ 30$

Double 30 is 60. 12×5 60

A. How can you calculate 12×6 by thinking of 6×6?

B. How can you calculate 12×12 by thinking of 6×12?

Try These

1. **a)** 6×7 **b)** 6×8 **c)** 6×9 **d)** 6×11
    12×7 12×8 12×9 12×11

2. Describe how to use doubling to multiply by 14.

3. Calculate using mental math.
    a) 14×3 **b)** 14×4 **c)** 14×5 **d)** 14×6

2 Equivalent Fractions

You will need
- grid paper
- pencil crayons

Goal Make models of fractions and name equivalent fractions.

Some food was left over after Liam's party.

? **What fractions are left?**

Liam's Fractions

I ate $\frac{1}{2}$ a sandwich. Grandad ate $\frac{2}{4}$ of a sandwich.

I left $\frac{1}{2}$. Grandad left $\frac{2}{4}$. These amounts are the same.

I can model the leftovers with a diagram.

I shade $\frac{1}{2}$. I draw a line to make fourths.

my sandwich   Grandad's sandwich

Both $\frac{1}{2}$ and $\frac{2}{4}$ represent the same amount of sandwich.

They are **equivalent fractions**. $\frac{1}{2}$ is equivalent to $\frac{2}{4}$.

$$\frac{1}{2} = \frac{2}{4}$$

The juice pitcher holds 12 glasses of juice.
There is half a pitcher of juice left.
I can model the pitcher by drawing a diagram with
12 sections. I shade $\frac{1}{2}$ to show the leftover juice.

$\frac{6}{12}$ servings are left.

$\frac{6}{12}$ is equivalent to $\frac{1}{2}$.

$$\frac{6}{12} = \frac{1}{2}$$

equivalent fractions

Fractions that represent the same part of a whole or the same part of a set

$\frac{2}{4}$ is equivalent to $\frac{1}{2}$.

$$\frac{2}{4} = \frac{1}{2}$$

Reflecting

1. Use this fraction model to explain how you know that $\frac{3}{4}$ and $\frac{9}{12}$ are equivalent fractions.

2. How can you divide up this fraction model to find another equivalent fraction for $\frac{3}{4}$?

Checking

3. Write two equivalent fractions for each picture. How do you know your fractions are equivalent?

   a)  b) 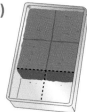 c)

Practising

4. Model and write two equivalent fractions for the yellow part.

   a) 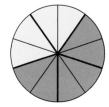 b)

5. Write a fraction to represent the blue area in each rectangle. Sketch a fraction model that shows an equivalent fraction for each blue area. Write the equivalent fraction.

   a)   b) 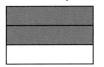 c)

6. Choose an animal sticker. Write two equivalent fractions for that fraction of all the stickers.

3 Comparing Fractions

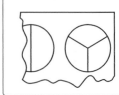

Goal Compare the size of fractions.

Every guest at Norman's party made a pizza. The pizzas were all the same size, but they were cut into different numbers of slices.

Monique   Norman   Karin   Aaron

? **If each guest eats two slices of his or her pizza, who will eat the most pizza?**

Monique's Pizza Fractions

Norman's two slices make $\frac{2}{8}$ of a pizza. $\frac{2}{8}$ is equivalent to $\frac{1}{4}$.

My pizza is cut into six slices. I can see that $\frac{2}{6}$ of my pizza is more than $\frac{1}{4}$ of a pizza. So $\frac{2}{6} > \frac{1}{4}$.

I will eat more than Norman.

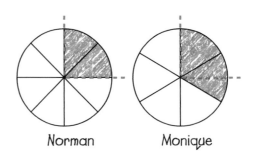

Norman   Monique

A. Use a fraction circle to represent Karin's pizza. What fraction of a pizza will Karin eat?

B. Compare the fraction for two slices of Karin's pizza with $\frac{1}{4}$. Who will eat more pizza: Karin or Norman? Explain.

C. Who will eat more pizza: Karin or Aaron?

D. Which of the four people will eat the most pizza?

Reflecting

1. What strategy did you use to compare the amounts of pizza Karin and Aaron will eat?

2. Suppose Karin and Aaron each eat four slices. Who will have eaten the most? How do you know?

3. a) Explain how you would compare two fractions with the same denominators, such as $\frac{2}{8}$ and $\frac{3}{8}$.
   b) Explain how you would compare two fractions with the same numerators, such as $\frac{2}{8}$ and $\frac{2}{10}$.

Checking

4. Compare the fractions of this pizza. Write > or <. Explain your strategy.

   a) $\frac{7}{12} \blacksquare \frac{9}{12}$ b) $\frac{5}{12} \blacksquare \frac{5}{6}$ c) $\frac{1}{2} \blacksquare \frac{4}{6}$

Practising

5. Alain's recipe calls for $\frac{2}{3}$ of a cup of oatmeal and $\frac{2}{5}$ of a cup of sugar. Is there more oatmeal or more sugar in the recipe? Explain your answer.

6. Compare. Write > or <. Explain your strategy.

   a) $\frac{2}{12} \blacksquare \frac{6}{12}$ b) $\frac{3}{12} \blacksquare \frac{3}{5}$ c) $\frac{3}{8} \blacksquare \frac{2}{10}$

7. Is each fraction more or less than $\frac{1}{3}$? Explain how you know.

   a) $\frac{1}{5}$ b) $\frac{2}{3}$ c) $\frac{3}{6}$

8. Four people each ate $\frac{1}{2}$ of a pizza plus one more slice.
   a) What fraction of a pizza did each person eat?
   b) Who ate the most pizza? Who ate the least? Explain your reasoning.

Juanita   Drake

Patrick   Camille

Mid-Chapter Review

 1. In a rectangle, $\frac{2}{3}$ of the squares are red.
   If there are 15 squares altogether, how many are red?
   If there are 30 squares altogether, how many are red?
   Show your work.

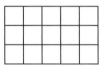

2. What fraction of each shape is coloured?
   Name an equivalent fraction for each picture.

   a)   b) 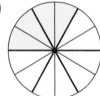   c)

3. A lasagna is cut into six equal pieces.
   Two pieces have been eaten.
   a) What fraction of the lasagna has been eaten?
   b) Write an equivalent fraction for this amount.

4. Compare. Write >, <, or =. Explain your strategy.

   a) $\frac{4}{8}$ ■ $\frac{7}{8}$ c) $\frac{1}{7}$ ■ $\frac{1}{9}$ e) $\frac{3}{5}$ ■ $\frac{4}{5}$

   b) $\frac{3}{4}$ ■ $\frac{7}{8}$ d) $\frac{3}{5}$ ■ $\frac{6}{10}$ f) $\frac{2}{3}$ ■ $\frac{3}{4}$

   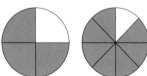      

5. Identify the greater part. Explain your strategy.
   a) $\frac{3}{5}$ or $\frac{3}{10}$ of this granola bar?   b) $\frac{3}{4}$ or $\frac{2}{3}$ of this flag?

      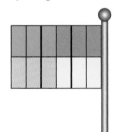

Curious Fractions

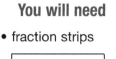

Jose knows that $\frac{1}{2} < \frac{2}{3}$ and $\frac{2}{3} < \frac{4}{5}$.

So he says $\frac{2}{3}$ is between $\frac{1}{2}$ and $\frac{4}{5}$.

Jose's Rule

When I look at the fractions,
I see that the 2 is between the 1 and the 4.
I see that the 3 is between the 2 and the 5.

$$\frac{1}{2} \longleftarrow \frac{2}{3} \longrightarrow \frac{4}{5}$$

I think I can always find a fraction between any two fractions by using denominators and numerators that are in between.

1 Sofia said, "I'm not sure about that. Is $\frac{2}{5}$ between $\frac{1}{2}$ and $\frac{9}{10}$?" Answer Sofia's question. What do you think about Jose's rule?

2 Find two fractions between $\frac{1}{2}$ and $\frac{9}{10}$ that follow Jose's rule.

3 Find two other fractions that don't follow Jose's rule.

4 Improper Fractions and Mixed Numbers

You will need

- fraction circles

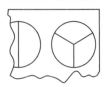

- grid paper

Goal Represent and rename improper fractions as mixed numbers.

Teresa is helping her dad roast a small chicken. It will take $1\frac{1}{4}$ hours to cook. She must baste it every quarter hour. She sets the timer to ring every 15 min.

? How many times will the timer ring until the chicken is cooked?

Teresa's Cooking Time

I can use a fraction circle with four parts to represent a clock.

I can count around the clock by quarter hours: $\frac{1}{4}, \frac{2}{4}, \frac{3}{4}, \frac{4}{4}, \frac{5}{4}$

The timer will go off five times, once for each of the five quarters.

Another name for the **mixed number** $1\frac{1}{4}$ is the **improper fraction** $\frac{5}{4}$.

$1\frac{1}{4}$ hours

mixed number

A number made up of a whole number and a fraction

improper fraction

A fraction with a numerator that is greater than or equal to its denominator

Reflecting

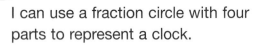

1. Why do you think Teresa used a fraction circle with four parts to represent a clock?

2. The improper fraction $\frac{8}{3}$ says there are eight parts and each part is $\frac{1}{3}$ of a whole. What mixed number is equivalent to $\frac{8}{3}$? How do you know?

Checking

3. **a)** Clock faces can be square.
   Draw a square on grid paper and show how
   to represent half an hour.
   b) A timer rings every half hour for $3\frac{1}{2}$ hours.
   Use your model to determine the number of rings.
   c) Write $3\frac{1}{2}$ as an improper fraction.

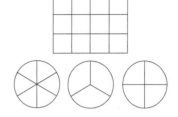

Practising

4. Draw a picture for each mixed number.
   Use fraction circles or grid paper for each.
   a) $3\frac{2}{3}$ hours   **c)** $1\frac{3}{4}$ cups
   b) $1\frac{5}{6}$ hours   **d)** $6\frac{1}{2}$ innings

5. Rename each mixed number in Question 4 as an
   improper fraction.

6. How many hours would be spent watching videos?
   Use fraction circles. Write your answers as improper
   fractions and mixed numbers.
   a) 8 videos, each $\frac{1}{3}$ hours long   **c)** 2 videos, each $\frac{3}{4}$ hours long
   b) 8 videos, each $\frac{1}{2}$ hours long   **d)** 7 videos, each $\frac{2}{3}$ hours long

7. One chocolate bar has eight squares.
   Write each number of bars as an improper fraction.
   Draw a model for each.
   a) $1\frac{5}{8}$ bars   **b)** $2\frac{1}{8}$ bars   **c)** 3 whole bars

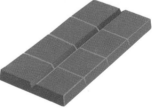

8. Jose spent $3\frac{1}{3}$ hours watching a
   video several times.
   a) How long could the video be?
   Explain your thinking.
   b) How many times did he watch it?

9. Write your own problem using an improper fraction and
   a mixed number. Explain the solution to your problem.

5 Relating Fractions to Decimals

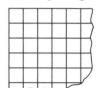

Goal Use the relationship between decimals and fractions to make comparisons.

Martin read that about 0.12 of people in the world are left-handed.
He found that 4 of the 16 members of his hockey team are left-handed.

? **How does the number of left-handed people on Martin's hockey team compare to the world average?**

Martin's First Step

I'll write $\frac{4}{16}$ as a decimal. Then I can compare $\frac{4}{16}$ to 0.12.

I need to write an equivalent fraction in tenths or hundredths to make a decimal.

I'll make a sketch to show $\frac{4}{16}$.
I see that $\frac{4}{16} = \frac{1}{4}$.
I can use a hundredths grid to show $\frac{1}{4}$.

A. Represent $\frac{1}{4}$ on a hundredths grid.

B. Write an equivalent fraction for $\frac{1}{4}$ in hundredths.
Write a **decimal equivalent** for $\frac{1}{4}$.

C. Calculate $1 \div 4$ on a calculator. How does your hundredths grid show $\frac{1}{4} = 1 \div 4$?

D. Compare your decimal for the number of left-handed people on Martin's hockey team to the world average.

decimal equivalent

A decimal that represents the same part as a fraction

$\frac{5}{10} = 0.5$

$\frac{5}{100} = 0.05$

Reflecting

1. How does it help to rename a fraction as tenths or hundredths when you want to write the decimal equivalent?

2. Why was it a good idea to change $\frac{4}{16}$ to $\frac{1}{4}$ to determine a decimal equivalent?

3. How do you write a decimal, such as 0.12, as a fraction?

4. How can you use a hundredths grid to calculate the decimal equivalent for $\frac{1}{5}$? How can you use a calculator?

Checking

5. On Anna's hockey team, $\frac{2}{20}$ of the players are left-handed.
   a) Represent $\frac{2}{20}$ on a hundredths grid and read it as a decimal equivalent.
   b) Compare $\frac{2}{20}$ to the world average of 0.12.

6. $\frac{3}{5}$ of the students in Martin's class play soccer. How does that compare with last year's average of 0.5? Show your work.

Practising

7. Write decimal equivalents and then list the landfill materials in order from least to greatest.
   a) $\frac{6}{25}$ of a landfill site is plastic
   b) $\frac{3}{50}$ of a landfill site is rubber and leather
   c) $\frac{2}{5}$ of a landfill site is paper

8. Compare these amounts of colour. Which is greater?
   a) $\frac{3}{10}$ blue or $\frac{2}{4}$ yellow
   b) $\frac{2}{5}$ red or $\frac{16}{20}$ yellow

9. Order these numbers from least to greatest.
   a) $\frac{1}{2}, \frac{3}{4}, \frac{2}{5}, \frac{7}{10}$
   b) $1\frac{3}{5}, 2\frac{1}{4}, 1\frac{8}{25}$

6 Solve Problems by Making Models

Goal Solve fraction problems by making models of the information.

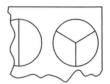

Heather helps coach a team of 12 basketball players. At halftime, the head coach asked her to get one piece of fruit for each player. She had to get apples for $\frac{1}{2}$ of the players, oranges for $\frac{1}{3}$ of the players, and pears for the rest.

? **What number of each fruit should Heather bring to the players?**

 Heather's Model

Understand

I need to get apples for $\frac{1}{2}$ of the 12 players, oranges for $\frac{1}{3}$ of the 12 players, and pears for the rest.

Make a Plan

I'll make a model. I'll use 12 counters to represent the players. Then I'll figure out how many players each fraction represents.

Carry Out the Plan

I use 12 green counters to show 12 players.

To represent players who want apples, I replace green counters with red counters until $\frac{1}{2}$ of the counters are red. 6 red counters make $\frac{1}{2}$ of 12.

To represent players who want oranges, I replace green counters with orange counters until $\frac{1}{3}$ of the counters are orange.

4 orange counters make $\frac{1}{3}$ of 12.

So 6 players want apples and 4 want oranges.

There are 2 players left, so I need 2 pears.

Reflecting

1. How did making a model of the team help Heather solve the problem?

Checking

2. If each person wanted $1\frac{1}{2}$ pieces of fruit, how many apples, oranges, and pears would Heather need to get?

Practising

3. Patrick used $1\frac{1}{2}$ cups of flour in a recipe and Helene used $\frac{4}{3}$ cups. Who used more flour? Use a model to solve the problem.

4. This triangle is $\frac{1}{4}$ of a larger shape. What could the whole shape look like?

5. Ben has a very unusual apartment. What fraction of the whole design does each colour represent? If his kitchen covers 25 m², what is the area of each of the other rooms?

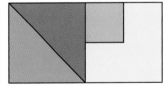

☐ kitchen
☐ living room
☐ bedroom
☐ bathroom

6. What fraction of the whole area of this triangle is covered by each shape? Show your work.
   a) triangles
   b) rhombuses
   c) trapezoids
   d) hexagons

7. Create a fraction problem that you can solve by using a model. Show how to solve your problem.

7 Ordering Fractions on a Number Line

Goal Use number lines to compare and order fractions.

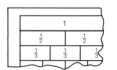

Marcus is hoping that Alain's snail will win the snail race.

Owner	Snail position
Alain	$\frac{3}{4}$ of the way to Finish
Monique	$\frac{2}{3}$ of the way to Finish
Karin	$\frac{3}{8}$ of the way to Finish
Dan	$\frac{6}{8}$ of the way to Finish
Yoshi	$\frac{1}{2}$ of the way to Finish
Liam	at Start

? **Whose snail is winning?**

Marcus's Number Line

I'll make a number line to compare the fractions. I can use fraction strips to make the number line.

The fractions are all from 0 to 1, so I can use a number line that goes from 0 to 1.

Liam's snail is at Start. I place his snail at 0.

Now I'll place Yoshi's snail. I can use a $\frac{1}{2}$ fraction strip to mark halves on my number line.

A. Use fraction strips to create a number line like Marcus's. Place Yoshi's snail.

B. Use a $\frac{1}{4}$ fraction strip to mark your number line. Place Alain's snail.

C. Use fraction strips to place the other snails.

D. Whose snail is winning the race? List the snails in order from first place to last place.

Reflecting

1. How could you tell before you placed all the snails that some of the snails were ahead of Yoshi's snail?

2. Whose snails are at the same place on the number line? How can they be at the same place when the fractions are different?

3. How is your fraction number line like a number line for whole numbers? How is it different?

Checking

4. This chart shows the positions of the snails later in the race.
   a) What extra fraction strip will you need to place the snails in their new positions?
   b) Use a different colour to mark the new positions of the snails on your fraction number line. Which snail hasn't moved?

Owner	Snail position
Alain	$\frac{5}{6}$ of the way to Finish
Monique	$\frac{4}{6}$ of the way to Finish
Karin	$\frac{3}{6}$ of the way to Finish
Dan	$\frac{7}{8}$ of the way to Finish
Yoshi	$\frac{5}{8}$ of the way to Finish
Liam	$\frac{1}{6}$ of the way to Finish

Practising

5. Nick put different amounts of water into identical glasses. He tapped the glasses to make musical sounds. Glasses with more water make lower sounds. Use a number line to order these glasses from lowest to highest sound.

   a) $\frac{1}{5}$ full, $\frac{1}{2}$ full, $\frac{3}{4}$ full, $\frac{3}{5}$ full

   b) $\frac{2}{3}$ full, $\frac{5}{8}$ full, $\frac{3}{4}$ full, $\frac{4}{6}$ full

   c) $\frac{1}{2}$ full, $\frac{3}{4}$ full, $\frac{2}{3}$ full, $\frac{3}{8}$ full

   d) $\frac{4}{5}$ full, $\frac{5}{8}$ full, $\frac{6}{8}$ full, $\frac{4}{8}$ full

Target 1

Number of players: 2
How to play: Spin to make a fraction.
Move counters on the game board until they are all on 1.

Step 1 Set up the game board. The red player puts a red counter at 0 on each of the six number lines. The blue player puts a blue counter at 0 on each line.

Step 2 The red player spins a fraction using both spinners. Spinner 1 gives the numerator and Spinner 2 gives the denominator. The red player records the spin fraction.

Step 3 The red player moves a red counter the same amount as the spin fraction (or an equivalent fraction) along one line. Counters can't go past 1. If the player can't move a counter, the player must pass.

Step 4 After the red player has moved or passed, the blue player spins.

The game ends when a player has a counter on 1 on every number line.

You will need

- spinners

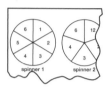

- game board

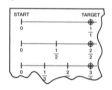

- a pencil and a paper clip
- counters

Spinner 1

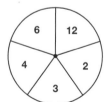

Spinner 2

Drake's Turn

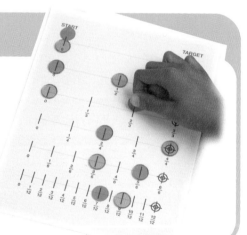

I spun 2 and 6, so I can move a red counter $\frac{2}{6}$.

My thirds counter is only at $\frac{1}{3}$.

I'll move that counter one mark to $\frac{2}{3}$.

Skills Bank

1

1. How many tiles in each rectangle are blue?

    a) A rectangle has 8 tiles. $\frac{1}{4}$ of its tiles are blue.

    b) A rectangle has 15 tiles. $\frac{2}{3}$ of its tiles are blue.

2. $\frac{2}{5}$ of the tiles in a rectangle are blue. How many tiles would be blue if the rectangle had 5 tiles? 10 tiles? 30 tiles?

2

3. What fraction of each picture is shaded?
Name the fraction in at least two ways.

    a)   **b)**   **c)**

4. Change each model to show the number of equal parts.

    a) tenths   **c)** sixths   **e)** ninths

    b) eighths   **d)** sixths   **f)** twelfths

3

5. Glynis, Anna, and Martin each ate five slices of pizza.
Which student ate half a pizza? Explain how you know.

       Glynis   Anna   Martin

6. Which fraction is greater? Explain your answers.

a) $\frac{5}{6}$ or $\frac{3}{6}$ 　　 b) $\frac{3}{5}$ or $\frac{3}{8}$ 　　 c) $\frac{1}{4}$ or $\frac{1}{12}$ 　　 d) $\frac{3}{8}$ or $\frac{1}{2}$

7. Name each shaded part as an improper fraction and as a mixed number.

a)

whole

b)

whole

8. It takes Carol $\frac{1}{3}$ of an hour to complete a riding trail on her horse. She rode the trail seven times on Saturday. Write an improper fraction and a mixed number to represent the total time she rode in hours.

9. Represent and write equivalent fractions using tenths or hundredths.

a) $\frac{1}{4}$ 　　 b) $\frac{4}{5}$ 　　 c) $\frac{3}{2}$ 　　 d) $\frac{1}{5}$ 　　 e) $\frac{1}{25}$

10. Represent and write equivalent decimals.

a) $\frac{1}{2}$ 　　 b) $\frac{3}{4}$ 　　 c) $\frac{3}{5}$ 　　 d) $\frac{17}{50}$ 　　 e) $\frac{7}{20}$

11. Simon said that $\frac{1}{4} = 0.4$. Is he right or wrong? Show how you know.

12. Order the nutritional information from greatest to least fraction.

protein	$\frac{3}{100}$	carbohydrates	$\frac{1}{5}$
fat	$\frac{1}{50}$	fibre	$\frac{1}{20}$

13. a) Make and label a number line to order these fractions from least to greatest: $\frac{1}{6}, \frac{2}{3}, \frac{5}{6}, \frac{1}{2}, \frac{1}{5}$

b) List all the equivalent fractions that you labelled on your number line.

$\frac{1}{2}$				$\frac{1}{2}$	
$\frac{1}{3}$		$\frac{1}{3}$		$\frac{1}{3}$	
$\frac{1}{5}$	$\frac{1}{5}$	$\frac{1}{5}$	$\frac{1}{5}$	$\frac{1}{5}$	
$\frac{1}{6}$	$\frac{1}{6}$	$\frac{1}{6}$	$\frac{1}{6}$	$\frac{1}{6}$	$\frac{1}{6}$

Problem Bank

1 1. Juanita planted 20 rosebushes. $\frac{3}{5}$ of the bushes were red. The rest were white. How many bushes of each colour did she plant? Show your work. Include a diagram.

2 2. Aaron baked two identical cakes. He cut one into 9 equal slices and the other into 18 equal slices.

a) Show that $\frac{2}{3}$ of the 9-slice cake gives the same number of pieces as $\frac{1}{3}$ of the 18-slice cake.

b) Which is greater: $\frac{2}{3}$ of the 9-slice cake or $\frac{1}{3}$ of the 18-slice cake? Use counters or pictures to explain your answer.

3 3. Which rectangle shows each fraction?

a) about $\frac{1}{3}$ c) about $\frac{5}{6}$ e) about $\frac{2}{5}$

b) about $\frac{1}{2}$ d) about $\frac{1}{6}$

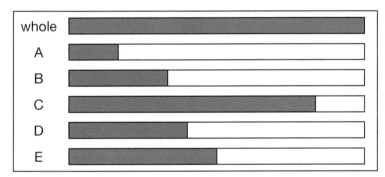

4. Jasleen saw a spinner at the Spring Fair. $\frac{1}{4}$ of the spinner was red, $\frac{5}{8}$ was green, and $\frac{1}{8}$ was blue. Write the colours in order from the most likely to the least likely to be spun. Explain your reasoning.

4 5. What are the next two fractions in each pattern? Explain.

a) $\frac{1}{3}, \frac{2}{6}, \frac{1}{4}, \frac{3}{12}, \frac{1}{5}, \frac{4}{20}$

b) $1\frac{2}{3}, 2\frac{3}{4}, 3\frac{4}{5}$

6. Write a fraction for the number of whole circles that are shaded. Show how you know.

7. Write a rule for this pattern.
Describe the next complete picture in the pattern.

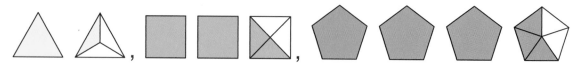

8. Sofia had 20 comic books and gave some of them to Heather. She used a calculator to figure out that she gave away 0.15 of her comic books. How many comic books did she give to Heather?

9. On a 10-slice pizza, $\frac{3}{10}$ has mushrooms, $\frac{7}{10}$ has extra cheese, and $\frac{2}{10}$ has eggplant. What is the least number of slices that have more than one topping on them? Show your work.

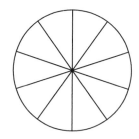

10. Drake had six coins worth 18¢. He gave $\frac{1}{3}$ of the coins to each of three friends. Each person got a different amount of money. How did Drake share the coins?

11. Match the Number Suspects to the clues. There may be more than one answer. Fractions may be used more than once.
   a) I am slightly greater than $\frac{1}{2}$.
   b) I am between $\frac{1}{2}$ and 1, but not equal to $\frac{3}{4}$.
   c) I am greater than 1.
   d) I am the least number listed.
   e) I am between $\frac{1}{5}$ and $\frac{2}{5}$.

Number Suspects

$\frac{4}{5}$ $\frac{3}{5}$ $\frac{1}{8}$

$\frac{9}{8}$ $\frac{1}{3}$ $\frac{6}{8}$

$\frac{3}{8}$ $\frac{7}{8}$ $\frac{2}{3}$

$\frac{5}{8}$

Chapter Review

LESSON

2 1. Write three fractions that are equivalent to $\frac{1}{2}$.
Use a diagram to show how you know you are right.

2. All the sections of this window are the same size.
Write two equivalent fractions to represent the part
that is blue.

3 3. Rewrite these statements using fractions and equivalent
fractions to describe the situation.
   a) In one month, 6 of 24 students in my class had
      the flu on the same day.
   b) I need to replace my broken shoelaces.
      I have 5 pairs of running shoes.
      2 laces are broken.

4 4. a) Draw a model to show $1\frac{3}{4}$ hours.
   b) Rename $1\frac{3}{4}$ as an improper fraction.

5. Represent each picture as a mixed number.
   Explain your answer.
   a)
   b)

5 6. Sofia surveyed students at her school
about the language they speak at home.
She got these results. Write decimal
equivalents for the fractions and order
the numbers from greatest to least.

English	$\frac{3}{4}$	French	$\frac{1}{10}$
Ukrainian	$\frac{1}{20}$	Chinese	0.02
Vietnamese	0.02	other	0.06

6 7. Dan baked enough peach pies for each of his 20 friends
to have $\frac{1}{8}$ of a pie. How many pies did he bake?
Show your work.

7 8. Order the following from least to greatest:
$\frac{3}{5}$, $\frac{6}{12}$, 0.8, $\frac{3}{4}$, 0.35

Chapter Task

Fractions in Your Life

Carmen says, "I sleep for 10 h each day, which is $\frac{10}{24}$ or $\frac{5}{12}$ of a day."

"I can hold my breath for 50 s or $\frac{50}{60}$ of a minute."

"I brush my teeth for 2 min or $\frac{2}{60}$ of an hour."

"I am almost 11 years old or $10\frac{363}{365}$ years old."

"I make up $\frac{1}{5}$ of my family. When my cousin comes over it is like having $\frac{6}{5}$ of the family together."

? **What are some of the fractions in your life?**

Part A: Record Your Activities

A. Make a chart of several activities in your life. Record your times using several different units: seconds, minutes, hours, days, and years.

Activity	in seconds	in minutes	in hours	in days	in years
sleep			10 h		
hold my breath	50 s				

B. Use fractions to create statements about each of your activities as Carmen did.

C. Record other fractions that describe you.

Part B: Tell a Fraction Story

D. Write a paragraph or a poem and draw a picture to represent the fractions in your life.

Task Checklist

☑ Did you explain your thinking?

☑ Did you use a model?

☑ Did you include diagrams?

☑ Did you use math language?

Probability

Goals

You will be able to

- describe and compare the probability of events using probability language

- use fractions to describe probabilities

- use tree diagrams to describe the results of probability experiments

- solve problems using probability

Playing letter games

Getting Started

You will need

• I Predict cards

1	2	3	4	5
6	7	8	9	10
1	2	3	4	5

I Predict

I Predict

Number of players: 2

How to play: Each player flips a card over and predicts whether the number on the next card will be greater, less, or the same.

Step 1 Shuffle the cards. Place them face down in a pile.

Step 2 Flip the top card over and predict whether the number on the next card will be greater, less, or the same.

Step 3 Flip the next card over to determine your score. Score 1 point for a correct prediction. Score 0 points for an incorrect prediction.

Step 4 Put both cards back in the pile and shuffle. Take turns. Each player takes 10 turns.

? **What strategies can you use to win the game?**

A. If your first card was 2, what prediction would you make? Why?

B. Play I Predict with a classmate. Record your data in a chart.

C. Look at your chart. Which happened more often: winning a point or not winning a point?

Drake's Score

First card	Prediction	Second card	Score
2	same	3	0
6	less	4	1
7	greater	10	1

D. When were you almost certain that you would win a point?

E. Which of the three possible predictions did you make least often? Why?

F. Describe a winning strategy for I Predict. Explain your thinking.

Do You Remember?

1. Sketch a **probability line**. Label it to show the probability of spinning each colour.

   a) red (**R**) **b)** blue (**B**) **c)** orange (**O**)

   impossible   certain

   less probable | more probable

   G

   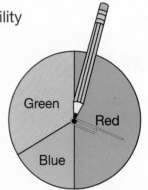

2. Sergei spun the spinner in Question 1 ten times. Which results are most likely from Sergei's spins?

   A.
   ```
   B B G R R
   G G G R B
   ```
   B.
   ```
   B B G G R
   B G R B R
   ```
   C.
   ```
   G R G B R
   G B R R R
   ```

3. **a)** You draw a tile from a bag like this without looking. Which colour of tile are you least likely to draw?

   b) Which colours are you **equally likely** to draw?

4. Make a **tree diagram** to show the possible combinations for ice cream cones with one flavour of ice cream.

   Pick a cone   Pick a flavour

   waffle   chocolate chip

   regular   banana fudge

                   vanilla twist

1 Using Probability Language

Goal Use probability language to describe predictions.

A new boy is joining Dan's class.
Dan is making guesses about him before he arrives.

His first name has 5 or more letters.

He is taller than 100 cm.

His birthday is in March.

He is 10 years old.

He has 7 brothers and 6 sisters.

He has been to school before.

? **Which predictions about the new student are most probable?**

A. Sketch a probability line.
Mark a position for each of these probability terms:

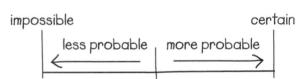

impossible   certain

less probable | more probable

- very likely (very probable)
- not very likely (not very probable)
- just as likely as unlikely

B. Which of Dan's predictions is least probable? Why?

C. Label your probability line to show the probability of each of Dan's predictions.

D. Make a prediction about the student to fit each description.
Place each prediction on your probability line.
- certain
- very unlikely, but possible
- almost certain
- impossible

1. Were some of Dan's predictions easier to place on the probability line than others? Why?

2. What everyday knowledge did you use when you made your own predictions?

3. How does using a probability line help you to describe and compare probabilities?

Mental Imagery

Creating Spinners

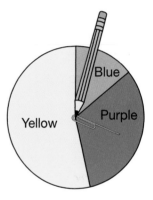

These probability statements are true about Spinner 1.
• You are more likely to spin yellow than blue or purple.
• You will likely spin yellow more than one half of the time.
• You will never spin orange.

A. What else can you say about the probability of spinning a colour on Spinner 1?

Spinner 1

Try These

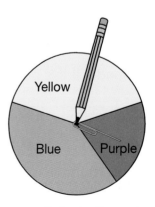

1. Write true probability statements about Spinner 2.

2. Create a spinner for which these statements are true.
   • You are just a bit more likely to spin blue than red or yellow.
   • You will likely spin red about the same number of times as yellow.

Spinner 2

2 Predicting Probabilities

Goal Predict the probability of events and test your predictions.

Karin's class is playing a word game called Lucky Letters. Each student draws a set of four letter cards from a bag.

? **What is probably true about a set of cards that a player draws from the bag?**

Karin's Strategy

Lucky Letters Cards

Letters	Quantity of each card	Value of each card
AEIOU	5	1
LNRST	4	2
BCDF GHKM PVWY	2	3
JQXZ	1	4

I draw sets of four cards from the bag and record the results in a chart.

My Cards

First set	A 1	E 1	N 2	R 2
Second set	L 2	B 3	C 3	E 1

My first set of cards has two vowels and two consonants. It is worth 1 + 1 + 2 + 2 = 6 points.

I wonder if this point total and number of vowels is common.

A. Draw a set of four Lucky Letters cards from a bag. Record the results in a chart like Karin's. Return the cards to the bag and mix them up. Repeat until you've drawn 10 sets.

B. Predict the probability of these **events**. Use your results from Part A. Show your predictions on a probability line.

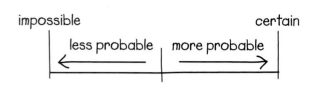

a. a set with two vowels

b. a set worth more than six points

c. a set worth six points or less

d. a set with more consonants than vowels

C. Test your predictions in Part B by choosing 10 more sets of Lucky Letters cards. Record your results.

Reflecting

1. Which of your predictions in Part B were reasonable? Which were not? Explain.

2. Why should you repeat the experiment many times before predicting the probability of an event?

Checking

3. **a)** Look at all of your Lucky Letters results so far. Which event happened more often:
   - two 1-point letters and two 2-point letters
   - four 2-point letters

   b) Predict which event is more probable if you pick 10 more sets:
   - two 1-point letters and two 4-point letters
   - four 2-point letters

Practising

4. **a)** Look at all of your Lucky Letters results so far. Predict which event is more probable if you pick more sets: a value of 10 or a value of 8.

   b) Choose 10 more sets of cards to test your prediction.

5. **a)** Look at the sets you have already picked. Predict which event is more probable if you pick more sets:
   - you can form a word with all four of your letters
   - you can't form a word

   b) Choose 10 more sets of cards to test your prediction.

3 Probabilities as Fractions

You will need
- a die

Goal Express the likelihood of an event as a fraction.

Sofia chose this poem for a poetry project. She is doing an experiment to determine where to put the chickens in her cover picture.

Last Night I Dreamed of Chickens

Last night I dreamed of chickens,
there were chickens everywhere,
they were standing on my stomach,
they were nesting in my hair,
they were pecking at my pillow,
they were hopping on my head,
they were ruffling up their feathers
as they raced about my bed.

They were on the chairs and tables,
they were on the chandeliers,
they were roosting in the corners,
they were clucking in my ears,
there were chickens, chickens, chickens
for as far as I could see ...
when I woke today, I noticed
there were eggs on top of me.

Jack Prelutsky

? **What fractions describe the probability of the places a chicken might be in Sofia's picture?**

Sofia's Idea

I used each number on a die to represent one event. An event is one place a chicken might be. I chose six places.

Then I rolled a die 12 times and recorded the results. I rolled ⊡ 3 times out of 12.

There's a $\frac{3}{12}$ probability the chicken will be on a stomach in the picture!

Places chicken might be	Roll	Number of times rolled
stomach	⊡ (1)	|||
hair	⊡ (2)	||
head	⊡ (3)	
chair	⊡ (4)	||
table	⊡ (5)	|||
chandelier	⊡ (6)	||

A. Which other event of Sofia's had a probability of $\frac{3}{12}$?

B. Write fractions for the probabilities of Sofia's other four events.

C. Roll a die 12 times. Record the results in a chart like Sofia's.

D. Use your data to write fractions for the probabilities of the six places the chickens might be in Sofia's picture.

Reflecting

1. Where were the chickens most likely to be in your experiment? Where were they least likely to be? What were the probabilities?

2. What is the least fraction that a probability can be in this experiment? What is the greatest?

Checking

3. a) Roll your die 12 more times. Combine the results with your results from Part C. Using these 24 rolls, write a fraction for the probability of each place a chicken might be.

   b) Were some places more probable with 24 rolls than with 12 rolls? Why might that happen?

Practising

4. Select six other places where the chickens might be. Choose a number from 1 to 6 to represent each place. Roll a die 10 times and record the results. Write the fraction for the probability of each possible place.

5. Roll a die 20 times. Record the results. Write the fraction for the probability of each event.
   a) rolling a 2
   b) rolling an even number
   c) rolling a number greater than 4
   d) rolling a number less than 4

6. You will roll a die 12 times. Predict an event that you think will have a probability between $\frac{3}{12}$ and $\frac{6}{12}$. Carry out an experiment to test your prediction.

Mid-Chapter Review

LESSON

1. **1.** Sketch a probability line. Label it to show the probability of each event.
   a) A Grade 3 student is a boy.
   b) A Grade 6 student is 10 years old.

2. A new student is joining your class. Describe events with probabilities that match letters A, B, and C.

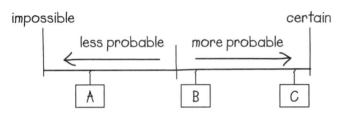

2. **3.** a) Turn to any page of a book and look at the first 10 words. Record the number of letters in each word.
   b) Predict which will be more probable if you choose a different page:
   - words with fewer than six letters
   - words with six or more letters
   c) Do an experiment to test your prediction. Describe the results.

3. **4.** Ian rolled a die 12 times. Use Ian's results to write a fraction for the probability of each event.
   a) rolling a 3
   b) rolling an odd number
   c) rolling a number greater than 5

   Ian's Rolls

   3 4 1 2 4 5 6 1 2 3 4 1

5. a) Roll a die 20 times. Record your results.
   b) Use your results to name an event with a probability greater than $\frac{4}{20}$.
   c) Use your results to name an event with a probability of $\frac{0}{20}$.

Sixty-Six

Number of players: 2 to 4

How to play: Predict whether the sum of two numbers will be greater than 66.

Step 1 Roll a die twice to create a two-digit number. The number from the first roll goes in the tens place and the number from the second roll goes in the ones place.

Step 2 Predict whether the sum of this two-digit number and the next two-digit number you roll will be greater than 66.

Step 3 Roll the die twice to make a second two-digit number. Add this to your first number.

Step 4 Score 1 point for each correct prediction.

Play until a player has 10 points.

Monique's Rolls

I rolled 4 first.
My second roll was 5.

That's 45.

$45 + \blacksquare = 66$
$66 - 45 = 21$

I need to roll 22 or greater to go past 66.
If my next roll is 2, I will probably go past 66.
I will definitely go past 66 if I roll 3, 4, 5, or 6.
I predict the sum will be greater than 66.

4 Modelling Probability Problems

You will need
• play coins

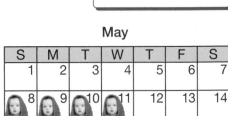

Goal Conduct probability experiments.

The first baby born in one hospital on each of the last four days was a boy.

? **What is the probability that the first baby born each day for the rest of the week will be a boy?**

May

S	M	T	W	T	F	S
1	2	3	4	5	6	7
8	9	10	11	12	13	14
15	16	17	18	19	20	21

Patrick's Strategy

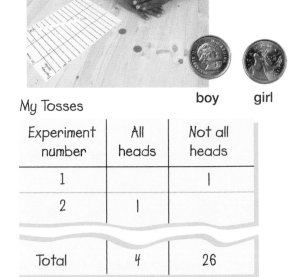

boy   girl

Heads and tails on a coin toss are equally likely. Boys and girls are about equally likely, too. I can toss coins to model the problem and estimate the probability.

Since there are three days left in the week, I'll flip three coins and record the results.

If I flip all heads, that will mean a boy was born first all three days. I'll flip the three coins 30 times.

I flipped all heads only 4 times out of 30. I estimate the probability that only boys will be born first for the rest of the week to be $\frac{4}{30}$.

My Tosses

Experiment number	All heads	Not all heads
1		1
2	1	
Total	4	26

I can show this information on a probability line.

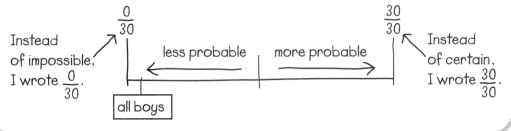

Instead of impossible, I wrote $\frac{0}{30}$.

$\frac{0}{30}$ less probable   more probable $\frac{30}{30}$

Instead of certain, I wrote $\frac{30}{30}$.

all boys

Reflecting

1. Why is $\frac{4}{30}$ an estimate of the probability that only boys will be born first for the rest of the week?

2. Why do you think Patrick used the labels $\frac{30}{30}$ and $\frac{0}{30}$ on the probability line?

3. Suppose Patrick wants to estimate the probability that only girls will be born first for the rest of the week. How can he record his data?

Checking

4. Patrick conducted his experiment again, but he made a different chart to record the data.
   a) Write a fraction for the probability of the event "all girls."
   b) Write a fraction for the probability of the event "2 boys and 1 girl."
   c) Show your answers for parts a) and b) on a probability line.

My Tosses

Experiment Number	3 H	2 H 1 T	1 H 2 T	3 T
1		✓		

| Total | 3 | 10 | 13 | 4 |

H = heads
T = tails

Practising

5. a) Conduct an experiment to estimate the probability that the first baby born in each of the next four days will be a boy.
   b) Was this probability greater or less than Patrick's probability? Did you expect this result? Explain.

6. Wendi and her sister get about the same number of phone calls from friends each evening.
   a) Use an experiment. Estimate the probability that the first two phone calls tonight will be for Wendi. Record the probability. Place it on a probability line.
   b) Repeat part a) for the first three phone calls.
   c) Suppose Wendi's friends always call her right after supper. Why would the experiment you used not be a good way to predict who will get calls first?

5 Using Tree Diagrams

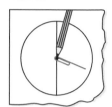

Goal

Use tree diagrams to record the outcomes of an experiment.

Glynis and Yoshi are playing Rock, Paper, Scissors. They both make their choices without following any particular strategy.

❓ **What is the probability of winning when you play Rock, Paper, Scissors?**

Glynis's Method

I made a tree diagram to show all of the possible results.
We played 10 times. I put a tally on the tree diagram to record the result each time.

Yoshi's choice	Glynis's choice	Results	
rock	rock	ll	tie
	paper	l	Glynis wins
	scissors		Yoshi wins
paper	rock	l	Yoshi wins
	paper		tie
	scissors	lll	Glynis wins

A. Copy and complete Glynis's tree diagram. Use the data in the chart. Record tallies to show how often each outcome occurred.

B. Play the game with a classmate 20 times without using a strategy. Use tallies on a tree diagram to record the results.

C. Use your data to determine the probability that you will win your next game.

Player	Games won	Ties
Yoshi	3	
Glynis	5	
Total	8	2

Reflecting

1. Why is your answer to Part C a fraction with a denominator of 20?

2. a) Use your data to determine the probability that your partner will win.
   b) Does this seem to be a **fair game**? Explain.

3. Why is a tree diagram useful for recording the results?

fair game
All players have an equal chance of winning

Checking

4. Play the game another 20 times. Use tallies on a tree diagram to record the results. Use your data to determine the probability of a tie.

Practising

5. a) Draw a tree diagram to show the possible results of spinning this spinner twice.
   b) Spin the spinner twice. Record the result with a tally on your tree diagram. Repeat 15 times.
   c) Use your data from part b) to determine the probability of spinning blue both times.

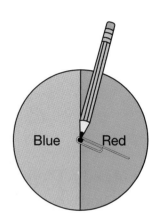

6. Sagitha and Jack are playing a game with the spinner from Question 5. They spin three times. Jack wins if all three spins are the same colour. Sagitha wins if the spins are different colours.
   a) Draw a tree diagram to show the possible results.
   b) Spin the spinner three times. Record the result with a tally on your tree diagram. Repeat 20 times.
   c) What is the probability of winning for each player?
   d) Does the game seem fair? Explain.

7. a) Design a spinner and an experiment to go with it. Think of an event for your spinner.
   b) Draw a tree diagram to show the possible results.
   c) Carry out your experiment. Record your results.
   d) What is the probability of your event?

6 Solve Problems by Considering All Possibilities

You will need
- a die

Goal Think about all of the possibilities when solving a problem.

Aaron rolls a die twice and multiplies the two numbers he rolls. Between his first and second rolls, Aaron predicts whether the product will be greater than 10.
He scores a point for each correct prediction.

? **What prediction should Aaron make to be more likely to score a point?**

Aaron's Solution

Make a Plan

To figure out what I should predict, I'll list all the possible products using a tree diagram.

Carry Out the Plan

Only 12 is greater than 10. I predict that the product will not be greater than 10.

	First roll	Second roll	Product
My first roll was 2.		1	2
		2	4
		3	6
	2	4	8
		5	10
		6	12

Look Back

I'll roll a die 20 times and multiply the number I get by my first number, 2.

The product was greater than 10 only $\frac{4}{20}$ of the time. My prediction was good.

Greater than 10	Not greater than 10
4	16

Reflecting

1. Why does Aaron need to look at only six possible products before making his prediction?

2. Why is it easier to predict whether the product will be greater than 10 after the first roll than before it?

3. How can a tree diagram help you make sure you have thought of all of the possibilities?

Checking

4. In another version of Aaron's game, a player rolls a die twice and predicts whether the sum will be greater than 7. What prediction should you make if the first roll is 2? Use Aaron's method.

Practising

5. You are playing a game in which you multiply a number on a blue card by a number on an orange card. You get a point for correctly predicting the product before you choose your cards.
   a) Use a tree diagram to list all of the possible products.
   b) Which predictions should you make? Why?

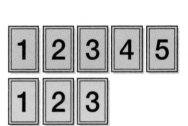

6. Two players each roll a die. Player 1 wins if the product of the numbers is even. Player 2 wins if the product is odd. If they play 20 games, how often is player 1 likely to win? Explain.

7. A triangle has a perimeter of 15 cm. All the side lengths are whole numbers of centimetres. How many possible triangles are there?

8. Create a problem that you can solve by listing all of the possibilities. Solve your problem.

Birthday Math

In a group of 23 people, there will be two people with the same birth day more than $\frac{1}{2}$ the time.

What can you say about the probability of two people having the same birth month?

Write the names of the 12 months on slips of paper. Put the slips in a paper bag. Draw a slip from the bag and record the month. Return the slip to the bag.
Keep doing this until you draw a month for the second time.

You will need

- slips of paper

- a paper bag

1 How many slips do you usually need to draw from the bag for a month to be drawn twice?

2 How is this like two people in a group with the same birth month?

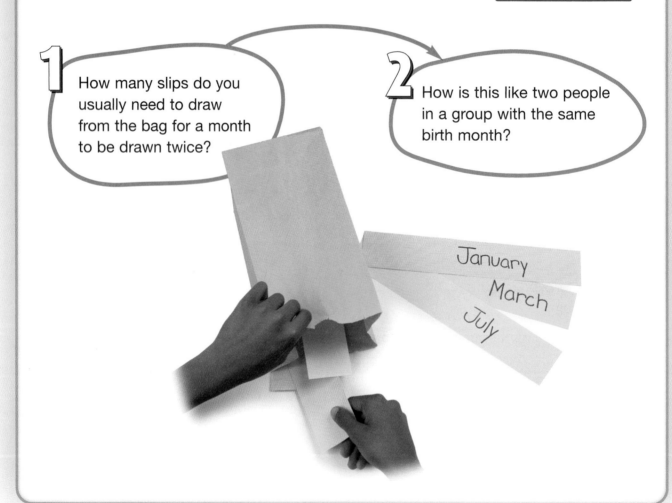

Skills Bank

1. Diane is drawing a tile from the bag without looking. Place the probability of drawing a blue tile on a probability line. Repeat for a purple tile and a white tile.

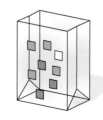

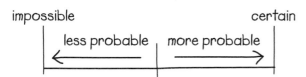

impossible   certain

less probable | more probable

2. Place each event on a probability line.
   A. A Grade 5 student has three sisters.
   B. A student in your class enjoys hockey.
   C. Your teacher is an adult.

3. Use your Lucky Letters.
   a) Choose a set of five letters and record the value of your set. Repeat 15 times.
   b) Look at your results. Predict which event is more probable:
      • a set worth more than 10
      • a set worth 10 or less
   c) Test your prediction with another 15 sets.

4. a) Turn to any page in your math book. Count the words that end in "e."
   b) How likely do you think it is that words will end with "e" on a different page? Show your prediction on a probability line.
   c) Test your prediction by checking 10 other pages.

5. Roll a die 20 times. Use your results to write a fraction for the probability of each event.
   a) rolling a 4
   b) rolling a 6
   c) rolling an even number
   d) rolling a number less than 5

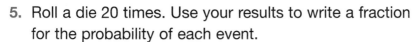

6. Write the days of the week on seven slips of paper and put them in a bag. Pick a slip, record the day, and put the slip back in the bag. Do this 15 times. Use your results to write a fraction for the probability of each event.
   a) picking Sunday   **b)** picking a day starting with T

7. Conduct an experiment to estimate the probability of each event. Use coins to model each situation. Repeat 15 times.
   a) The three Grade 5 students who win a contest are all girls.
   b) The first two customers who enter a bookstore are both male.

8. Place your results from Question 7 on a probability line.

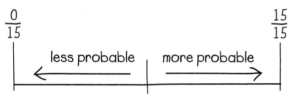

$$\frac{0}{15} \qquad\qquad\qquad \frac{15}{15}$$

less probable   more probable

9. a) Draw a tree diagram to show the possible results of spinning this spinner twice.
   b) Spin the spinner twice. Record the result using a tally on your tree diagram. Do this 20 times.
   c) Use your results. What is the probability that the product is even? What is the probability that the sum is less than 10?

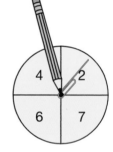

10. The numbers from two spins of the spinner will be added. You win a prize if you correctly predict whether the sum will be less than 10. Use your tree diagram from Question 9.
   a) Make a prediction for a first spin of 2.
   b) Test your prediction by spinning 10 times to get the second number.
   c) Repeat parts a) and b) for a first spin of 4.

Problem Bank

1 1. A new Grade 2 teacher is coming to your school. Make a prediction about the teacher to match each letter on the probability line. Explain your thinking.

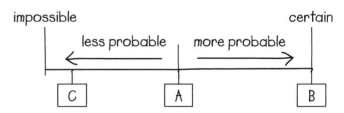

4 2. A survey shows that two out of every three Canadians think that cats should be on leashes when they are outdoors. Suppose you survey eight people for their opinions.

a) Spin the spinner eight times to model the problem. Repeat 15 times.

b) Estimate the probability that four of the eight people will say that cats should be on leashes. Use your data.

5 3. You are using a tree diagram with 12 branches to show the possible outcomes of a probability experiment. What might the experiment have been?

4. a) Spin this spinner three times and add the numbers. Use an experiment and a tree diagram to determine the probability that the sum will be greater than 10.

b) Show your answer on a probability line. Include fractions with your labels.

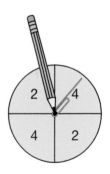

6 5. You will divide one of the numbers 12, 13, 14, 15, and 16 by either 2 or 3.

a) Use a tree diagram to show all of the possible results.

b) Predict whether it is more likely that there is a remainder or that there is no remainder.

c) Test your prediction. Write the numbers 12 through 16 on five slips of paper. Put the five slips in a bag. Put two more slips of paper with a 2 and a 3 in another bag. Choose a slip from each bag. Check whether there is a remainder. Repeat 20 times.

d) Was your prediction reasonable? Explain.

Chapter Review

1

1. Place the probability of each event on a probability line.
   A. an event that is slightly more probable than not
   B. an event that is fairly likely
   C. an event that is almost impossible
   D. a professional baseball player is nine years old
   E. a teacher went to high school
   F. a student in Grade 3 is eight years old

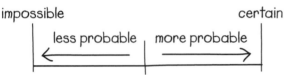

2

2. You are taking three I Predict cards from a deck.
   The deck has four of each number card from 1 to 10.
   a) Take three cards without looking.
      Record whether or not the numbers are all different.
      Put the cards back in the deck. Repeat 15 times.
   b) Predict the probability that the numbers on the next
      10 sets of cards you take will all be different.
   c) Test your prediction with an experiment.

3

3. Sam rolled a die 20 times. The results are shown in
   the chart. What is the probability of each event?
   a) rolling a 4
   b) rolling a 1
   c) rolling an even number
   d) rolling an odd number greater than 2

   Sam's Rolls

   4 5 1 2 3 6 1 2
   5 4 3 1 6 1 2 5
   3 2 4 1

4

4. Jane has two e-mail pen pals, Meghan and Kaycee.
   They each write her several times a day at
   unpredictable times.
   a) Flip a coin twice to model the first two e-mails
      Jane gets from her pen pals on a typical day.
      Repeat 20 times.
   b) Use your results to estimate the probability that the
      first two e-mails on a typical day are from Kaycee.

5. Draw a tree diagram to show the possible results for each experiment.

a) Three coins are tossed.

b) This spinner is spun twice.

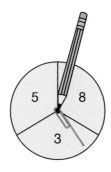

6. a) Conduct an experiment. Toss three coins and record the result on your tree diagram from Question 5 a). Repeat 15 times.

b) What is the probability of tossing two heads and one tail?

7. a) What are the even numbers between 1 and 5?

b) What are the odd numbers less than 6?

c) You multiply an answer from part a) by an answer from part b). How many products are greater than 5?

8. A rectangle has side lengths that are whole numbers of centimetres. The perimeter is 30 cm. How many different sizes of rectangles are possible? Which sizes of rectangles have areas greater than 40 cm^2?

perimeter = 30 cm

9. The first roll of a die is a 3. You will roll the die a second time and add the two numbers.

a) Draw a tree diagram to show all of the possible sums.

b) Predict how likely it is that the sum of two rolls will be greater than 5.

c) Do an experiment to test your prediction.

Chapter Task

Fair Games

Juanita and Liam are playing a game.

They each roll a die.
Liam calculates the sum of the two numbers.
Juanita calculates the difference between the two numbers.
Then they add the sum and the difference to get a final sum.

Liam gets a point if the final sum is 6 or less.
Juanita gets a point if the final sum is greater than 6.

$1 + 4 = 5$
$4 - 1 = 3$

Final sum: $5 + 3 = 8$
Juanita wins.

? How can you change the rules to make this game more fair?

A. Create a tree diagram to show all of the possible results of the dice rolls.

B. Roll the dice 20 times. Tally the results beside the tree diagram.

C. Which is more likely: Liam will win or Juanita will win?

D. Change the rules to make the game more fair.

E. Play the game with a classmate to decide if your rules make the game more fair.

Task Checklist

☑ Did you use a tree diagram to keep track of the results?

☑ Did you play enough times to come to a conclusion?

☑ Did you organize your work so it is easy to follow?

☑ Did you explain your thinking?

☑ Did you use math language?

Patterns and Motion in Geometry

Goals

You will be able to

- tile an area using transformations

- describe tiling patterns using math language

- describe translations, reflections, and rotations

- identify and model transformation pattern rules

- model congruent and similar shapes using transformations

Polygon tiles

Getting Started

Extending Transformation Patterns

You will need

- pattern blocks

- pattern block grid paper

- pencil crayons

? **How many hexagons and triangles are in six rows of this scarf?**

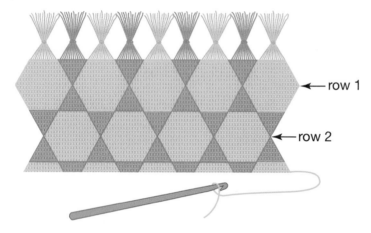

← row 1

← row 2

A. Model the scarf pattern. Use pattern blocks.

B. What attributes change in this pattern?

C. Extend your model for two more rows.

D. Describe the scarf pattern. Use words like **reflection** (flip), **rotation** (turn), and **translation** (slide).

E. Make a table to record the number of hexagons and triangles for rows 1 to 4.

F. What is the number pattern in each column?

G. Use the number patterns to predict the number of shapes in rows 5 and 6.

H. What is the total number of hexagons and triangles in six rows of the pattern? Show your work.

Row	⬡	▲
1		
2		
3		
4		

Do You Remember?

1. Use the word reflection, rotation, or translation to describe how the trapezoid changes in each pattern.

   a)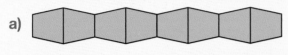

   b)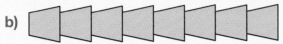

   c)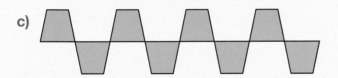

2. Name the new coordinates.

   a) The blue star at A5 moves 2 right and 3 down.

   b) The yellow star at B2 moves 2 right and 2 up.

   c) The green star at D5 moves 1 left and 4 down.

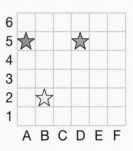

3. What is the **counterclockwise** (CCW) angle of rotation?

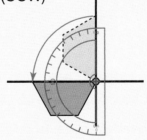

4. Copy the shape and the line of reflection. Draw the shape's reflection.

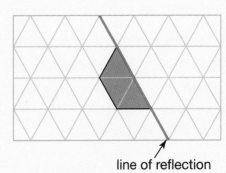

line of reflection

1 Tiling an Area

You will need
• drawing software

 Goal Tile an area using software.

Glynis is making a title page for her report on shapes.

Glynis's Cover Design

I'll use congruent triangles to cover the title page.
I'll use computer software to translate, reflect, or rotate the triangle.

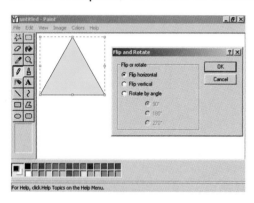 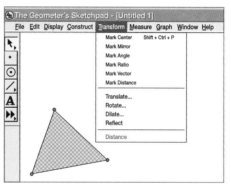

? How can you rotate, reflect, and translate congruent triangles to cover a rectangle?

A. Draw a rectangle to show the area you will **tile** with triangles. Use software.

B. Draw one triangle.

C. Copy the triangle and rotate, reflect, or translate it. Repeat to cover the rectangle completely.

tile
Use repeated congruent shapes to cover an area without gaps or overlaps

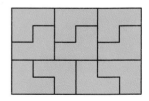

Reflecting

1. Describe how you used the software to tile the area.

Which Shapes Tile?

Rectangles can be used to tile an area.

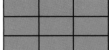

1 Can this pentagon be used to tile an area? Explain.

Rotating Shapes

You will need
- square dot paper

Each time you rotate this square 90° counterclockwise (CCW), the colours appear in different positions.

A. Show where the colours will be after the square is rotated another 90° CCW.

centre of rotation

90° CCW

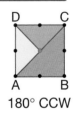

180° CCW

Try These

1. Sketch these shapes as they are repeatedly rotated 90° clockwise (CW). Use dot paper.

a)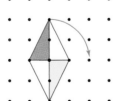

b)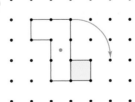

2 Describing Tiling Patterns

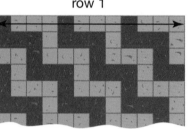

Goal Describe tiling patterns.

A driveway is tiled with 13 rows of dark and light bricks that make a pattern.

? **How many dark and light bricks are needed to tile the driveway?**

row 1

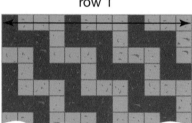

Martin's Model

I used square tiles to make a model of the driveway.

I can describe the **tiling pattern** by its rows.

The **pattern rule** for row 1 is, "Start with one dark tile and three light tiles beside it. Repeat two more times."

I can use a table to see if there is a pattern in the numbers of tiles in the rows.

tiling pattern

A pattern of repeated congruent shapes that fit together with no gaps or overlaps

Row	◼	◻
1		
2		
3		

A. Describe the pattern in row 2. Write the pattern rule.

B. How is the pattern in row 3 like the pattern in row 1? How is it different?

C. Complete the 13 rows of the driveway pattern. Use square tiles. Record the number of dark and light tiles in each row. Use a table.

D. How many dark and light tiles are needed to tile the driveway? Show your work.

Reflecting

1. Why do rows 1 and 3 have different pattern rules, even though the numbers in the table are the same?

2. How does the pattern let you predict that the numbers in the table will be multiples of 3?

Checking

3. Karin wants to describe the tiling pattern by its columns.
   a) Describe the tiling pattern in column 3.
   b) Which columns have a different pattern?
   c) Write the pattern rules for columns 3 and 4.

column 3

Practising

4. a) How many different row patterns are in pattern A?
   b) How many different row patterns are in pattern B?
   c) Write all the different pattern rules for the rows in patterns A and B.

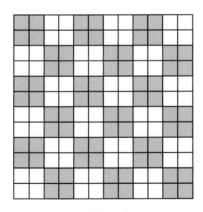

pattern A   pattern B

5. a) Create your own tiling pattern for a kitchen wall. Use dark and light square tiles.
   b) Describe the pattern by row or by column.
   c) Write a pattern rule for your pattern.

3 Extending Tiling Patterns

Goal Write a pattern rule to extend a pattern.

You will need

- grid paper

- pencil crayons

- a transparent mirror

- drawing software (optional)

Camille's mother designs rugs by starting with a two-by-two block and making copies of it to extend a pattern.

? **What is the pattern rule for this rug pattern?**

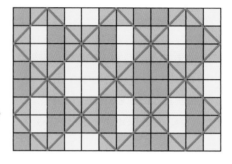

 ## Camille's Pattern

The pattern starts with a square block.

The block is copied and rotated 90° counterclockwise (CCW) about the **centre of rotation**.

centre of rotation

Then the pattern continues by rotating each new block 90° CCW.

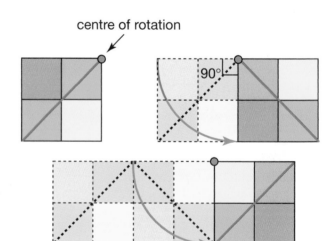

The second row of blocks is a reflection of the first row. Each new row is a reflection of the row above.

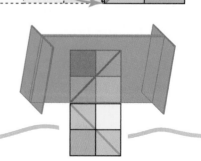

I can write the pattern rule.

Start with the square design.

Go to the right by rotating 90° CCW about the top right corner. Continue the pattern.

Go down by reflecting each row. Continue.

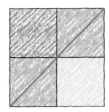

Reflecting

1. Describe the second row of blocks using rotations. Describe the centre of rotation.

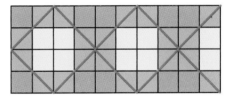

2. Is there more than one correct way to write a pattern rule? Explain.

Checking

3. a) How is this rug the same as Camille's rug? How is it different?

   b) Write a pattern rule for the rug. Start with the block at the top left.

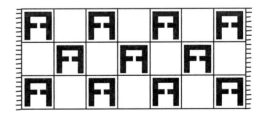

Practising

4. a) Write a pattern rule for this rug pattern based on the letter F.

   b) Make a pattern using another letter of the alphabet. Write a rule for your pattern.

5. a) Write a pattern rule for the rug made with this square.

   b) Change the pattern rule to make a new rug.

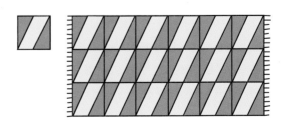

4 Translating Shapes on Grids

You will need
- grid paper

- a ruler

Goal Identify the rule for translating a shape.

Marcus is translating and tracing shapes to create a piece of art. He moves a shape on grid paper. The red translation arrow shows the direction and distance he moves the quadrilateral.

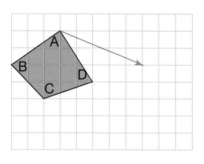

? **How can Marcus describe the translation?**

Marcus's Translation

The red translation arrow goes from vertex A to the new position of vertex A. The new vertex is 5 units right and 2 units down.

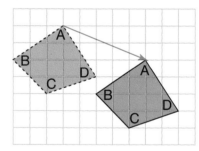

I check that the same rule applies to the new positions of vertices B, C, and D.

My translation rule is that the position of every new point is 5 units right and 2 units down.

I notice that the translation arrows are parallel and that they are all the same length.

The **orientation** of the shape stays the same.

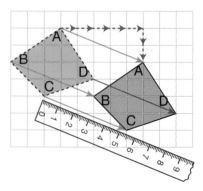

Reflecting

The direction around a shape when you name the vertices in order

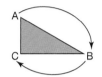

triangle ABC with clockwise orientation

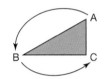

triangle ABC with counterclockwise orientation

1. Compare the size and shape of Marcus's original and translated quadrilaterals. What math word describes how these shapes compare to each other?

2. How does Marcus know that the orientation of the shape doesn't change?

3. What does the length of one translation arrow tell you about every point in the translated shape?

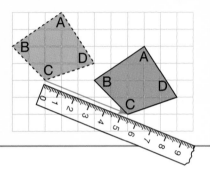

Checking

4. Draw another shape on a grid. Use Marcus's translation rule to locate the translated vertices. Draw the translated shape.

Practising

5. Copy the triangle in the middle of a grid. Each rule below describes the new position after a translation. Show the result of each translation. Draw a translation arrow for each.

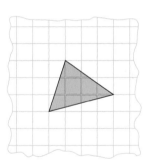

   a) right 3, up 2   c) left 3, down 2
   b) right 3, down 2   d) down 5

6. Write a translation rule to describe the new position of any point after each translation.

   a)
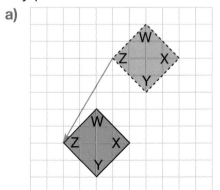

   b)
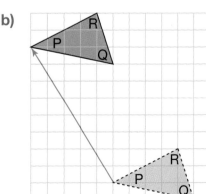

LESSON

Mid-Chapter Review

1

1. **a)** Trace the triangle. Use the tracing to tile any area.
   b) Which transformations did you use to tile the area? Explain.

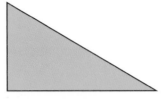

2

2. **a)** Describe the tiling pattern.
   b) How many dark and light tiles are needed to make 18 rows?

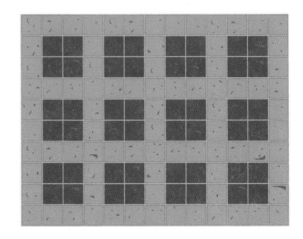

3

3. **a)** Write a pattern rule for this tiling pattern that uses the letter F.
   b) Extend the pattern for two more rows.

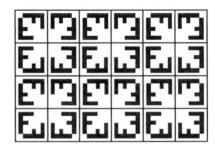

4

4. Write the translation rule.

   a)

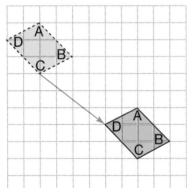

   b)

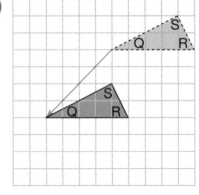

The Tiling Game

Number of players: 4 (2 teams of 2 players)
How to play: Teams take turns placing pattern blocks on a pattern block grid to tile the area.

Step 1 Each player chooses one type of pattern block as a playing piece.

Step 2 Roll a die to determine the number of pattern blocks a team can place on the game board in a turn. A team skips a turn when they cannot place a pattern block on the grid.

Step 3 Make a chart to keep track of the number of blocks placed. Determine the area covered by your blocks. Use the triangle as one unit.

Step 4 When no more pattern blocks can be placed on the game board, calculate the total area covered by your team's blocks.

The team that covers the greater area wins.

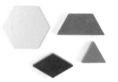

You will need

- a die

- 4 types of pattern blocks
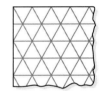

- pattern block grid paper

Teresa's Team

I chose the trapezoid and Dan chose the hexagon.

We rolled 3. We decided to place two hexagons and a trapezoid on our first turn.

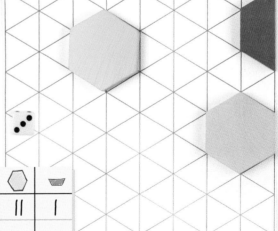

	⬡	⬯
Number of blocks	II	I
Area		

5 | Rotating Shapes

You will need
- a protractor

- square dot paper
- tracing paper

Goal **Rotate shapes in a pattern.**

Drake is making a logo by rotating triangles in a pattern.

? **What could the logo look like?**

Drake's Logo

I can describe how to make my logo with a pattern rule:

> Start with an isosceles right-angled triangle.
>
> Rotate it 45° CCW seven times. Alternate colours.

Step 1 Make triangle PQR. P is at the centre of rotation.

Step 2 Draw a 45° angle at P from line segment PR.

Step 3 Rotate triangle PQR 45° CCW about point P. Draw the rotated triangle.

Step 4 Repeat Steps 2 and 3 six more times.

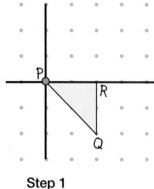

Step 1

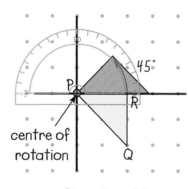

Steps 2 and 3

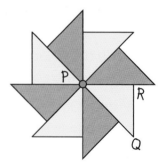

Step 4

Reflecting

1. How can you describe how to make Drake's logo with a clockwise (CW) rotation?

2. How would the logo look if Drake used reflections instead of rotations?

Checking

3. Trace one of these shapes to make your own logo.

   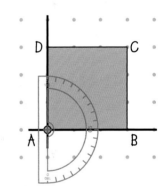

   a) Rotate your shape using Drake's pattern rule. Use a protractor.
   b) Sketch each rotated shape on square dot paper.
   c) Label the angles of rotation.

Practising

4. a) Predict the shape of the logo using Jake's pattern rule.

   > Start with square ABCD.
   >
   > Rotate it 90° CW three times about point A.
   >
   > Alternate colours.

   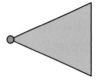

   b) Make the logo using the pattern rule.
   c) Label the centre of rotation and the angles of rotation.
   d) How close was your prediction? Explain.

5. a) Predict the shape of the logo using Fatima's pattern rule.

   > Start with isosceles triangle ABC.
   >
   > Rotate it 72° CCW four times about point A.
   >
   > Alternate colours.

   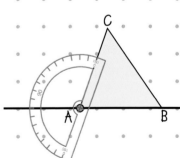

   b) Make the logo using the pattern rule.
   c) Label the centre of rotation and the angles of rotation.
   d) How close was your prediction? Explain.

6. Create your own logo using your own shape and 60° rotations.

6 Communicate About Transformations

Goal Describe transformations using math language.

Anna is explaining how some **transformations** (reflections, rotations, and translations) are alike and how they are different.

? **How can Anna describe the effects of the transformations?**

transformation
A rule that results in a change in a shape's position, orientation, or size

Anna's Transformations

I translated the pink triangle and coloured it yellow.
I reflected the pink triangle and coloured it blue.
I rotated the pink triangle and coloured it green.

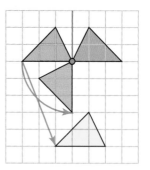

When I do a translation, nothing really changes except the position. If there was a point at the top, it stays on top. If there was a horizontal line, it stays horizontal.

When I do a reflection, the shape turns backward. Points move to the other side of the line of reflection. The new points are the same distance from the line of reflection as the original points.

When I do a rotation, there is one point that doesn't move. Other points move in a circle.

A. Identify some strengths of Anna's description. Use the Communication Checklist.

B. How would you improve Anna's description?

Communication Checklist

☑ Did you use math language?

☑ Did you include diagrams?

☑ Did you show the right amount of detail?

Reflecting

1. How does each transformation affect the orientation of a shape? Draw and label a triangle and use examples to explain your answer.
   a) translation   b) reflection   c) rotation

2. How did Anna describe a change in orientation?

3. Anna described the distance of the vertices from the line of reflection. What happens to points *on* the line of reflection?

Checking

4. Which statement is correct? Rewrite the incorrect ones.
   a) Triangle A is a reflection of the red triangle in a horizontal flip line.
   b) Triangle B is a 90° clockwise rotation about point O of the red triangle.
   c) Triangle C is a translation of the red triangle that moves points 4 units left and 2 units down.

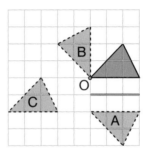

Practising

5. What kind of transformation is described? How do you know?
   a) Bruce: My transformation changed the orientation of a triangle.
   b) Linda: My transformation changed the position of every point.
   c) Marian: For my transformation, each vertex of a square moved clockwise to the next vertex.

6. a) Copy the diagram on grid paper. Reflect it in the line of reflection.
   b) Describe the effect of the reflection on each vertex.

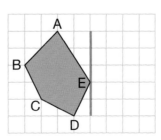

7 Modelling Congruence with Transformations

Goal Show congruence using transformations.

Norman saw this collage called Morning Traffic in a gallery. He wants to make one just like it.

? **How can Norman find all the congruent shapes he needs to cut out to make the collage?**

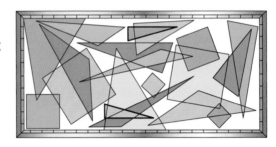

Norman's Congruent Shapes

I traced the green triangle.

I translated the tracing to the edge of the blue triangle. I saw that the blue triangle is a reflection of the green triangle.

If I reflect it, the green triangle covers the blue triangle exactly. They are congruent.

I used a translation and a reflection to find congruent shapes.

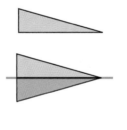

You will need

- Morning Traffic

- tracing paper

- Dancing Rectangles

- a transparent mirror

- a protractor

- grid paper

A. Choose another shape. Copy the shape using tracing paper.

B. Use transformations to find other shapes congruent to it.

C. Repeat Parts A and B to find every set of congruent shapes.

Reflecting

1. How do you know when two shapes are congruent?

2. Explain why translations, reflections, and rotations are sometimes called congruence transformations.

Checking

3. Norman saw this painting called Dancing Rectangles.
   a) Trace a rectangle.
   b) How many other rectangles look congruent to the rectangle you traced?
   c) Describe the transformations you can use to check congruence.
   d) Find other congruent rectangles in the picture. Describe the transformations you can use to check.

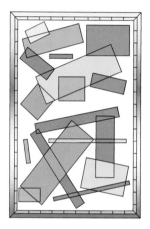

Practising

4. Which shapes are congruent? Explain how you know. Use transformation language.

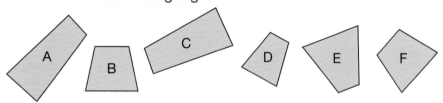

5. The painting has two congruent triangles of the same colour. Which two triangles are congruent? How do you know? Describe the transformations you can use to check.

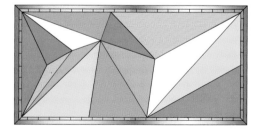

6. a) Make an abstract art picture. Use transformations and congruent shapes. Draw it on grid paper.
   b) Describe the transformations you used to make the picture.

8 Exploring Similarity

You will need

- elastics
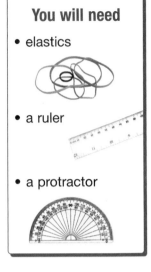
- a ruler
- a protractor

Goal Identify similar figures using transformations.

Similar shapes can be enlargements or reductions.

? **How can you make similar shapes?**

Step 1 Draw any polygon.

Step 2 Tie two identical elastic bands together.

similar

Identical in shape, but not necessarily the same size

Step 3 Hold the end of the bands at one vertex with your finger. Stretch the bands so the knot is over another vertex. Mark a point at the other end of the elastic. Repeat for the other vertices.

 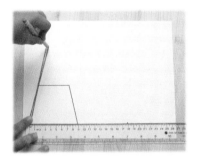 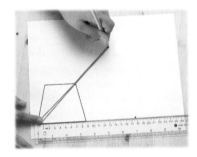

Step 4 Join the new vertices.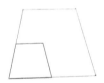

These two trapezoids are similar.

A. Use a ruler to draw three different polygons. Use your pencil and elastics to enlarge them.

B. Compare all the angles in the original and the enlargement.

Reflecting

1. How can you show that two shapes are similar?

Skills Bank

LESSON

1
1. How many hexagons like this one can fit inside the rectangle in a tiling pattern? Estimate first and then try it.

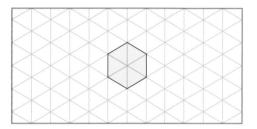

3
2. Linda wants to make this beaded bookmark.
   a) Describe the pattern.
   b) State the pattern rule for row 1 and row 2.
   c) Record the number of triangles, hexagons, and trapezoids in this beaded pattern. Use a table.

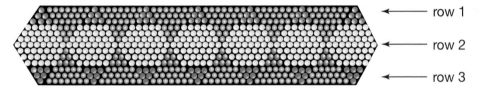

← row 1
← row 2
← row 3

4
3. Write the translation rule to describe the new position of any point after the triangle is translated as shown.

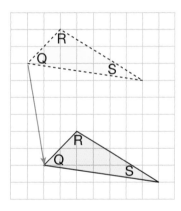

5
4. Make a logo using rotations.
   a) Copy this hexagon.
   b) Rotate it about point B, 45° CW seven times.
   c) Predict the shape of the logo if it were rotated about point C.
   d) Rotate it about point C, 45° CW seven times.

5. This logo was created by rotating a shape.
   a) What is the angle of rotation?
   b) Name the centre of rotation.
   c) State the pattern rule for creating this logo.

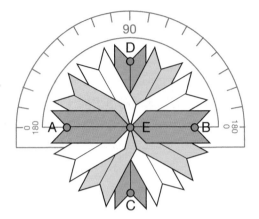

6. Identify two pairs of congruent shapes.
   Describe the transformations you can use to check.

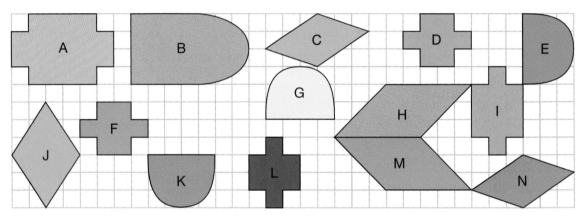

7. Which shapes are similar? Show your work.
   a)

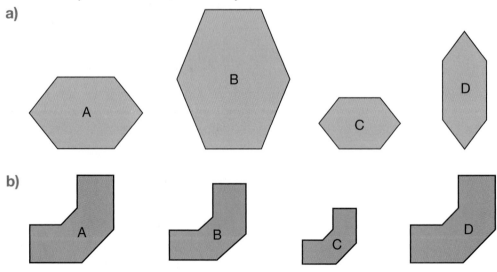

   b)

Problem Bank

1

1. The area to tile is 72 square units. Each shape covers 3 square units. Which shape will tile more of the area without going over the edges? Explain your choice.

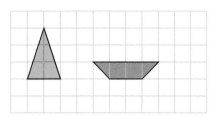

3

2. Which tiling block was used to design this beaded bracelet? Explain your choice. Describe the transformations used.

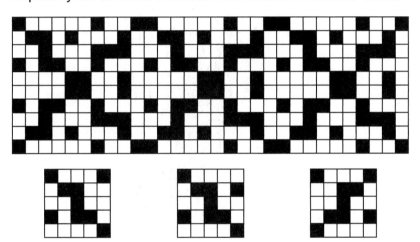

block A   block B   block C

5

3. **a)** Describe a translation that moves point A to point B.
   b) Sketch a rotation that moves point A to point B.
   c) Sketch a line of reflection that moves point A to point B.

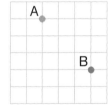

8

4. A "reptile" is a tile made up of smaller congruent tiles. The large tile is similar to the small tile.
   a) What transformations do you see in the reptile?
   b) Use four trapezoid pattern blocks to make another reptile. Name the transformations you used to create the new reptile.

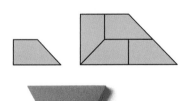

Chapter Review

1 1. **a)** How many rhombuses like this one can you fit on the grid without going over the edges?
   b) Which transformations did you use?

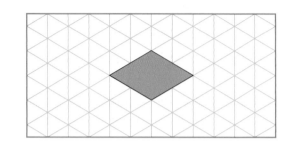

2 2. **a)** Describe the pattern for each column.
   b) How is the pattern rule for column 2 different from the pattern rule for column 4?
   c) Record the number of yellow and white squares in a table.
   d) How many yellow and white squares are needed to make 20 columns?

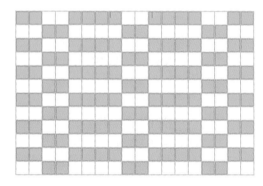

3 3. This tile was used to create the wall mosaic. Write a pattern rule for the wall mosaic.

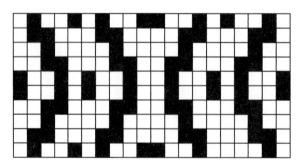

4 4. Jessica translated a triangle using the rule 3 units right and 2 units down. She drew the second triangle in another colour. Which triangle was the original? Explain.

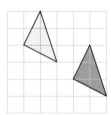

404

5 5. **a)** Trace the shape. Make a logo using Maria's pattern rule.

> Rotate the shape 60° CW
> about the red point.
> Repeat four more times.

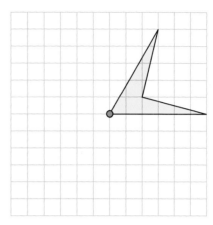

   b) Label the angles of rotation and centre of rotation on your sketch.

6 6. Use Devon's description to identify the transformation as a translation, reflection, or rotation. Explain how you know.

> The size and shape stay the same.
> The orientation doesn't change.
> A horizontal line becomes vertical.

7 7. **a)** Describe sets of congruent shapes in the border pattern.
   b) Explain how you can check for congruent shapes using transformations.

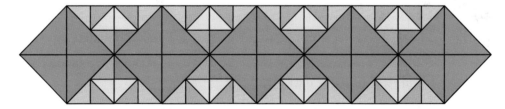

8 8. Which white shape is similar to the green shape? Explain your answer.

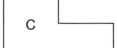

Chapter Task

Tiling a Patio

Stones For You sells these stones for tiling a patio.

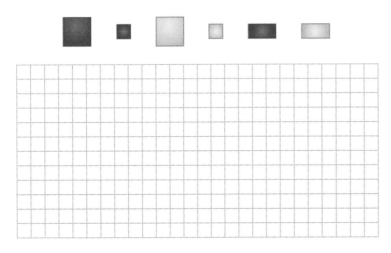

Inventory for *Stones for You*

Tile	Quantity	Price
	100	$2.00
	100	$2.00
	200	$1.50
	200	$1.50
	300	$1.00
	300	$1.00

? **What tiling pattern can you make with these stones?**

Part A

A. Make a block with the stones.

B. Transform the block to create a tiling pattern. Use the patio grid.

C. Write instructions for making your tiling pattern. Use transformation language.

Task Checklist

☑ Did you include diagrams?

☑ Did you use math language?

☑ Did you show the right amount of detail?

Part B

D. Does *Stones For You* have enough of each stone to complete the patio? Show your work.

Cumulative Review

Cross-Strand Multiple Choice

1. Which pair of fractions describes the **blue** part?
   A. $\frac{4}{5}, \frac{8}{10}$
   C. $\frac{2}{3}, \frac{8}{12}$
   B. $\frac{9}{12}, \frac{2}{3}$
   D. $\frac{8}{12}, \frac{3}{4}$

2. Which set of fractions is in order from least to greatest?
   A. $\frac{3}{6}, \frac{5}{6}, \frac{1}{4}, \frac{2}{3}$
   C. $\frac{1}{4}, \frac{3}{6}, \frac{3}{4}, \frac{7}{8}$
   B. $\frac{3}{6}, \frac{2}{3}, \frac{1}{2}, \frac{9}{10}$
   D. $\frac{1}{2}, \frac{1}{3}, \frac{2}{3}, \frac{7}{8}$

0     $\frac{1}{2}$ 1

3. Monique spun this spinner 18 times and recorded the results. What fraction describes the probability of spinning an odd number?

   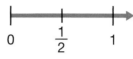

   My Spins

   5 8 5 7 9 8 7 8 7

   9 5 7 5 9 8 7 9 5

   A. $\frac{14}{18}$ B. $\frac{10}{18}$ C. $\frac{17}{18}$ D. $\frac{4}{18}$

4. Rowan is playing a game where he rolls a die to see how many squares to move on a grid. Then he takes a card to see which direction to go. How many different moves are possible with a regular die and these cards?

   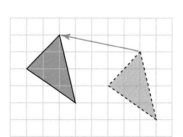

   A. 4   B. 12   C. 24   D. 18

5. Which describes the position of the triangle after the translation?
   A. right 5 down 1
   C. left 4 up 2
   B. left 5 up 1
   D. right 4 up 1

   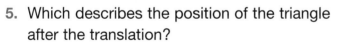

6. Which describes the transformation from the blue shape to the black shape?
   A. 45° CCW rotation about the centre of rotation
   B. 90° CW rotation about the centre of rotation
   C. reflection across the red line
   D. 90° CCW rotation about the centre of rotation

   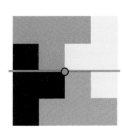

Cross-Strand Investigation

Amusement Park

Akiko, Norman, and Karin went to an amusement park.

7. a) Draw the Zoom Pond on grid paper. Draw the bottom of a Zoom boat on the pond. Use transformations to draw your boat in two other positions. Describe the transformations.

   b) Are your boat drawings congruent? Tell how you know.

   c) There are 25 rides at the park. Karin went on $\frac{20}{25}$ of them, and Norman went on 0.64 of them. Who went on more rides? Use a hundredths grid to show how you know.

   d) In the game Double Six, you toss a giant die 6 times. If you toss 2 sixes, you win. Play the game 10 times and keep track of the numbers you roll. Is someone who plays this game likely or unlikely to win? Explain.

   e) Create a problem about an event at the amusement park that you can solve by flipping a coin or tossing a die. Solve your problem.

8. a) The Sea Dragon ride goes forward 3 m and then back 1 m. It travels a total of 28 m forward and back as it goes around the track and returns to where it started. Show one way to determine the distance around the track.

   b) Sea Dragon tickets cost $1.50 each, $7.00 for 5, or $10.50 for 8. Karin wants 15 tickets. How should she buy them? Explain.

Glossary

Instructional Words

calculate: Figure out the number that answers a question; compute

clarify: Make a statement easier to understand; provide an example

classify: Put things into groups according to a rule and label the groups; organize into categories

compare: Look at two or more objects or numbers and identify how they are the same and how they are different (e.g., Compare the numbers 6.5 and 5.6. Compare two shapes.)

construct: Make or build a model; draw an accurate geometric shape (e.g., Use a ruler and a protractor to construct an angle.)

create: Make your own example

describe: Tell, draw, or write about what something is or what something looks like; tell about a process in a step-by-step way

draw: 1. Show something in picture form (e.g., Draw a diagram.)
2. Pull or select an object (e.g., Draw a card from the deck. Draw a tile from the bag.)

estimate: Use your knowledge to make a sensible decision about an amount; make a reasonable guess (e.g., Estimate how long it takes to cycle from your home to school. Estimate how many leaves are on a tree. Estimate the sum of 3210 and 789.)

evaluate: Determine if something makes sense; judge

explain: Tell what you did; show your mathematical thinking at every stage; show how you know

explore: Investigate a problem by questioning, brainstorming, and trying new ideas

extend: 1. In patterning, continue the pattern
2. In problem solving, create a new problem that takes the idea of the original problem further

justify: Give convincing reasons for a prediction, an estimate, or a solution; tell why you think your answer is correct

list: Record thoughts or things one under the other

measure: Use a tool to describe an object or determine an amount (e.g., Use a ruler to measure the height or distance around something. Use a protractor to measure an angle. Use balance scales to measure mass. Use a measuring cup to measure capacity. Use a stopwatch to measure the time in seconds or minutes.)

model: Show an idea using objects and/or pictures (e.g., Model a number using base ten blocks.)

predict: Use what you know to work out what is going to happen (e.g., Predict the next number in the pattern 1, 2, 4, 8, ….)

reason: Develop ideas and relate them to the purpose of the task and to each other; analyze relevant information to show understanding

record: Put work in writing or in pictures

relate: Show a connection between objects, drawings, ideas, or numbers

represent: Show information or an idea in a different way (e.g., Draw a graph. Make a model. Create a rhyme.)

show (your work): Record all calculations, drawings, numbers, words, or symbols that make up the solution

sketch: Make a rough drawing (e.g., Sketch a picture of the field with dimensions.)

solve: Develop and carry out a process for finding a solution to a problem

sort: Separate a set of objects, drawings, ideas, or numbers according to an attribute (e.g., Sort 2-D shapes by the number of sides.)

validate: Check an idea by showing that it works

verify: Work out an answer or solution again, usually in another way, to show that the original answer is correct; show evidence of correctness

visualize: Form a picture in your mind of what something is like; imagine

Glossary

Mathematical Words

acute angle: An angle that measures less than 90°

45°

acute-angled triangle: A triangle with only acute angles

addend: A number that is added to another number

algorithm: A series of steps you can use to carry out a procedure (e.g., add, subtract, multiply, or divide)

analog clock: A clock that measures time using rotating hands

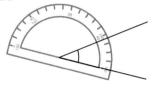

angle: An amount of turn measured in **degrees**

area: The amount of space a surface covers, measured in square units

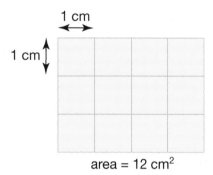

1 cm

1 cm

area = 12 cm²

array: A rectangular arrangement of objects or pictures in **rows** and **columns** (e.g., An array can show why 2 × 3 and 3 × 2 have the same product.)

This array shows 2 rows of 3 or 2 × 3.
It also shows 3 columns of 2 or 3 × 2.
In both cases, the product is 6.

attribute: A characteristic or quality that can be used to describe and compare things (e.g., Some common attributes of shapes are size, colour, texture, and number of edges.)

average: One piece of data that is a good overall representative of all of the pieces of data in a set; there are different types of averages. (See also **mean** and **mode**.)

axis (plural is **axes**): A horizontal or vertical line in a graph, labelled with words or numbers to show what the lines, bars, or pictures in the graph mean

B

bar graph: A way to show and compare data that uses horizontal or vertical bars

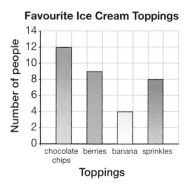

Favourite Ice Cream Toppings

base: 1. The **face** on which a 3-D shape is resting
2. The face that determines the name and the number of edges of a **prism** or **pyramid**
3. The **line segment** at the bottom of a 2–D shape

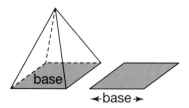

base ten blocks: Blocks that represent numbers as hundredths, tenths, ones, tens, hundreds, thousands, and so on

Thousands	Hundreds	Tens	Ones
2	3	5	4

biased results: Survey results for part of a group that are not likely to apply to the rest of the group

broken-line graph: A graph in which data points are connected point to point

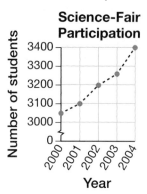

Science-Fair Participation

C

capacity: The amount that a container will hold; common units of measurement are **litres (L)** and **millilitres (mL)**

cell: A box in a spreadsheet or table (e.g., Cell A4 is in column A and row 4.)

	A	B
1	Garage sale prices	
2		sm?
3	Number of items	
4	1	$
5	2	$

centimetre (cm): A unit of measurement for **length**; one hundredth of a metre (e.g., A fingertip is about 1 cm wide.)
1 cm = 10 mm, 100 cm = 1 m

centre of rotation: The point that a shape rotates around (e.g., Point O is the centre of rotation for the triangle.)

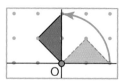

century: A unit of measurement for time; 100 years

certain outcome: A result that will always occur (e.g., If you roll a die with a 3 on every face, rolling a 3 is a certain outcome.)

chance: The likelihood that a particular event will occur. (See also **probability**.)

circle: The curve formed by a set of points that are all the same distance from the centre

centre

circle graph: A way to show data that uses parts of a circle to represent parts of the set of data (e.g., A circle graph can be used to show how students spend their days.)

My Day

school | sleep
watch TV
play outside | eat
homework

circumference: The distance around a **circle**

circumference

clockwise (CW): The direction the hands of an analog **clock** move

closed: Having no **endpoints** (e.g., A square is a closed shape.)

column: A set of items lined up vertically (See also **row**.)

column

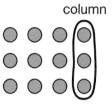

concave: Curved or pointed inward (e.g., A concave **polygon** has one **vertex** that points inward.)

vertex

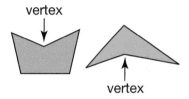

vertex

congruent: Identical in size and shape

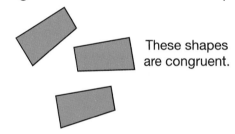

These shapes are congruent.

convex: Curved or pointed outward (e.g., A convex **polygon** has all of its **vertices** pointing outward.)

vertex   vertex

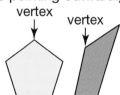

coordinate grid: A grid with horizontal and vertical lines numbered in order

coordinate pair: A pair of numbers that describes a point where a **vertical** and a **horizontal** line meet on a coordinate grid; the coordinate from the horizontal axis is always written first (e.g., Point A has the coordinates (3, 4).)

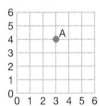

counterclockwise (CCW): The opposite direction from **clockwise**

cube: A 3-D shape with six **congruent** square faces

cubic centimetre (cm³): A unit of measurement for **volume**; the volume occupied by a cube with edges all 1 cm

data: Information gathered in a survey, in an experiment, or by observing (e.g., Data can be in words, such as a list of students' names; in numbers, such as quiz marks; or in pictures, such as drawings of favourite pets.)

decade: A unit of measurement for time; 10 years

decimal: A way to describe fractions and mixed numbers using place value; a **decimal point** separates the ones place from the tenths place

decimal equivalent: a decimal that represents the same part of a whole or the same part of a set as a fraction or another decimal
$$\frac{5}{10} = 0.5 \text{ and } \frac{5}{100} = 0.05 \text{ and } 0.5 = 0.50$$

decimal point: A dot used to separate the whole number part from the fractional part in a decimal

decimetre (dm): A unit of measurement for **length**; one tenth of a **metre** (e.g., A tens rod from a set of **base ten blocks** is 1 dm long.)
1 dm = 10 cm, 10 dm = 1 m

degree (°): A unit of measurement for angle size

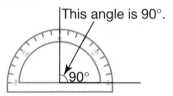

This angle is 90°.
90°

degree Celsius (°C): A unit of measurement for temperature (e.g., Water freezes at 0°C and boils at 100°C.)

denominator: The number below the bar in a **fraction** symbol that represents the number of parts in the whole or set. (See also **numerator**.) (e.g., The denominator of $\frac{3}{4}$ is 4.)

$$\frac{3}{4} \longleftarrow \text{denominator}$$

diagonal: In a 2-D shape, a line segment that joins any two **vertices** that are not next to each other; in a 3-D shape, a diagonal joins any two vertices that are not on the same **face**.

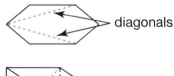

diagonals

diagonal

difference: The result when you subtract; the amount by which one number is greater than or less than another number

$$\begin{array}{r} 93 \\ -45 \\ \hline 48 \end{array} \longleftarrow \text{difference}$$

digit: One of the ten number symbols from 0 to 9; in the base-ten system, the position of a digit shows its value (e.g., the digit 3 in the number 237 represents 3 tens; in 5.03, it represents 3 hundredths.)

dimension: A way to describe how an object can be measured (e.g., A line has only length, so it is one-dimensional. Area is two-dimensional (2-D). Volume is three-dimensional (3-D).)

dividend: The number that is divided into equal parts in a division operation

$$9 \div 3 = 3$$
$$\uparrow$$
$$\text{dividend}$$

divisible: Can be divided with no remainder (e.g., 30 is divisible by 6 because you can make exactly 5 groups of 6 from 30.)

divisor: The number you divide by in a division operation

$$24 \div 3 = 8$$
$$\uparrow$$
$$\text{divisor}$$

double: To multiply a number by 2

edge: The **line segment** formed where two **faces** meet on a 3-D shape

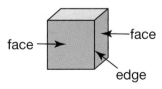

endpoint: The point at which a **line segment** begins or ends

equally likely outcomes: Results that have an equal chance of occurring (e.g., In flipping a coin, heads and tails are equally likely outcomes.)

equation: A mathematical sentence in which the left side is equal to the right side (e.g.,
$$4 + 2 = 6$$
$$5 + 3 = 4 + 4)$$

equilateral: In a triangle, having all sides equal in length

equivalent: Having the same value (e.g., Equivalent fractions are two fractions that represent the same number, such as $\frac{2}{6}$ and $\frac{1}{3}$.)

equivalent decimal: See **decimal equivalent**

equivalent fractions: Fractions that represent the same part of a whole or the same part of a set

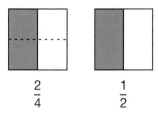

$$\frac{2}{4} \qquad \frac{1}{2}$$

$\frac{2}{4}$ is equivalent to $\frac{1}{2}$.

$$\frac{2}{4} = \frac{1}{2}$$

estimate: A reasoned guess about a measurement or answer

even number: A number that is **divisible** by 2 (e.g., 12 is even because 12 ÷ 2 = 6.)

event: A set of **possible outcomes** of a **probability** experiment (e.g., When rolling a die, you could decide that an event is rolling an even number, such as 2, 4, or 6.)

expanded form: A way to write a number that shows the value of each digit (e.g., In expanded form, 2365 is 2000 + 300 + 60 + 5 or 2 thousands 3 hundreds 6 tens 5 ones.)

face: A 2-D shape that forms a flat surface of a 3-D shape

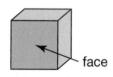
face

fact: An addition, subtraction, multiplication, or division **equation** (e.g., In Grade 5, we learn multiplication facts to 12 × 12 = 144.)

fact

fact family: A set of addition and subtraction or multiplication and division facts; all facts in the set use the same numbers

3 × 2 = 6   6 ÷ 3 = 2
2 × 3 = 6   6 ÷ 2 = 3

factor: One of the numbers you multiply in a multiplication operation

2 × 6 = 12
factor   factor

fair game: A game that all players have an equal chance of winning

flip: See **reflection** (See also **transformation.**)

fraction: Numbers used to name part of a whole or part of a set (e.g., $\frac{3}{4}$ is a **proper fraction**; $\frac{4}{3}$ is an **improper fraction**; 0.2 is a **decimal** fraction; $5\frac{1}{2}$ is a **mixed number.**) (See also **numerator** and **denominator**.)

gram (g): A unit of measurement for **mass** (e.g., 1 mL of water has a mass of 1 g.) 1000 g = 1 kg

graph: A way of showing information so it is more easily understood; a graph can be concrete (e.g., boys in one line and girls in another), pictorial (e.g., pictures of boys in one row and girls in another), or abstract (e.g., two bars on a bar graph to show how many students are boys and how many are girls)

greater than (>): A sign used when comparing two numbers (e.g., 10 is greater than 5, or 10 > 5.) (See also **inequality signs.**)

h: The symbol for **hour**

halve: To divide a number by 2

heptagon: A **polygon** with seven sides

hexagon: A **polygon** with six sides

horizontal line: A line across a page that is **parallel** to the bottom edge, or a line that is level with the floor

hour: A unit of measurement for time; the symbol for hour is **h**
60 min = 1 h

impossible outcome: A result that cannot occur (e.g., If you roll a die with a 3 on every face, rolling a 5 is an impossible outcome.)

improper fraction: A fraction in which the **numerator** is greater than the **denominator** $\left(\text{e.g., } \frac{4}{3}\right)$

inequality signs: The symbols > and < that are used to make comparisons (e.g., 8 > 5 is read as "Eight is greater than five." 5 < 8 is read as "Five is less than eight.") (See also **greater than** and **less than**.)

interval: The distance between two endpoints on a graph scale; intervals in a graph should be equal (e.g., If the scale axis is numbered 0, 5, 10, 15, …, then the intervals are 5.)

isosceles: In a triangle, having two sides equal in length

kilogram (kg): A unit of measurement for **mass** (e.g., A math textbook has a mass of about 1 kg.)
1 kg = 1000 g

kilometre (km): A unit of measurement for **length**; one thousand metres
1 km = 1000 m

kite: A quadrilateral that has two pairs of equal sides with no sides parallel

legend: A feature on a map or graph that explains what colours or symbols mean

length: The distance from one end of a **line segment** to the other end

The length of this line segment is 2 cm.

less than (<): A sign used when comparing two numbers (e.g., 5 is less than 10, or 5 < 10.) (See also **inequality signs**.)

like denominators: Equal denominators (e.g., $\frac{3}{8}$ and $\frac{7}{8}$ are both in eighths; they have like denominators.)

likely outcome: A result that can easily occur (e.g., If you roll a die with a 3 on all the faces but one, rolling a 3 is a likely outcome.)

line of symmetry: A line that divides a 2-D shape into halves that match when the shape is folded on the line of symmetry

line of symmetry

linear pattern: A pattern in which the difference between each item and the next is always the same (e.g., 2, 4, 6, 8, 10, ... is linear because it always increases by 2. 98, 96, 94, 92, 90, ... is linear because it always decreases by 2.)

line segment: Part of a line with two **endpoints**

○———————○

line segment

litre (L): A unit of measurement for **capacity** 1L = 1000 mL

mass: The amount of matter in an object; common units of measurement are grams (g) and kilograms (kg)

mean: A type of average; the amount that results when all the amounts in a set of data are distributed evenly; the sum of a set of numbers divided by the number of numbers in the set (e.g., The set 3, 4, 5, 2, 2, 3, and 2 has seven numbers that add to 21. The mean is 21 ÷ 7 = 3.)

metre (m): A unit of measurement for **length** (e.g., 1 m is about the distance from a doorknob to the floor.) 1000 mm = 1 m, 100 cm = 1 m, 1000 m = 1 km

millennium: A unit of measurement for time; 1000 years

millilitre (mL): A unit of measurement for **capacity**; 1000 mL = 1 L

millimetre (mm): A unit of measurement for **length** (e.g., A dime is about 1 mm thick.) 10 mm = 1 cm, 1000 mm = 1 m

min: The symbol for **minute**

minute: A unit of measurement for time; the symbol for minute is min 60 s = 1 min, 60 min = 1 h

mixed number: A number made up of a **whole number** and a **fraction** (e.g., $3\frac{1}{2}$)

mode: A type of average; the number that occurs most often in a set of numbers

2, 2, 2, 3, 3, 4, 5

The mode of these numbers is 2.

multiples: The products found by multiplying a whole number by other whole numbers (e.g., When you multiply 10 by the whole numbers 0 to 4, you get the multiples 0, 10, 20, 30, and 40.)

nearest (unit): The closest when rounding a number or a measurement; less than half a unit is rounded down to a lesser value; more than half a unit is rounded up to a greater value (e.g., 4.6 cm^2 rounded to the nearest square centimetre is 5 cm^2.)

net: A 2-D shape you can fold to create a 3-D shape

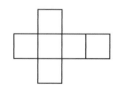

This is a net for a cube.

nonlinear pattern: A pattern in which the difference between each term and the next does not stay the same (e.g., 1, 3, 6, 10, 15, ... is nonlinear because the differences are 2, 3, 4, and so on.)

nonstandard unit: A unit of measurement that is not part of a customary system (e.g., A desk is about 5 juice cans wide.)

number line: A diagram that shows ordered numbers or points on a line

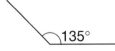

0 1 2 3 4 5 6 7 8 9 10

number sentence: A mathematical statement that shows how two quantities are related (e.g., $3 \times 8 = 24$; $3 < 8$). (See also **equation**.)

numeral: The written symbol for a number (e.g., 148, $\frac{3}{4}$, and 2.8)

numerator: The number above the bar in a **fraction** symbol. (See also **denominator**.)

$$\frac{3}{4} \leftarrow \text{numerator}$$

obtuse angle: An angle that measures greater than 90° and less than 180°

135°

obtuse-angled triangle: A triangle with one obtuse angle

octagon: A **polygon** with eight sides

odd number: A number that has a remainder of 1 when it is divided by 2 (e.g., 15 is odd because $15 \div 2 = 7$ R1.)

open sentence: A **number sentence** containing at least one unknown number (e.g., $2 \times \blacksquare = 8$)

ordinal number: A way of describing an item's place in a numbered sequence (e.g., 1st, third, 15th)

organized list: The problem-solving strategy of following an order to find all possibilities

orientation: The direction around a shape when you name the vertices in order

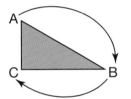 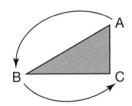

triangle ABC with clockwise orientation

triangle ABC with counterclockwise orientation

outcome: A single result (e.g., If you roll a die, the possible outcomes are 1, 2, 3, 4, 5, and 6; 7 is an impossible outcome.)

parallel: Always the same distance apart

parallelogram: A **quadrilateral** with equal and **parallel** opposite sides (e.g., A **rhombus**, a **rectangle**, and a **square** are all types of parallelograms.)

pattern: Something that follows a rule while repeating or changing

pattern rule: A description of how a pattern starts and how it continues

pentagon: A **polygon** with five sides

perimeter: The total length of the sides of a shape

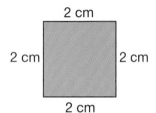

The perimeter of this square is 8 cm.

pictograph: A **graph** that uses pictures or symbols to represent quantities

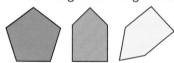

How Old Are You?

7 ☺☺☺☺
8 ☺☺☺☺☺☺☺☺
9 ☺☺☺☺☺☺☺
10 ☺☺☺

Each ☺ means 5 people.

place value: The value given to a digit based on its position in a numeral (e.g., The 3 in the number 237 represents 3 tens, while in the number 5.03 it represents 3 hundredths.)

polygon: A closed 2-D shape with sides made from straight line segments

possible outcome: Any result that can occur (e.g., If you roll a die, the possible outcomes are 1, 2, 3, 4, 5, and 6.)

precision: A way to compare tools and measurements (e.g., A measurement made with a ruler divided in millimetres is more precise than a measurement made with a ruler divided in centimetres.)

prism: A 3-D shape with opposite **congruent bases**; the other faces are parallelograms (e.g., a triangle-based prism)

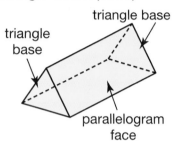

triangle base

triangle base

parallelogram face

probability: How likely it is that a particular result will occur

probability line: A way to show probabilities of several outcomes

impossible   certain

less probable   more probable

product: The result when you multiply

$$2 \times 6 = 12$$

product

proper fraction: A fraction in which the **denominator** is greater than the **numerator** $\left(\text{e.g., } \frac{1}{2}, \frac{5}{6}, \frac{2}{7}\right)$

properties: The features of a shape that describe it (e.g., The properties of a square are four equal sides, four equal angles (all right angles), two pairs of parallel sides, and four lines of symmetry.)

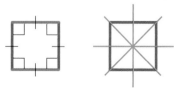

protractor: A tool used to measure **angles**

pyramid: A 3-D shape with a polygon for a base; the other faces are triangles that meet at a single **vertex** (e.g., a rectangle-based pyramid)

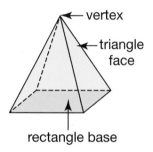

vertex

triangle face

rectangle base

quadrilateral: A polygon with four straight sides. (See also **kite**, **parallelogram**, **rectangle**, **rhombus**, **square**, **trapezoid**.)

quotient: The result when you divide, not including the **remainder**

$$12 \div 5 = 2 \text{ R2}$$

quotient

range: The **difference** between the greatest and least values in a set of data (e.g., For the numbers 1, 2, 5, 7, 9, 11, 12, the range is 12 − 1 or 11.)

rectangle: A **quadrilateral** with four square corners

reflection: A flip of a 2-D shape; each point in a 2-D shape flips to the opposite side of the line of reflection, but stays the same distance from the line. (See also **transformation**.)

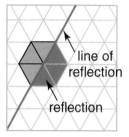

line of reflection

reflection

regroup: Trade 10 smaller units for 1 larger unit, or 1 larger unit for 10 smaller units

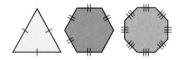

regular polygon: A polygon with all sides equal and all angles equal

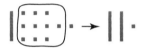

remainder: The number of items left over after division

$$14 \div 4 = 3 \text{ R2}$$

remainder

rhombus: A **quadrilateral** with four equal sides

right angle: The angle made by a square corner; a right angle measures 90°

90°

right-angled triangle: A triangle with one right angle

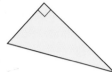

rotation: A turn of a shape; each point in the shape must stay an equal distance from the **centre of rotation**. (See also **transformation**.)

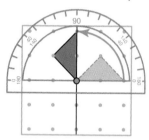

This is a 90° counterclockwise rotation about the centre of rotation.

round: To approximate a number to a given place value (e.g., 8327 rounded to the nearest hundred is 8300.)

row: A set of items lined up horizontally (See also **column**.)

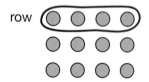

s: The symbol for **second**

scale: 1. Numbers and marks arranged at regular intervals that are used for measurement or to establish position (e.g., the markings on the side of a measuring cup, or on the **axis** of a graph) 2. The size of a model compared with what it represents (e.g., If the scale of a model is "1 cm represents 1 m," a real object that is 1 m tall would be 1 cm tall in the model.)

scale model: A model that is larger or smaller than the real object, but is the same shape; a model is **similar** to the real object

scalene: In a triangle, having no two sides equal in length

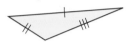

second: A unit of measurement for time; the symbol for second is **s** 60 s = 1 min

set: A collection of items or numbers; Each item in the set is called a "member" of the set

shape: 1. A geometric object (e.g., A square is a 2-D shape. A cube is a 3-D shape.) 2. The **attribute** that describes the form of a geometric object (e.g., Circles and spheres both have a round shape.)

side: One of the line segments that forms a polygon

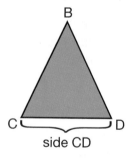

side CD

similar: Identical in shape, but not necessarily the same size. (See also **congruent**.)

These are similar rectangles.

skeleton: A 3-D shape that has only edges and vertices

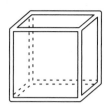

skip count: To count without using every number, but according to a set pattern or rule (e.g., counting to 100 by fives)

slide: See **translation**. (See also **transformation**.)

square: A **quadrilateral** with four equal sides and four right angles

square centimetre (cm^2): A unit of measurement for **area**; the area covered by a square with sides all 1 cm

square corner: See **right angle**

square metre (m^2): A unit of measurement for **area**; the area covered by a square with sides all 1 m

square unit: A unit of measurement for **area**

standard form: The usual way in which we write numbers (e.g., 23650 is written in standard form.) (See also **expanded form** and **numeral**.)

standard unit: A unit of measurement that is part of an accepted measurement system (e.g., metres, kilograms, litres, and square metres are all standard units.) (See also **nonstandard unit**.)

stem-and-leaf plot: A way to organize data in groups according to place value; The stem shows the beginning of a number and the leaf shows the rest of the number (e.g., The circled leaf in this stem-and-leaf plot represents the number 258.)

Stem	Leaves
24	1 5 8
25	2 2 3 4 7 ⑧ 9
26	0 3
27	
28	8

sum: The result when you add

$$14 + 37 = 51$$

sum

survey: 1. A set of questions designed to obtain information directly from people 2. To ask a group of people a set of questions

T

2-D shape: A shape that has the dimensions of length and width

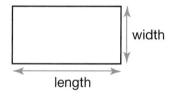

3-D shape: A shape that has the dimensions of length, width, and height

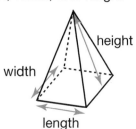

12 h clock: A method of naming the hours of the day from 1 to 12, along with the notation a.m. and p.m.; The symbol for **hour** is **h** (e.g., 2:00 p.m. is equivalent to 14:00.)

24 h clock: A method of naming the hours of the day from 0 to 23; (e.g., 14:00 is equivalent to 2:00 p.m.)

tally: A way to keep track of data using marks

//// //// /

tally chart: A chart that uses tally marks to count data (e.g., If you are surveying students about favourite flavours of ice cream you could use a tally chart like this one.)

Favourite Ice Cream Flavours	
vanilla	//// //// /
chocolate	//// //// //// //// ///
strawberry	////

t-chart: A way to organize related information in a chart with two columns; both sides of the t are labelled

Weeks	Days
1	7
2	14
3	21

tetrahedron: A 3-D shape with four **faces** that are **polygons**

A triangle-based pyramid
is a tetrahedron.

tile: Use repeated congruent shapes to cover an area without gaps or overlaps

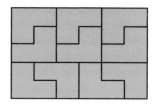

tiling pattern: A pattern of repeated congruent shapes that fit together with no gaps or overlaps

tonne (t)**:** A unit of measurement for **mass** (e.g., A small car has a mass of about 1 t.) 1 t = 1000 kg

transformation: A rule that results in a change of position, orientation, or size; transformations include **translations**, **rotations**, and **reflections**

translation: A slide of a shape; the slide must be along a straight line. (See also **transformation**.)

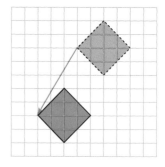

trapezoid: A **quadrilateral** with only one pair of **parallel** sides

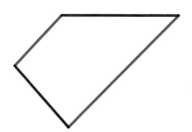

tree diagram: A way to record and count all combinations of **events** (e.g., This tree diagram shows all the three-digit numbers that can be made from the digits 1, 2, and 3.)

trend: The general direction of data presented in a graph; the data can increase, decrease, or stay the same over time

increase

decrease

stays about the same

triangle: A **polygon** with three sides

turn: See **rotation**. (See also **transformation**.)

unlikely outcome: A result that has little chance of occurring (e.g., If you roll a die with a 3 on all the faces but one, rolling a number other than 3 is an unlikely outcome.)

Venn diagram: A way of showing the relationship(s) between collections of objects or numbers

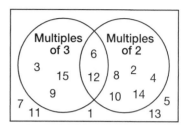

This Venn diagram shows that 6 and 12 are both **multiples** of 2 and multiples of 3.

vertex (plural is **vertices**): The point at the corner of an angle or a shape (e.g., A cube has eight vertices. An angle has one vertex.)

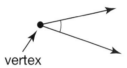

vertex

vertical line: A line that goes up and down a page parallel to the side edge, or straight up and down from the floor

volume: The amount of space occupied by an object; a common unit of measurement is the **cubic centimetre (cm^3)**

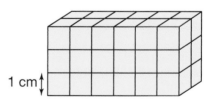

1 cm

The volume of this box is 36 cm^3.

whole numbers: The counting numbers that begin at 0 and continue forever; 0, 1, 2, 3, ...

Index

and pictographs, 70–71
place value charts,
     252–253, 256–257
problem-solving lessons,
     162–163, 290–291
regrouping, 252–253, 255,
     256–257
working backward,
     290–291

Nearest square centimetre,
224
Net (of 3-D shape)
     congruence, 304–305
     definition, 304
     drawing, 304–305
     matching with 3-D shape,
          306–307
Number facts
     in multiplication, 158–159
Number lines
     and comparing, ordering,
          34–35, 348–349
     decimal, 42–43, 46–47
     in division, 288–289
     fractions, 348–349, 350
     math game, 350
     mental math, 164–165
     metre stick, 42–43
     in multiplication, 164–165
     in rounding, 36–37, 46–47
Number patterns. *see*
patterns, number
Numerators. *see* fractions

Obtuse angle, 194
Obtuse-angled triangle, 195
Open sentences, 97
Ordering, comparing. *see*
comparing, ordering
Orientation
     definition, 391
     reflections, 396–397
     rotations, 396–397
     translations, 390–391

Pattern rules. *see also*
     patterns, 2-D shape;
     patterns, 3-D shape;
     patterns, number
     chapter task, 406
     and spreadsheets, 14–15
     tiling an area, 386–389
Patterns, 2-D shape
     in Braille alphabet, 11
     chapter task, 22, 406
     and charts, tables, 4–5
     curious math, 11, 13
     tiling, 386–389
Patterns, 3-D shape, 12–13
Patterns, geometry. *see*
     patterns, 2-D shape;
     patterns, 3-D shape
Patterns, number
     chapter task, 22
     and charts, tables, 4–7
     curious math, 277
     in decimal quotients, 277
     solving problems with, 8–9
     and spreadsheets, 14–15
Pentagon
     tiling, 385
Perimeter
     and area, 225, 226–229, 231
     chapter task, 154
     curious math, 225
     estimating and measuring,
          134–135, 138–139, 154
     of rectangle, 138–139,
          226–229
Pictographs
     communicating about, 80
     estimating numbers
          represented in, 70–71
     scale in, 70–71, 80–81
Pie (circle) graphs. *see* circle
Place value charts
     in addition, 108–109
     base ten blocks, 252–253,
          256–257, 278–283
     and decimal tenths,
          hundredths, 114–115,
          252–253, 256–257,
          274–276, 278–283

in division, 174–175,
     274–276, 278–283
in multiplication, 252–253,
     256–257
in reading and writing
     numbers, 28–29
and regrouping, 174–175,
     252–253, 256–257,
     274–276
in subtraction, 114–115
tens, ones, 274–276
and thousands, hundreds,
     28–29
Polygon
     angles in, 202–207
     chapter task, 216
     classifying, sorting by
          properties, 204–207
     definition, 202
     enlargement, reduction,
          similarity, 400
     estimating, measuring area,
          222–223
     estimating, measuring
          perimeter, 134–135,
          138–140
     regular, 203
Precision in measurements,
278
Predictions. *see* probability
Prism
     cross-sections, 311
     curious math, 311
     drawing, building, 302–303
     mental imagery, 313
     net (of 3-D shape),
          304–308
Probability
     chapter task, 380
     comparing, ordering,
          360–361
     curious math, 374
     estimating, 368–369
     fair games, 370–371, 380
     and fractions, 364–365,
          368–369, 370–371
     illustrations: bar graphs,
          circle graphs, 77
     illustrations: probability
          lines, 360–363, 368–369

Units of measure
area, 224, 226, 232
capacity and volume, 312–317
curious math, 137
length, 128–131, 137
mass, 318–321
time, 144–147

Vertex in 2-D shapes, 197
Vertex in 3-D shapes
mental imagery, 313
solid models, 302
Volume
cubic centimetre (cm^3), 314
describing, 308–309
measuring and comparing, 314–315
relating to capacity, 316–317

Working backward in problems, 290–291

Credits

This page constitutes an extension of the copyright page. We have made every effort to trace the ownership of all copyrighted material and to secure permission from copyright holders. In the event of any question arising as to the use of any material, we will be pleased to make the necessary corrections in future printings. Thanks are due to the following authors, publishers, and agents for permission to use the material indicated.

Front Cover: Wayne R. Bilenduk/Image Bank/Getty Images
Back Cover: Tom Walker/Image Bank/Getty Images

Chapter 1: Opener Page 1 top left to right, Corbis/Magma, © Gerald and Buff Corsi/Visuals Unlimited, © Hal Horwitz/ Corbis/Magma, © Pat Jerrold; Papilio/Corbis/Magma, © Mark Cassino/Superstock, © Priscilla Connell/Index Stock Imagery, C Squared Studios/Photodisc Green/Getty Images; Page 8: "Strawberry Seeds" by Gregory Tang which appeared in THE GRAPES OF MATH. Text copyright © 2001 by Gregory Tang. Published by Scholastic Inc.

Chapter 2: Opener Page 23: © AFP/Corbis/Magma; Page 30: © Duomo/Corbis/Magma; Page 32: Business Wire; Page 34: Jerry Kobalenko/First Light; Page 49: © AFP/Corbis/Magma; Page 56: © Darrell Gulin/Corbis/Magma

Chapter 3: Page 60: HARRY POTTER AND THE ORDER OF THE PHOENIX by JK Rowling (Bloomsbury). Cover illustration by Jason Cockcroft; A SERIES OF UNFORTUNATE EVENTS #10: THE SLIPPERY SLOPE by Lemony Snicket and illustrated by Brett Helquist. Cover Copyright © 2003 by Brett Helquist. Used by permission of HarperCollins Publishers.; CHARLIE AND THE CHOCOLATE FACTORY by Roald Dahl, illustrated by Quentin Blake, copyright © 1998 by Quentin Blake, illustrations. Used by permission of Puffin Books, A Division of Penguin Young Readers Group, A Member of Penguin Group (USA) Inc., 345 Hudson Street, New York, NY 10014. All rights reserved; THE CHRONICLES OF NARNIA: THE LAST BATTLE by C.S. Lewis and illustrated by Pauline Baynes. Reprinted by permission of HarperCollins Publishers Ltd. Copyright © 1956 C.S. Lewis Pte. Ltd. Copyright renewed 1984 C.S. Lewis Pte. Ltd.; THE HOBBIT by J.R.R. Tolkien. Reprinted by permission of HarperCollins Publishers Ltd. Copyright © J.R.R. Tolkien.; Page 70: CP Picture Archive; Page 72: top right, Mark Tomalty/Masterfile, centre right, © Darrell Gulin/Corbis/Magma; Page 88: © Lynda Richardson/ Corbis/Magma; Page 92, left to right: Photodisc, © Brandon D. Cole/ Corbis/Magma, John Foxx/Fotosearch

Chapter 4: Opener Page 93: right, Al Harvey/The Slide Farm; Page 98: CP Picture Archive; Page 103 top: NASA, centre, David Madison/Photodisc Red/Getty Images; Page 106: top right, © Theo Allofs/Corbis/Magma: centre right, © Tim Zurowksi/ Corbis/Magma, bottom right, © Paul Souders/Corbis/Magma; Page 112: © MacDuff Everton/Corbis/Magma

Chapter 5: Page 128 top, Corel, centre left, Kristiina Paul Bowering, centre right, Corel; Page 143: centre, CP Picture Archive, bottom, Corbis/Magma; Page 153: Matthew Fearn/ CP Picture Archive

Chapter 6: Page 157, Daniel Bosler/Stone/Getty Images; Page 158 top, Photo Bank Yokohama/First Light, bottom, Mark Tomalty/ Masterfile; Page 178, Jules Frazier/Photodisc Green/Getty Images; Page 181 top, © Lowell Georgia/Corbis/Magma, centre, Yellow Dog

Productions/The Image Bank/Getty Images; Page 182, Courtesy of the Gabriel Dumont Institute (www.gdins.org); Page 184, Picture Arts/First Light

Chapter 7: Opener Page 187, © Diana Ong/Superstock; Page 194, Kristiina Paul Bowering; Page 204 left to right: Photodisc/ Photodisc Green/Getty Images, S. Solum/PhotoLink/Photodisc Green/Getty Images, Kristiina Paul Bowering, Kristiina Paul Bowering, Kristiina Paul Bowering; Page 213 left to right, Kristiina Paul Bowering, S. Solum/PhotoLink/Photodisc, Kristiina Paul Bowering, Photodisc/Photodisc Green/Getty Images

Chapter 8: Opener Page 219: © Lowell Georgia/Corbis/Magma; Page 224: Richard H. Johnston/Taxi/Getty Images; Page 232, © Gunter Marx Photography/Corbis/Magma; Page 235, © Lowell Georgia/Corbis/Magma; Page 244: Illustration from EARLY CIVILIZATIONS, 2001, Courtesy of Duval House Publishing.

Chapter 9: Page 248, Courtesy of MSSS Crafts Website, url: www.mssscrafts.com; Page 251, © Michael Newman/Photo Edit; Page 253, top right, © Huguette Rainforth/Magma, centre right, © Myrleen Ferguson Cate/Photo Edit Inc.; Page 254: Davies & Starr/Image Bank/Getty Images; Page 264, G. K. & Vikki Hart/Image Bank/Getty Images

Chapter 10: Opener Page 269, © Duomo/Corbis/Magma. Page 271, © Richard Cummins/Corbis/Magma; Page 272, © Kevin R. Morris/Corbis/Magma; Page 281, © Keren Su/Corbis/ Magma; Page 283, Kristiina Paul Bowering; Page 284, bottom, Zoran Milich/Masterfile; Page 286, Kristiina Paul Bowering; Page 287, Ron Watts/First Light; Page 288, centre right, Darryl Dyck/CP Picture Archive, bottom right, Andrew Parsons/CP Picture Archive; Page 289, Wayne R. Bilenduk/Image Bank/Getty Images; Page 290, Kristiina Paul Bowering; Page 291, Richard Hartmier/First Light; Page 292, Kristiina Paul Bowering; Page 293 top right, Burke/Triolo Productions/Brand X Pictures/ Getty Images, centre right, Alan & Sandy Carey/Photodisc Green/Getty Images; Page 296 centre, NHMPL/StoneGetty Images, bottom right, © Joel W. Rogers/Corbis/Magma; Page 297, Ryan McVay/Photodisc Green/Getty Images

Chapter 11: Page 302, Imagestate/First Light; Page 303, www.firstlight.ca; Page 323 centre left, Ryan McVay/Photodisc Green/Getty Images, centre right, Photodisc Collection/Photodisc Blue/Getty Images, bottom left, C Squared Studios/Photodisc Green/Getty Images; Page 325 left, © David Young-Wolff/Photo Edit, centre, Rommel/Masterfile, right, www.firstlight.ca; Page 327 centre left, Ryan McVay/Photodisc Green/Getty Images, centre, Digital Vision/Getty Images, centre right, Thinkstock/Getty Images, bottom left, Ryan McVay/Photodisc Green/Getty Images, bottom right, Photodisc Collection/Photodisc Blue/Getty

Chapter 12: Page 344, © Dennis MacDonald/Index Stock Imagery; Page 345, www.firstlight.ca; Page 349, © Owen Franken/ Corbis/Magma

Chapter 13: Page 364, "Last Night I Dreamed of Chickens" by Jack Prelutsky from SOMETHING BIG HAS BEEN HERE by Jack Prelutsky. TEXT COPYRIGHT © 1990 BY JACK PRELUTSKY. Used by permission of HarperCollins Publishers; Page 377, G.K. & Vikki Hart/Photodisc Green/Getty Images

Chapter 14: Opener Page 381, © Christine Osborne/Corbis/Magma